Labor at the Polls

Union Voting in Presidential Elections, 1952-1976

Jong Oh Ra

University of Massachusetts Press   Amherst 1978

Acknowledgment is made to the following for permission to reprint copyrighted material:

Harper & Row, for "Demographic Division of Presidential Preferences" (table 1A) and "Democratic Vote in 1952 and 1960, by Religion and Class" (table 1B), from *Elections in America: Control and Influence in Democratic Politics* by Gerald M. Pomper. Copyright © 1968 by Dodd, Mead & Company, Inc.; and for material from *The Future of American Politics* by Samuel Lubell. Copyright © 1951, 1952 by Samuel Lubell. Used by permission of Harper & Row Publishers, Inc.

V. O. Key, Jr., for table 17, copyright © 1956.

Prentice-Hall, for material from Edwards, Reich, Weisskopf, *The Capitalist System: A Radical Analysis of American Society,* pp 213, 236–37. Copyright © 1972. Reprinted by permission of Prentice-Hall, Inc., Englewood Cliffs, New Jersey.

The Southern Political Science Association and the Luella Gettys Key Trust, for material from *The Journal of Politics* 17:1 (1955), pp. 3–18.

Holt, Rinehart and Winston, for material from *The Semi-Sovereign People: A Realist's View of Democracy in America* by E. E. Schattschneider. Copyright © 1960 by E. E. Schattschneider. Reprinted by permission of Holt, Rinehart and Winston.

The University of Utah, for table 47. Reprinted with permission.

Transaction, Inc., for material published by permission of Transaction, Inc. from *Transaction,* Vol. 7, no. 2. Copyright © 1969 by Transaction, Inc.

For My Mother and Father

To Gus & Marie —

To a pair of friends whose insatiable curiosity and boundless inquisitiveness have animated my own posture toward self-discovery.

Love,
Gary R

Contents

List of Illustrations

Tables

Preface

That labor union voting behavior arouses the interest of students of American politics is not difficult to explain. The study of labor unions in politics and the analysis of voting behavior are two of the most prominent concerns of political scientists during the last half century. Pluralism, the New Deal realignment, bargaining, incrementalism, and consensus politics—these are but a few of the most familiar subjects that have spawned voluminous literature since Bentley formally introduced the group basis of American politics, and labor unions occupy a central place in group politics. No less impressive is the attention given to voting behavior research. Ranging from early rudimentary, descriptive investigations to the current series of analytic and quasitheoretical attempts, research in this area has left unscathed few census records, poll results, or, indeed, tawdry electronic gadgets.

Though the size of the literature in these fields is overwhelming, the search for even a modest bibliography on labor union voting behavior is challenging. This paucity, more than anything else, provided the initial incentive for the present study. Not that a paucity of literature should cause discomfort; in political science, it is commonplace. But the poverty of the literature in this field seemed a symbol of disjointed efforts that have so long plagued the discipline—normative, structural, historical, and descriptive (and largely that) on the one hand, and empirical, behavioral, individual, and quantitative (and largely that) on the other. Predictably, outcomes of these atheoretical attempts have often been less important than interesting.

This book is, in a narrow sense, a study of how American labor union members and their families voted in seven recent presidential elections, 1952–1976. Substantive findings in this regard should help equip us with additional insights about the origin, development, and present makeup of the New Deal coalition. In a broader sense, however, it is an exercise in theory building, bringing together plural levels of descriptions and analyses in order to *explain* why they vote the way they do.

To be sure, limitations abound in this book: the very nature of the data, the way they were assembled for our purpose, the pitfalls of a secondary analysis in general. Nevertheless, my basic purpose in this study is to demonstrate how I manipulated the data in order to account for a model—one that points out the convergence of as well as the tension between writings in philosophy, history, and social psychology, and one that presents situation-specific generalizations. I believe this is a worthwhile attempt. As a student of philosophy of science, I have often been frustrated with the dearth of applications; as a political scientist, with the oversupply of middle-range theories. I am convinced that this is a way to make a study *important* and hence useful.

Many people, friends, students, and colleagues, helped me with this project. Fred Coombs, Marvin Weinbaum, Philip Monypenny, Robert Weissberg, and the late Kern Dickman read parts of the earlier draft and forced me to rethink several aspects of my reasoning. Rod Eslinger provided countless hours of computer assistance and my brother, Jong Mann, devoted one of his otherwise colorful summer vacations to helping me with the tedious coding chore. Judy Gallistel, Cathy Reisner, and Rhonda Grierson typed the manuscript with competence and tolerance. I am profoundly grateful to all of them. Of course, I alone am responsible for the contents of this work.

I am especially grateful to my wife, Carol, who has been an editor and critic of my work. I owe her my deepest intellectual debt. Most of all, I thank her for her unwavering moral support and warm encouragement throughout the preparation of this manuscript. Without her, this book would not be.

Finally, I wish to express my most heartfelt gratitude to my mother and father who originally inspired my academic work, and have since steadfastly stood by me through many difficult periods of my career, painlessly forgetting their own problems. They continue to be a most important source of my strength, and their meaning for my life looms larger as I grow. To them, this book is dedicated.

J. O. R.
July 1977

1   Introduction: Scope and Method

The American Voter in the Political Universe

Studies of voting behavior in America have prospered since the 1930s when political scientists launched their first quantitative analyses of the existing aggregate data.[1] Despite their multifarious variety and accelerating volume, these studies have followed a certain chronological pattern: first, a period of aggregate or demographic investigations; second, a stage of microlevel studies; and third, the recent emphasis on systemic analysis of voting behavior.[2]

Early studies of voting behavior scarcely amounted to more than an application of some of the novel methodological tools to the existing aggregate data.[3] Depending on the extent to which the methods fit the data and the ingenuity with which the data were used, the quality of the results ranged from instances of outright abuse[4] to significant contributions to political science as a scientific discipline.[5] Though largely descriptive, the contributions made by these aggregate or demographic approaches provided profound insights into the foundation of our political process.[6]

Geographical identifications of party strength often revealed equally elaborate and detailed sources of partisan allegiance, in terms that had never previously engaged the attention of either historians or political scientists.[7] Again, insights rarely reached even the crudest level of analysis;[8] the disclosure of the elements underlying the geographical regularity, however, was a revelation, if not a revolution, for the discipline.[9] The now familiar bimodal distribution of the demographic data along the continuum of affiliation with the Democratic and Republican parties dates from this period.[10]

Despite the crudeness of tools employed, or because of their simplicity, the focal point became what the central thrust of research should have been all along—the political and systemic implications of voting patterns. In other words, the party system itself was the most prominent of the independent variables, and when the order of variables was reversed so that the act of voting was viewed as an independent variable, the purpose of the investigation was to assess the systemic impact for which the election was held responsible.[11] Thus examinations of stability and change were far different from the ahistorical or apolitical overtones of analysis practiced by most of today's behaviorally oriented social scientists. The question, then, is not so much *whether* researchers indulged in a trend analysis as *how* they performed their tasks.

The following period saw the mushrooming of new survey techniques, statistical tools, public opinion studies, and other sociological and psychological research that permeated political science. Aided by these develop-

Table 1A Demographic division of presidential preferences
(In percentages of national opinion)

	1964		1960		1952	
	Goldwater	Johnson	Nixon	Kennedy	Eisenhower	Stevenson
Occupation						
Professional business	44	56	55	45	66	32
White collar	31	69	54	46	61	37
Skilled workers	19	81	39	61	45	52
Unskilled workers	12	88	45	55	31	63
Farmers	39	58	66	34	59	35
Sex						
Men	33	67	48	52	50	48
Women	29	71	52	48	54	43
Education						
College	45	55	64	35	71	28
High school	29	71	46	53	55	44
Grade school	18	81	48	52	46	48
Religion						
Protestant	42	58	61	39	57	39
Catholic	21	79	20	80	46	53
Jewish	30	70	10	90	23	77
Party						
Democrat	13	87	23	76	27	73
Independent	44	56	50	49	67	33
Republican	80	20	93	7	96	4

Source: Gerald M. Pomper, *Elections in America: Control and Influence in Democratic Politics* (New York: Dodd, Mead and Company, 1968), p. 72.
Note: Some of the categories originally included in Pomper's table have been omitted.

Table 1B Democratic vote in 1952 and 1960, by religion and class
(In percentages)

	1952			1960		
	Catholic	Protestant	Total	Catholic	Protestant	Total
Manual	64	52	56	85	47	60
Nonmanual	38	28	34	75	29	45
Total	55	42		81	38	
Total class difference		22%				15%
Total religious difference		13%				43%

Source: Gerald M. Pomper, *Elections in America: Control and Influence in Democratic Politics* (New York: Dodd, Mead and Company, 1968), p. 82.

ments, social scientists pooled their resources and skills to delve past the aggregate level to the social psychological determinants surrounding the individual voter's decision-making process.[12]

An impressive repertory of what we know today about the environmental and psychological factors behind a voter's decision was established during this period. These findings now pervade all levels of political scientists' concern. Today, for example, in an introductory American government textbook we find the following profile of the American voter:

1. Participation in voting in the United States is relatively low.
2. The American electorate has a low emotional involvement in national elections.
3. Many voters lack familiarity with the leading issues, government policy toward them, and party position on them.
4. Ideological positions are weak among American voters.
5. Party identification is the most important factor affecting a voter's behavior over time.
6. Despite the importance of party identification, the voting decisions of many Americans—and indeed their party identification as well—are heavily affected by psychological and group-membership factors.[13]

On several accounts, however, findings about the voter were often little more than discrete and hence mundane accumulations of census data. In his chapter on the profile of the American voter, Gerald Pomper takes exhaustive stock of research findings to refute two of his three models: the "philosophical citizen" and the "manipulated subject." [14] What is illuminating for our purpose is not the success or failure of his undertaking so much as the startling contradiction that he must risk in order to validate his third and final model, "the meddling citizen." [15]

Pomper counters the first model of the autonomous philosophical citizen by illustrating the cogent influence of reference groups—religious, ethnic, occupational—with the body of data that displays the demographic division of presidential preferences (see Table 1A). Also cited as a factor militating against autonomous decision making is pervasive party identification. However, in order to reject simultaneously the "manipulated subject" model in terms of individuality, Pomper is forced to conjure up the image of the "responsible electorate," [16] the effete influence emanating from group demands,[17] overlapping membership,[18] the very nature of the sociological categories,[19] and finally the varying extent of group influence from election to election.

His subsequent attempts to refute both models in terms of issue awareness and policy choices juxtapose two equally contradictory sets of findings.[20] What these attempts reveal is the limits imposed on Pomper's analysis by the almost exclusively social psychological approaches on which his summary depends. In other words, the paucity of an analytic schema in the studies with which he dealt critically curtailed his ability to leap from the mere presentation of mutually inconsistent data to adoption of the third model *in ways that are theoretically significant as well as empirically relevant.*

Thus when Pomper presents and validates his third model of the meddling citizen, the emerging characterization becomes at best anticlimactic and at worst useless.

The evidence of the voting studies confirms neither the theory of the philosophical citizen nor that of the manipulated subject. Voting is not an isolated act but neither is it fully determined by sociological membership or party identification. Voters do not have broad factual knowledge or an integrated ideology, but they do react to the parties in terms of the group benefits they provide and their records in office.[21]

Much conflict inevitably ensued between the aggregationists and the survey researchers. The former criticize the latter for their failure to acknowledge the limitations of an ahistorical and episodic method, and for their unwillingness to focus their attention upon matters of genuine substantive concern to students of politics.[22] "The survey researchers, on the other hand, insist that survey research alone can study the primary psychological and motivational building blocks out of which the political system itself is ultimately constructed."[23] Consequently the most recent literature on voting behavior attempts to view the voter and all levels of the political system in the context of mutually influencing components of the political universe.[24] The survey researchers seem to be paying increasing attention to the need to specify conditions under which a same set of certain characteristics of the voter may produce different partisan alignments. On the other hand, the students of the aggregate voting behavior "are turning to the data and methods of survey research to explore the structure and characteristics of contemporary public opinion. A convergence is clearly under way."[25] Likewise, Campbell et al. join this trend when they note that "this sort of commerce between survey and historical analysis is likely to be increasingly common."[26]

Objectives

Harry M. Scoble bemoans the lack of "a full description of what it is in fact that labor unions *do* in elections and ... systematic analysis of such activity" despite the importance for the American political party system of the entrance of organized labor into electoral activity.[27] Detailed reviews of the related literature are deferred to Chapter 2, but some illustrations of the references to which Scoble alludes are in order. On a more general level, there appear to be few empirical studies that either support or modify the traditionally accepted functions of interest groups in the American political process.[28] Closer to our concern is Scoble's criticism of both the poverty of and inconsistencies among the findings relating to the labor unions' political participation.[29] Scoble's admonition applies uniformly to the labor unions' relationship to (1) the national convention and legislative recruitment, (2) the party apparatus, (3) the financing of politics, and (4) the members in the electoral process. About this last area of inquiry, Scoble writes: "Labor unions have carried out registration drives and get-out-the-vote drives in both primary and general elections and have done everything else that a political party does. . . . At the level of description, facts abound; but *at the level of analysis knowledge remains fragmented, shadowy, and highly unsystematic.*" [30]

We suggest that the reasons underlying the inadequacies of past investigations may be found in three areas. First, the analytic approach to research on voting behavior is a relatively recent development and no concerted systematic effort has yet begun in this direction. Second, where an analysis is attempted, the investigator immediately begins with a simple convergence of or commerce between two levels of data and consequently leaves a great many lacunae in our understanding of American politics.[31] Change over time is a common trap. Much as some historians engage in a post hoc description and connection of events, so political scientists often force connectives and relationships out of their utilitarian sense of the current need.[32] Political implications that were drawn were largely open ended beyond any possible combination of analytic schema simply because their investigations did not begin with one such definitive constriction.[33] Nor did the social psychological approaches, as a rule, supply their own microlevel theories.[34]

Distinct trends and characters earmarked each school of scholars: the orientation to system stability and continuity on the part of the social psychologists[35] and to change and cycles on the part of the aggregate analysts.[36] Each school offers its own explanation of its roots. Although all involved recognize this difference and the need to minimize it, they seldom pursued mutual reliance *in terms of theory building.*

Finally, and perhaps most important, with the possible exception of model building,[37] the deductive approach from a theoretical foundation seldom materialized. Again, both sides have neglected theory. Empirical data were never used to test historical patterns that were delineated; empirical findings, on the other hand, were barely more than fragments of evidence to support an isolated hypothesis.

This last point best describes how past studies faltered, and it is particularly relevant to our objective—to study the voting behavior of labor union members and their families. For generalizations about the psychology and sociology of a group need to be investigated in the light of hypotheses that may be derived from a handful of both normative and empirical theories of the American political process, e.g., the group basis of American politics. It would indeed be a triviality if, for instance, findings about the impact of a reference group were separated from the system as a whole. Nor does simply merging the two levels accomplish the explanatory purpose. The data to generate the theory about the system do not exist; rather, they are assembled and catalogued in such a way as to account for the theory from which the entire undertaking begins.

Such a theory of labor union members' voting behavior—or, for that matter, the voting behavior of a member of any politically involved secondary group—would first require an analytic framework whose theoretical structure demands a unique taxonomy of related independent variables and then would predict the outcomes of their interaction with the voting behavior. The laws relating them must be developed or borrowed and assembled.[38]

Descriptions and variables are plentiful in the existing literature; equally fortunate for our purpose is an existing body of provocative theories attempting to explain the makeup of American politics. Our task is first to arrange the relevant empirical data in terms that are significant according to our theoretical structure, and second, to provide the linkage that suits our purpose.[39] Such an undertaking will lend some perspective to the existing literature, and the resulting arrangement of data will be important as well as interesting. More important, such an arrangement will produce a justifiable reinforcement for a prediction and an assertion based on it.

Summary

Three broad categories of inquiry are made in this study: how the labor union members and their families vote; why they vote the way they do; and, finally, the systemic implications of these findings for American politics. We do this in two ways. First, a theory of labor union voting behavior is carefully arrived at based on insights drawn from plural levels of inference and tested with evidence thought to be *generally* representative of American voters including labor union members and their families—the data from the presidential elections of 1952, 1956, 1960, and 1964. Near the end of this book, we test some concrete hypotheses deduced from our theory, using the election data from the presidential contests of 1968, 1972, and 1976, which both individually and collectively represent a period of more erratic and bewildering partisan behavior on the part of the masses.

In Chapter 2 we first reconstruct the historical pattern of the *organizational* involvement of labor unions and their leaders in American party politics. For this, we rely mainly on past studies that investigated the labor unions in politics and later as party apparatus. The second part of the chapter reviews research on the labor union members' voting behavior in order to summarize the empirically confirmed social psychological expectations.

Given the different historical periods of the unions' organizational affiliations on the one hand, and a set of behavioral expectations of the rank-and-file members in a peculiar group setting of different periods on the other, we will be able to list the individual political behavior (e.g., voting) consonant with both history and social psychology.

Chapter 3 introduces the theoretical structure underlying this study. Three different levels of thought [40] are described—speculative, organizational, and social psychological—with the focus on the nature of the relationship among status, class, economy, and polity in an industrialized society. In explaining the political behavior of an individual or a group, many social scientists have borrowed their analytic schemata from speculative (and often normative) schools of thought. We do essentially the same thing in an attempt to deduce a set of testable hypotheses from these thoughts. For example, we may pose questions such as the following: What portion of the Marxian class analysis successfully explains the persistence of economic factors influencing political choice? How is it inadequate to predict some of the noneconomic determinants? What modifications must be introduced, and from whose ideas?

For the historical perspectives, we return to the descriptive material in Chapter 2 to identify the expected correlates on the individual level. However, before we test the hypotheses deduced from these two levels of thought, we digress a bit to reexamine with our data the inadequacies of the economic explanation, in this case, the thesis of embourgeoisement. Does an explanation based on purely economic assumptions in fact fail to predict today's political behavior and change of the union members? If so, in what way and why?

We emphasize this last line of inquiry because we believe that those factors—in this case, the relative deprivation theory—contributing to the failure of the economic explanation not only explicitly suggest the ultimate understanding that we seek but further enable us to integrate all three classes of variables so that we can present a *theory* of labor union voting behavior.

In Chapter 4 we investigate the impact of the relation between union membership and political behavior. Our purpose is to specify the extent to which union membership can explain the variance in the presidential votes of the members. The results of the hypotheses tested are catalogued in such a way that they both meet the demand for descriptive data on the national scene[41] and suggest the areas in which temporal changes must be examined.

Change itself—i.e., whether changes have occurred—is the primary focus of Chapter 5. In this chapter we trace the origin and development of some of the empirical studies dealing with the thesis of embourgeoisement and actually test some of the related hypotheses with our data. We search the income measurement tools and their rationale in order to find reasons for the failure of the embourgoisement thesis. In Chapter 6 we investigate the remaining question on the direction of the change: What new or additional factors may be determinants of union voting behavior? In accounting for the particular direction of change, we return to the summary of the evidence in Chapter 5 to introduce the relative deprivation theory as it indirectly relates to our search for a theory.

To conclude the first set of inquiries, we ask: What is the systemic consequence for the two-party dominance of American politics implied by the changing interests of labor unions and their members? What specific meaning do these expanded areas of interest have for the alliance between the labor unions and different sectors of the American party world? What accommodations must the political parties make in order to adapt to the qualitatively different set of demands waged by a much wider and diversified constituency? These and other questions on the implications of our theory for the system will be our topic in Chapter 7.

Methods

The evidence for this study comes from the data on the presidential elections of 1952, 1956, 1960, and 1964 gathered by the Center for Political Studies of the University of Michigan.[42] The findings from these data in turn are compared with comparable portions of previous reports on union members' voting behavior.

Two separate formats of these data are used: (1) a single data set consisting of all four election data pyramided on sixty-seven variables that are present in each one of the four decks and (2) four separate bodies of data with their full inventory of variables originally included. The pyramided decks constitute the primary—not the exclusive—evidence for the analysis in Chapter 4, while the four individual data sets are used primarily for the inferences made in Chapters 5 and 6. For the causal inferences that we draw in Chapter 6, however, the merged deck is the most useful evidence. In the remainder of this section we shall limit our discussion to the rationale for this scope and arrangement of the evidence.

The *general* evidence chosen for this study comes from a period during which the political attitudes of the American electorate were relatively unstable *at a given election time;* however, we believe that the mean level of the voters' performance, viewed in the context of all four years as a period, approximates the normal standard.

The presidential contests of 1952 and 1956 are "deviating elections" [43] in which the basic partisan loyalties were not seriously disturbed but in which the short-term effect of attitude on the vote determined the outcome.[44] They were deviant in that they represented a temporary change in the period of long-term Democratic dominance.[45] The criterion used to classify elections is party identification, which is not subject to a radical shift except in a period of realignment [46] or in a "critical election." [47] This is important because all that a deviant election denotes for the Center's classification is the fact of deviation, not the extent. But by the extent of its deviation, the election of 1952 stands out as a "landslide" in which the American electorate expressed their lack of confidence in the previous administration and in which the decline in strength of the party in power also permeated most social, economic, and geographical divisions in a "spectacular fashion" [48] (see Table 2).

The peculiarities of the two elections in our data contrast with the characteristics of the elections of 1960 and 1964 which, according to the Center's standard, qualify as "reinstating elections." [49] In these presidential contests the normal pattern of party identification is restored by the electorate who reinstate the dominant party. By the twin standards of the electoral outcomes and the voters' movement across social economic classes, it may very well be that the 1964 election was a landslide.[50] The contrasts between the elections of 1952 and 1956 and those of 1960 and 1964 assure us of two general and useful groups of characteristics. First, viewing the voting behavior of the American electorate one election at a time brings out the social psychological and environmental factors that affected the individual decision for that election and made it unique. When the data for all four elections are merged, because of the assumptions given previously, they depict a *typical* (or general) American electorate during the post–New Deal period of Democratic dominance. The first group of character-

Table 2   Partisan divisions in presidential elections of 1948 and 1952 by income levels (In percentages)

	Voted			
	Republican	Democratic	Other	Did not vote
1952				
Under $2000	30	23	*	47
$2000–2999	36	31	1	32
$3000–3999	40	35	1	24
$4000–4999	41	41	1	17
$5000 and over	59	28	1	12
1948				
Under $2000	16	28	2	54
$2000–2999	17	38	6	39
$3000–3999	35	34	5	26
$4000–4999	36	33	6	25
$5000 and over	53	25	4	18

Source: Angus Campbell, et al., *The Voter Decides* (Evanston: Row, Peterson, 1954), p. 73.
*Less than 1 percent.

istics accentuates change over time while the latter supplies descriptive statistics about the American electorate.

On the statistical side, the rationale for the pyramided samples is more our need than its statistical soundness.[51] The hazards of using a small sample size to specify and elaborate an initial generalization are familiar to those who have had a modicum of dealings with quantitative analysis. When the population in question—labor union members—is a subsample in the first place, and when its compositional diversity necessitates even the simplest partition design to proceed at least two or three times to permit drawing a useful inference, the diminishing cell sizes make it all but impossible to say something significant about a group—for example, young residents in the West who are unskilled industrial union members. With each additional control variable, the problem grows increasingly insoluble.

Not only the problem of inference but that of the sampling error limits any meaningful operation on a small sample. Sampling error is not uniform across all variables, and when the interaction between two or more variables must be made, the compounded sampling error may become prohibitive. Increasing the total sample size reduces the sampling error as well.

However, a mere increase in the size of the sample, in this case by the pyramiding technique, does not automatically insure a sound statistical basis for inference because the law of large numbers is predicated on repeated random sampling and hence independent selection of samples—both individual sampling units and group sampling units.[52] Our data violate these requirements somewhat. For example, since the samples for the 1956 and 1960 elections were for a panel design, they were not independently selected; nor is the total sample a strict EPSEM sample.[53] The Center's data for the national presidential elections are selected through a multistage process—that is, we first divide them geographically, then stratify them according to social and economic characteristics, and finally determine clusters within these geographical, stratified samples.[54] As a result, it would be incorrect to claim that the benefits accruing from the increased sample size are proportionate to the increase factor.

Some of these limitations may not be detrimental if pyramiding is performed on variables that remain relatively immune to such short-term factors as campaigns, candidates, and issues. Thus there is cogent reason to believe that some of the variables reflecting social psychological dimensions of the voter are more stable than those representing temporally unique responses to ephemeral environmental variables. Examples of these stable variables include party identification, religious affiliation, sense of political efficacy, feelings of citizen duty, political participation, and attentiveness to mass media. If the temporal, environmental factors such as candidates or campaigns bring out these latent elements, they have more to do with eliciting than determining these latent elements. In addition there are variables that represent dimensions embedded in one's life cycle and which are relatively more stable—number of children, marital status, age, level of education.

Particularly in our case, we believe that aggregation presents fewer risks than usual since we treat the samples from different election years as distinct units when we are interested in the dimensions of change. Thus when we ask about the change due to short-term forces as they vary from election to election for votes in different income categories, we measure the change in each of the four years and compare the results. Even where changes occur conspicuously in a given variable over a period of time, aggregation will not prove harmful if the changes are monotonic.

In the remainder of this book, we test some of the central themes in our theory against the presidential elections of 1968, 1972, and 1976. The results should be both substantively interesting from the perspective of American partisan politics and theoretically important in view of our theory verified for the previous four elections. At this writing, however, the 1976 election data from the Center for Political Studies have not been made available. As a result, our analysis of the 1976 election is intended as speculation about future union voting behavior.

Ever since American labor unions came into existence, many studies have concentrated on the unions' political role. Most historical approaches to this question concern the *external* aspect, that is, the political impact of labor unions in terms of their organization (and hence leadership) affiliations. On the other hand, a few social scientists have recently examined the way in which the organizational activities of local unions influence the political orientation and behavior of their members.

In this chapter we will deal with both topics: first, the pattern of the unions' organizational involvement in American national politics since the turn of the century, and second, some of the results from the voting behavior studies on the members of various local labor unions and their families. Our purpose is simply to identify two of the sources from which we will infer concrete hypotheses in Chapter 3.

Organized Labor in National Politics: 1906–1964 [1]

One of the most visible and permanent changes resulting from industrialization in the late nineteenth and the early twentieth century was the sheer growth of the industrial labor force—from 29 million in 1900 to 53 million some forty years later, an increase of about 85 percent.[2] Without property or capital, this massive new class found itself largely at the mercy of the entrepreneurial community and the plutocracy. For them, organized collective action was the only channel of expression.

The general condition for the rise of the laboring class was not entirely unfavorable, however.

The American industrial laboring class emerged in an ideological climate superficially hospitable to political action. Doctrines of political equality and of the right of self-government seemed to pave the way for the new toiling masses to grasp power and to mold the state to suit their wishes. Moreover, while American workers were increasing in number, socialist ideas were blossoming around the globe. Heady doctrines were being proclaimed: workers should unite and take what was justly theirs. Furthermore, if they merged the ideas of socialism and democracy, they would not have to take what they wanted—all they had to do was to vote for it. He who would understand politics in the large may ponder well the status of labor: a numerically great force in a society adhering to the doctrine of the rule of numbers, yet without proportionate durable political power as a class.[3]

The ups and downs of the American labor unions in national politics from the early 1900s to the 1960s can be traced through five distinct stages:

(1) the pre-1906 period, (2) 1906–1922, (3) 1922–1928, (4) 1928–1955, and (5) 1955–1964.

Until the turn of the century, the policies of American unions on national politics conformed closely to the doctrine of laissez-faire. This conservative stand resulted both from environmental factors that hampered the growth of the labor movement itself and from deliberate actions undertaken by the union leadership to preserve the mutual neutrality of labor and politics.

According to some, one of the most formidable obstacles to labor's collective action was the conspicuous absence of a European class consciousness among the working class in America.

That American unions have appreciated the full gravity of this problem [of organization] ... is shown by several practices, which they have carried to a much further extent than unionists in other countries. It would seem as though, through these practices, they have tried to make up for the lack of a spontaneous class solidarity, upon which European unions could always reckon with certainty. These practices are ways of ruthlessly suppressing "dual" unions and "outlaw" strikes.[4]

A plethora of reasons have been offered for this absence: interclass mobility;[5] the dominant myth of unlimited opportunity associated with the availability of free land and with the lack of inherited feudal institutions and class separations;[6] the steady stream of immigrants who made themselves available for the more menial tasks in the labor force; the generally rising level of income among laborers, owing to labor shortages during this era;[7] the ethnic and racial heterogeneity of the American workers;[8] and universal white male suffrage which eliminated a source of political alienation.[9]

In addition, the solidarity and effectiveness of labor's activity was slowed by the imposing strength and hostility of private property. The threat that labor unions' incompatible objectives posed to the propertied class inhibited labor's cohesion.[10]

Employers in no other country, with the possible exception of those in the metal and machine trades of France, have so persistently, so vigorously, at such costs, and with such a conviction of serving a cause opposed and fought trade unions as the American employing class. In no other Western country have employers been so much aided in their opposition to unions by civil authorities, the armed forces of government and their courts.[11]

Governmental antiunion measures were administered on all levels—state, local, and federal [12]—and took such diverse forms as court injunctions, executive interventions, and congressional apathy.[13] In turn, this plutocratic repression of the late nineteenth and the early twentieth century rendered a sense of legitimacy to the antiunion attitudes of the property class and hence further dampened any significant labor movement on a wide scale. This inevitably insured relative isolation of the early labor unions from the political arena.

If labor's posture of political neutrality was an imposed one—largely to leash some of the rebellious rank-and-file membership—neutrality could not have been more suited to the deliberate designs of some of the labor leadership. In other words, the illusion of "voluntarism" and preoccupation with organizational survival on the part of the labor leaders[14] as well as their failure to define and articulate specific political objectives accounted for much of their separation from the partisan politics. To them, the key to an effective organizational strategy that both maximizes the possibility of achieving their goals and insures their survival was labor's strict separation from politics. What was clear was the central voluntarist tenet to oppose "all compulsion and paternalism either by government in economic life or by the [union] with regard to the affairs of its affiliates." [15]

This doctrine of laissez-faire was understandable given the hostile and inhibitive governmental interventions. The message was clear: "Let the state leave labor alone; it would care for itself through organization, collective bargaining, and the strike." [16] The activities of the state invariably compete for union members' allegiance "such as protection for collective bargaining, medical insurance, minimum-wage and maximum-hour laws (for privately employed adult males), and unemployment insurance." [17] Often they were viewed as outright antiunion measures. Thus Gompers' justification of his opposition to most social-insurance programs was that they coerced workers under "a special bureaucratic administration—not contemplated under a government made up of free and equal citizens." [18]

Neutrality has proved a persistent theme to this day. It is not uncommon to hear about the virtues of nonpartisanship on the part of union organizations.[19] Even when union activities tangentially concerned politics before 1906, they were largely negative legislative activities. Unions simply demanded that the states cease their intervention so that they might freely encounter and fight employers on more equal terms.[20] Frequently, they would ask for restrictions on competing sources of labor such as immigration, the repeal of contract prison labor, or the abolition of the track system of wage payment. In addition, they called for "a mechanics' lien law which would give a worker a prior lien upon property for the payment of wages, the repeal of conspiracy laws . . . and the enforcement of sanitary laws in mines and factories." [21]

The political results of all these were predictable. While the American Federation of Labor occasionally expressed concern for political problems,

there was considerable hesitation when it bordered on political entangle-
ment. In 1881 a number of delegates to the first AFL convention resisted
even the discussion of political questions. In 1886 the first convention of
the reorganized federation endorsed independent political action, although
the idea of organizing a third party was summarily rejected.[22] Thus
"Gompers always argued that the worker should be concerned with politics and legislation," but he wanted no explicit partisan affiliations.[23] Political awareness and involvement were desirable; partisan loyalty was
prohibited. Section 8, Article IV of the AFL's constitution under Gompers
decreed that "party politics, whether they be Democratic, Republican, So-
cialistic, populistic, prohibition, or any other, should have no place in the
convention of the American Federation of Labor." [24]

Much of this laissez-faire doctrine has been attributed to the dominant
role that the building trades played in the formation of the AFL policies,[25]
to the leaders' determination to resist the attempts by leaders of ideological
movements to capture the union, and, finally, to the influence of the Roman
Catholic clergy.[26]

With its 1906 promulgation of the historic "nonpartisan" policy of re-
warding its friends and punishing its enemies, the AFL took a markedly
different course of political activism—that of favoring one party over the
other in an election or on issues. The immediate stimulus for this decision
was congressional apathy to labor's "Bill of Grievances," an inventory of
labor legislation and political–economic reforms pursued by the AFL.[27]
However, more fundamental impetus for this shift came both from the external environment and the internal change within the AFL.

When governmental regulation of railroad rates became inevitable as
the industry occupied a strategically important position in nonprivate sectors of the national economy, its impact on the workers' wage structure
left the railroad brotherhoods (both independent of and affiliated with the
AFL) little choice but greater political involvement.[28] Further, the hostility
of the railroads after World War I forced employees to rely on methods
more powerful than economic power and organizational front.[29]

The sheer growth of the AFL was another decisive factor.[30] It meant that
organizational survival was less a threat and that its members' voting power
could be used as leverage to gain allies in national politics. What persistent
governmental hostility there was—e.g., the courts' antistrike injunctions—
justified their political alignment that much more (Table 3).[31]

The important point here is that the labor community as a whole began
to see the limits of purely economic channels of solution and started in
earnest to forge the connection between politics and economy. At the mini-
mum level, therefore, the labor unions sought much broader legislative

goals: hour legislation for women, wage and hour legislation for government workers, child labor laws, old age pensions, women's suffrage, direct
election of senators, a public works program, nationalization of communication industries, and governmental ownership of public works and util-
ities.[32] Thus:

In spite of what appeared to some as overcautious leadership, by virtue of
certain phases of its program the Federation was a part of the progressive
forces of the country. It supported movements for democratic reform and was
an ally of the farmers and liberal middle class. It was affiliated with the International Federation of Trade Unions in token of its declared faith in the
brotherhood of the workers of all lands and in the cause of peace between
nations. To many observers the Federation seemed on the threshold of a new
era of development along industrial and social lines when the World War
broke.[33]

However, labor's political activism was much more than an intensified
version of the earlier nonpartisan political involvement. In 1908, when
labor's legislative programs[34] met with an unfriendly reception by the
Republican party, Gompers decided to support the Democratic presidential candidacy of Bryan.[35] Thus "the 1906 election set a pattern that, with
variations from election to election, continued until at least 1922." [36] The
Democratic endorsement was never an official stand expressed by the AFL
convention, but the message was unmistakable.[37]

The other side of labor's partisan activities took distinct and significant
forms of campaign techniques: printing political editorials, organizing
speaking tours, distributing campaign literature.[38] In the late 1910s, however, the external political and economic climate slowly began to change.
Democratic leaning toward conservative politics dampened labor's enthu-
siasm for them. This decline of labor's courtship with the Democratic party
culminated in labor's outright rejection of the 1920 Democratic platform
which expressed friendship to the business community more than any other
sector.[39]

Weakened by their political allies, the unions were further seriously
threatened by adverse court decisions during this period. The court decisions rendered during the relatively short period from 1917 to 1922 testify
to the grave setbacks that labor was experiencing. In 1917, for example,
two decisions severely restricted labor's strike activities.[40] After 1919 the
courts intensified their antiunion decisions even more. The second child
labor law of 1919 was declared invalid;[41] in 1921 picketing was virtually
barred as a legitimate labor activity unless carried out under conditions so
narrowly specified as to greatly dilute its political effectiveness.[42] During

Table 3   Reported average membership of the American Federation of Labor 1897–1906

| Year | Average annual membership | Increase or decrease over preceding year | |
		Membership	Percentage
1897	264,825	—	—
1898	278,016	+ 13,191	+ 5.0
1899	349,422	+ 71,406	+25.7
1900	548,321	+198,899	+56.9
1901	787,537	+239,216	+43.6
1902	1,024,399	+236,862	+30.1
1903	1,465,800	+441,401	+43.1
1904	1,676,200	+210,400	+14.4
1905	1,494,300	−181,900	−10.9
1906	1,454,200	− 40,100	− 2.7

Source: Report of the Proceedings of the Fifty-Second Annual Convention of the American Federation of Labor, 1932, in Lewis L. Lorwin, *The American Federation of Labor* (Washington, D.C.: The Brookings Institution, 1933), p. 484.

Table 4   Reported average membership of the American Federation of Labor 1920 -1932

| Year | Average annual membership | Increase or decrease over preceding year | |
		Membership	Percentage
1920	4,078,740	+818,672	+25.1
1921	3,906,528	−172,212	− 4.2
1922	3,195,635	−710,893	−18.2
1923	2,926,468	−269,167	− 8.4
1924	2,865,799	− 60,669	− 2.1
1925	2,877,297	+ 11,498	+ 0.4
1926	2,803,966	− 73,331	− 2.5
1927	2,812,526	+ 8,560	+ 0.3
1928	2,896,063	+ 83,537	+ 3.0
1929	2,933,545	+ 37,482	+ 1.3
1930	2,961,096	+ 27,551	+ 0.9
1931	2,889,550	− 71,546	− 2.4
1932	2,532,261	−357,289	−12.4

Source: Report of the Proceedings of the Fifty-Second Annual Convention of the American Federation of Labor, 1932, in Lewis L. Lorwin, *The American Federation of Labor* (Washington, D.C.: The Brookings Institution, 1933), p. 484.

the 1920s case after case presented the labor community with an increasing menace of injunctions.[43]

In addition, employers' campaigns to vie for employee loyalty accompanied their expanded antiunion strategies and again threatened the power of the union as the protector of the laboring class. "Later in the decade management began to compete for worker loyalty through welfare capitalist plans like grievance procedures, health and safety programs, employees' stock purchases and company unions." [44] To make matters worse, the Republican triumph in the presidential race all but sealed any hope for an immediate remedy.

Internally the unions (the AFL, for example) were experiencing a crisis (Table 4). The sharp decline in membership was accompanied by an increased level of homogeneity:

... the Federation became more homogeneous in spirit than it had ever been before. Conservatives, progressives, and socialists within the Federation were drawn more closely together to combat the communists and "left-wingers." At the conventions of 1923–24 there were no contests for office. In other ways, too, the 1924 convention showed a harmony which appeared to many as listlessness. There were no extended debates and not a single roll-call. The turbulent era which began with the World War was coming to an end.[45]

Consequently, the broadened progressive political goals that labor once pursued were replaced by a revived economic voluntarism which redefined the union essentially as an agency for economic ends—distinct from political goals—and reemphasized the need for cooperation and harmony between capital and labor.[46]

An all too familiar extension of this outlook was the increasing emphasis by the AFL on nonpartisanship. Taft observed:

Differences between the American Federation of Labor and the railroad unions over political action were on the increase. The American Federation of Labor, while entertaining no illusions about the real attitude of members of Congress to organized labor, approached political questions largely from the historical and pragmatic points of view. The railroad unions believed that they, more than the rest of the labor movement, had a tremendous stake in the kind of administration in control of the government. To a greater extent than perhaps other industries, their members were at this time subject to government regulation and control. Consequently, they sought to devise methods by which they could exercise more direct influence upon Congressional opinion and Congressional action.[47]

Viewing their function largely as that of negotiating with the two major parties, labor leaders in the Non-Partisan Political Company Committee appeared before both the Democratic and Republican parties to present their case,[48] a move that did not diminish their sense of alienation from both parties. In 1924, at the AFL's Executive Council meeting to determine a policy for the presidential campaign, Gompers delivered a vitriolic criticism of the Democratic and Republican platforms as well as the candidates. He went one step further to lead the AFL to endorse La Follette's independent candidacy.

I was against them [John W. Davis and Calvin Coolidge] and made up my mind if it takes the last bit of energy. I have to put it in the campaign for La Follette. The situation is entirely different from the previous campaigns. Here we have practically no choice, one is no nearer to us than the other. You look at the platforms of 1908, 1919, 1916 and you will find nothing in any of them in the platforms of 1924. The Republican convention, they have got hold of the boodle and where they cannot make excuses they have not said a thing. The Democrats say they want honesty. There must be something more than honesty—something more than an indictment of crooks. Here is something where we may help. It is at least a protest and perhaps something better.[49]

It was a brief flirtation; more than that, it was a reaction to the apathy of the two major parties and not an active endorsement of a third party. To prevent any significant schism from developing internally, the Executive Council had to emphasize that its approval of the records of the independent candidates was in no way a formal endorsement of an independent party movement or a third party, adding that it could not be "so construed as support for such a party group or movement, except as such action accords with our non-partisan policy." [50]

The brief strain in the labor–Democratic relationship lasted only until the 1928 election, in which several important issue areas served as a basis for electoral realignment. Al Smith's candidacy as a Catholic helped to introduce an ethnic electoral alignment on an unprecedented scale; his stand on prohibition and his origin as "a child of the streets of New York" successfully pitted urban voters against rural residents and Catholic followers against Protestant skeptics who did not believe that the Vatican would not dominate the White House. In the words of the opposing candidate, the new cleavage represented a division between "the growing left-wing movement, embracing many of the 'intelligentsia'" and "the American system, as opposed to all forms of collectivism." [51]

V. O. Key's study of the aggregate data of the 1928 election confirms the demographic characteristics of this new alignment. His study of the voting pattern of twenty-nine towns and cities having the sharpest Democratic increases, 1920–1928, and that of the thirty towns and cities having the most marked Democratic loss, 1920–1928, revealed the expected differences.[52] "Urban, industrial, foreign-born, Catholic areas made up the bulk of the first group of towns, although an occasional rural Catholic community increased its Democratic vote markedly. The towns with a contrary movement tended to be rural, Protestant, native-born. The new Democratic vote correlated quite closely with a 1930 vote on state enforcement of the national prohibition law. . . ." [53] Key noted that the great reshuffling of voters in the 1928 election was perhaps the final stage in a process that had been under way for some time (Figure 1).

Later research based on detailed data showed that Key's hunch was essentially correct. MacRae's principal component analysis on the aggregate election data[54] from 1888–1958 showed that in both 1896 and 1928 a "critical election" was but a manifestation of the general trend of a "critical period" and that "third party votes have functioned as a 'half-way house' in transitions of voters between the two major parties." [55]

The La Follette campaign in 1924, which the AFL had explicitly supported, contributed significantly to the erosion of Republican support. More significant perhaps, the AFL's unofficial and fluctuating support for the Democrats from 1906 onward appears to have anticipated at the institutional or organizational level a parallel development in the electorate, that is, the massive reorientation of partisan attitudes, which had begun at least in 1922. In other words, trade unions as organizations began to shift to the Democrats in 1906 much as individual workers began to shift in the early 1920s.[56]

When the New Deal era arrived, many notable changes occurred both within the labor community and in the relationship between labor and government. Of all the changes, Milton Derber observed:

Perhaps the most significant aspect of the labor movement in the New Deal period was its growth and expansion. At the height of national prosperity in 1929, union membership was estimated at only about 3.4 million. This represented an estimated decline of about 1.7 million from the post World War I peak, and was the first extended period in which union membership had failed to advance during a time of general economic prosperity. With the onset of the Great Depression, union membership fell further, to a point below 3 million in 1933. By 1939, however, the membership was estimated at over 8 million, and the stage was set for a doubling of this figure in the sixteen war and postwar years which followed.[57]

Four million of these members belonged to the newly founded Committee of Industrial Organization.[58]

Equally important was the distribution of new union membership. Although initial growth was most marked in the mining communities[59]

Figure 1 Persistence of electoral cleavage of 1928 in Massachusetts: mean Democratic percentage of presidential vote in towns with sharpest Democratic gains, 1920–1928. (From V. O. Key, Jr., "A Theory of Critical Elections," in Donald G. Herzberg and Gerald M. Pomper, *American Party Politics* (New York: Holt, Rinehart and Winston, 1967), p. 426.

Percent

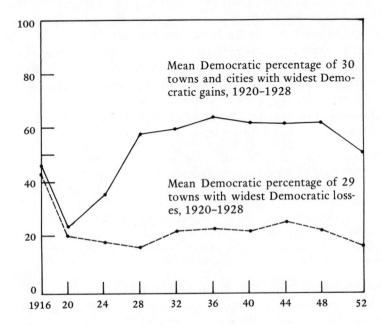

and among garment workers,[60] the most phenomenal movement by far was the unionization of "factory workers, service workers, and other groups which had previously been outside union ranks." [61] It was apparently a spontaneous reaction to the depression and an inevitable outcome of the increasing class consciousness, waning confidence in employers, and abundant grievances.[62] The rise of unionism in the large mass-production industries as well as in trucking, maritime, mining, and other nonmanufacturing industries tended to inculcate members' consciousness which transcended the traditional craft–noncraft classification and introduced a broadened basis for their membership—the common status of wage earners. Thus ethnic barriers were reduced. Instead, a noticeable geographical pattern of the membership emerged: the urban areas of the Northeast, the Pacific coast, and the Midwest rather than the traditional strongholds of the AFL in small towns and cities.[63]

Over the long term, the structural transformation of the American labor unions, especially the CIO, has broadened the traditional AFL concern for narrow job unionism and its preoccupation with *economic* improvement through economic means—bargaining, strikes, and the like.

Giant corporations could not so readily be coerced by the strike and threat of strike as could the smaller employers with whom AFL unions had characteristically dealt. . . . In its concern with legislation of general interest to workers, the CIO introduced a range and intensity of activities alien to the AFL. The younger CIO leadership, liberally sprinkled with intellectuals, attempted far more to improve the status of the working class generally by legislation than did the old-time leadership of the AFL. The CIO, in fact, came to be interested in about every major government policy: budgets, foreign trade, the level of domestic investment, the rate of interest—these and other matters affect the health of the economy and the CIO worried about all of them.[64]

The militancy of the CIO was a direct product of the entire New Deal period. What Perlman refers to as "dynamic job consciousness" was acutely intensified at this time.[65] With 25 percent of the entire work force unemployed in 1932 and workers receiving low wages for seven-day work weeks,[66] the whole labor movement was much more vulnerable to radical leadership[67] whose leverage thrived on the endless spiral of strikes and the growing sense of class solidarity.[68]

The growth of the workers' sector of the American electorate, whose outward solidarity seemed intensely class conscious, was such a lure to vote-seeking politicians[69] that one scholar virtually dismisses any discernible *organizational* influence of the unions on New Deal labor policies. Instead, any New Deal sensitivity to labor interests is attributed to the vote power of the workers seeking an identical political palliative.[70]

Whatever their motive, the New Deal's Democratic administration concentrated on assistance programs for lower-income groups and wage earners. These included work relief programs, income tax reform, social insurance system, old age pension and unemployment compensations, public housing for the low-income groups, low-cost public power, federal reserve and its guarantee of small banking accounts, and protection for home owners.[71]

The labor organizations, on the other hand, were at once enticing and responding to the New Deal government by politically institutionalizing their resources for the Democratic party.[72] The AFL's support for Roosevelt's reelection in 1936 went much further than Gompers' "nonpartisan" political activities. Under the initiative of the CIO leadership, the AFL actively participated in the campaign through Labor's Non-Partisan League.[73] Voter mobilization became especially lively in such industrial states as New York, Illinois, Pennsylvania, and Ohio, but this time labor did not limit its efforts to union members alone.[74] Large-scale financial contributions added impetus for a liberal platform.[75]

Labor's partisan role developed steadily and gained intensity especially in the mid 1940s.[76] Labor's campaigning in the 1944 and 1948 elections marked its full-fledged entry into the national party system as a Democratic campaign organization, and this working relationship peaked in the first half of the 1960s during the first six years of the Kennedy–Johnson administrations.[77]

Labor's all-out organizational affiliation involved two related phenomena: the AFL's abandonment of laissez-faire and its subsequent shift left, and the CIO's decline of militancy with its shift to the center of the political spectrum, until the organizational merge of the AFL–CIO in 1955. Commenting on the "slowing dynamo" of the New Deal in terms of the CIO's diminishing activism Samuel Lubell writes:

The same photographs of Franklin Roosevelt and Frank Murphy hung on the wall but it was hard to believe that it was the same place. When I first visited Chrysler Local Seven of the United Automobile Workers a few days after Roosevelt's third term victory, the scene was one of belligerent activity. Bulletin boards bristled with photographs of police clubbing strikers and of tear gas riotings. When the union's educational director heard that I was analyzing the election for the *Saturday Evening Post,* he stiffened suspiciously and seemed about to have me thrown out. Then, he began boasting freely of how class conscious the auto workers were and how ready they were to vote for Roosevelt a fourth or a fifth term. He wore a lumber jacket. With his feet on his desk and a buzzer by his hand, he looked the very picture of newly arrived power.

Returning eight years later, after Truman's victory, the whole atmosphere of the local had changed. The strike photographs had come down from the bulletin boards and had been replaced by idyllic snapshots of the union's annual outings and sporting events. An honor roll listed fifty-nine union members who had been killed in the war. Nearby stood a cabinet filled with loving cups and other trophies won in city-wide UAW tournaments. The "class-conscious" educational director was gone—ousted in the UAW-wide fight against Communists which Walter Reuther led. On their desks, the new officers had propped the slogan, "UAW Americanism for Us." They were wearing green jackets and green silk legion caps.

In 1940 the flavor of the local was one of street barricades and sit-down strikes; eight years later it was almost like a lodge hall.[78]

Some interpreted this erosion of the New Deal militancy as a crisis in the labor movement, particularly when the disturbing membership decline became quite obvious in the late 1950s.[79] Others have pointed out the resilience of organized labor and its ability to withstand open challenges. On the basis of his evidence on occupational recomposition and automation, Philip Taft concludes that "the American labor movement with all its defects and limitations fights harder, better, and more successfully than any in the world." [80]

To be sure, whether a crisis in fact exists has not yet been satisfactorily determined. The two most often cited reasons for the alleged crisis are the lack of class consciousness and the decline of militancy on the one hand, and the so-called embourgeoisement of American labor on the other. The truth or falsity of such an observation must be empirically established. Further, we must determine how labor's political organizations and the membership's political attitudes are related to one another at a given time.

The need for such an empirical undertaking is especially acute because those who have studied the organizational pattern of labor's partisanship on the leadership level tell us that the labor–Democratic partnership peaked in the 1960s. They point to the AFL-CIO's first formal endorsement of the candidacy of Adlai Stevenson in 1952;[81] they exhibit their stepped-up voter mobilization effort, especially in recent times;[82] and they show the impressive financing record of American labor in the electoral arena (Table 5).

Labor's campaign expenditures increased about six times between 1956 and 1968, approximately 4 percent of the total national spending. Most importantly for our purpose, labor's contribution to the 1968 election doubled since 1956 in labor's percentage of the Democratic total spending —from approximately 30 percent in 1956 to almost 60 percent in 1968.[83]

Studies of Labor Union Voting Behavior

To date, a handful of studies have been conducted on union members'
voting behavior as it is influenced by their group membership.[84] All these
studies either implicitly or explicitly borrow their analytic schema from
the now-familiar application of the secondary reference group theory to
the political attitudes of the group members.[85] Briefly, the model is represented by a triad of relationships among (1) individual members, (2)
secondary groups that they either belong to or identify with, and (3) the
political world. Research questions are, therefore, largely concerned with
the relationship between combinations of these components. Most of the
findings defy a generalized pattern of relationship on a given level.

For example, the degree to which union members identify with their
union in general is not quite clear. One consensus appears to be that the
temporal variation of the level of identification is not in general extremely
strong. A study of the United Auto Workers in Detroit in the 1952 election
included a "Union Attachment Rating," a scale designed to measure the
members' identification with the union.[86] A little over one-third of the
members were strongly attached, while 21 percent were in the weak identification category. Joel Seidman and others found a similar result in their
survey of a local union and added that "the membership as a whole gives
support to the local at critical times, but otherwise shows little active
interest in union affairs." [87]

Some exceptions of strong identification were found among coal miners,
the Teamsters, the Packing House Workers, the Garment Makers Union,
and among unions of craftsmen such as printers and plumbers. An average
coal miner's strong identification was explained in the following way:

For most of the miners unionism was a normal and natural part of the environment in which they grew up, an institution to be accepted and identified
with in almost the way that one's church is accepted. Loyalty to the union
developed much as did loyalty to one's country, as a result of accepting and
internalizing the standards of behavior, the values and ideals, to which one is
exposed in one's family and community.[88]

There seems to be fairly consistent variation in the members' identification from place to place and from union to union. Strongly identified
members account for anywhere from 25 percent to 35 percent of the
membership while the weak identifiers range from 20 percent to 30 percent, the largest number of members occupying the middle category.

The members' perception of the degree to which the union as an organization is related to politics also varies. Newer unions such as those in

the CIO, as expected, generally have a much higher percentage of members who believe the union does have political interests. For example, a large number of the UAW members in the Detroit study recognized the relationship.[89] Moreover, unionists said, four to one, that they would trust the recommendations of the union leadership on voting matters. This finding was confirmed by Sheppard and Masters in their follow-up study of UAW members in theDetroit area for the 1956 election.

A majority . . . indicate that they (a) trust the voting recommendations of labor groups; (b) believe that labor should be accorded more influence in government; (c) think that it is permissible for labor to endorse candidates; and (d) are members of the Democratic party or Independent with Democratic leanings.[90]

However, the "business union" mentality still exists in many unions. Sidney Lens writes:

The plain fact is that the average worker does not see very clearly the connection between politics and his union. When his leaders call on him to strike he sees immediate advantages—higher wages, improved working conditions. When they call on him to support Truman or Dewey or Eisenhower . . . or some local politician, he does not see how the candidate's election affects his living conditions, except in a nebulous way.[91]

One important way in which those members recognize the connection between unions and politics concerns the scope of the political issue in which they perceive that the union's activities are related to politics. If they see the union's political connections with economic issues (or job related issues), then they are most likely to recognize the union's concern over the social issues (or issues that are not exclusively related to jobs and working conditions) as well. This "extension" of labor's political affiliation seems to be increasing, although the rate of expansion and intensity of the social concerns vary with personal circumstances.[92]

What about the union's internal communication pattern? Factors cited as inhibitors of an effective communication system are lack of leadership involvement in the process (paucity of union literature on a given political issue or election); unclear cues from the leadership (an overt sign of divided leadership on an issue or election); and receptivity of the members as a function of their initial low level of involvement and their membership in other secondary groups.

There seems to be a consensus on the increased organizational effort to mobilize not only union members but also the general electorate. Accompanying this, recent findings reveal that union members rate union literature as a major source of information and trust it more than any of the other mass media.[93]

On the question of the solidarity of political attitudes among the union leadership, studies of pre-1960 elections show varying degrees of internal schism with regard to candidate support. Among the more recent examples are the abortive attempt by John L. Lewis to support Wilkie in the 1940 election and the departure of the Teamsters Union from Green of the AFL in 1948.

Even clear cues must be heard in order to produce any effect. But what evidence exists in this regard demonstrates the propensity of earlier union members not to hear their leaders. Despite an active campaign on a major issue by the leaders of a union, a dismally low proportion of members mentioned even hearing of it.[94] The proportion declined sharply as the salience of the issues dropped. Seidman and others reported similar results from their Chicago study. They concluded that "political activity as the union carried on was largely undertaken by leaders and active members leaving the 95 percent or more of inactive members uninvolved and almost completely untouched." [95]

A union member's "overlapping membership" is one of the most important influences on his political attitude. Many union members belong to various groups outside their union. Jack Kroll, the first director of the PAC, expressed the problem that his organization faced when he noted: "Labor union members are also church members. They belong to athletic clubs, to social organizations, to ethnic groups. They are subject to diverse social pressures, many of them much stronger than the pressure of the union." [96] Calkins attributes the failure of the PAC effort in the Ohio election of 1950 to overlapping membership.

The average Ohio CIO member lived in the same political environment as his non-union neighbor. He was often subject to their vague fear of Communism with no precise definition of that term. He held their suspicions about all authorities whether they were factory bosses, political bosses, or labor bosses.[97]

Varying degrees of systematic differences in the members' political attitudes surfaced, depending on their extraunion group membership and the sociological categories to which they belong—social class, income, education.

According to most of the literature, party identification represents one of the most powerful barriers to vote manipulation. Bernstein in 1941 recognized this as a major factor in the failure of John L. Lewis to sway the votes of the CIO when he commented, "No last minute effort, even one so dramatic as that of Lewis, can basically change these voting habits." [98] Berelson and others reached the same conclusion:

Many union men were themselves registered Republicans; in fact, there were as many registered Republicans as Democrats among labor leaders in Elmira. For labor to team up with the Democratic party organization would immediately have antagonized important elements in Elmira unions.[99]

Joseph Rosenfarb summed up the situation well when he noted:

Men live by symbols. In politics these are called party labels. If labor wants to muster mass support, it cannot keep shifting that mass from one party to the other. The inertia is too great. Labor's voters, no less than others, need conditioning symbols.[100]

Summary and Conclusion

A brief perusal of the descriptive literature dealing with the history of labor's involvement in national politics led to the identification of five distinct periods in the history of the labor movement. Among the conditions that affected the degree of the unions' partisan involvement were external political and economic factors and internal pressures due to the size and composition of the membership (Figure 2).

For our purpose, the most important thesis arising from this historical observation is this: There is a very strong relationship between the breadth of issues with which the labor organization is concerned at a given time and the extent to which the labor unions function as an electoral organization *within* the Democratic party. Thus, as unions became a campaign apparatus of the Democratic party, especially after the AFL-CIO merger in the mid 1950s, their political activities were aimed at a far broader constituency than union members. Consequently, the union leaders' support for social issues not directly related to jobs is construed as an outcome of labor's *organizational* partnership with the Democratic party and broadened constituency.

Empirical studies of the union members' voting behavior show variation in the members' political behavior from union to union and from place to place. All these investigations seem to rest on an analytic schema of a triad —the union members, the union, and the political world. However, while the variation of political behavior exists, a systematic description of this variation was wanting for understandable reasons.[101] More importantly, since these attempts are largely ahistorical, they unfortunately fail to interpret the individual's attitudes in a group setting defined at a given historical juncture. For example, a question that could have been investigated would concern not only degrees of issue awareness among the members—with the

Table 5   Campaign financing 1956–1968

	1956	1960	1964	1968
Democratic committees				
Total spending	$6,492,634	$11,800,979	$13,348,791	$13,577,715
Democratic percentage of national spending	29.2	42.0	34.6	21.6
Labor committees				
Expenditures	$1,805,482	$2,450,944	$3,816,242	$7,631,868
Labor percentage of national spending	8.1	8.7	9.9	12.2

Source:*Congresssional Quaterly* 27 (Dec. 5, 1969), p. 2435. For a breakdown of labor contributions into individual labor groups see also pp. 2457-2459.

Figure 2   Historical pattern of labor's partisan involvement

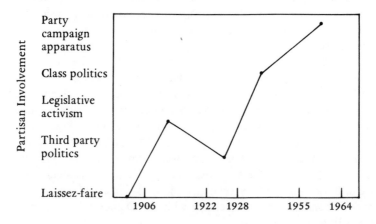

continuum of their union identification as an independent variable—but the kind of issues that most influence their voting decisions.

Similarly, historical studies would have examined the underlying reasons for the members' political attitudes. The studies too often seem to neglect psychological and sociological factors that contribute to a certain relationship. If individual voting behavior can be interpreted in a historical context which defines the group interest at that particular time, then it may be far easier to make a predictive statement of systemic importance. It is, in other words, the connection between levels of analysis that is lacking from both the historical literature and the empirical studies. Our national election data will be analyzed according to the theoretical foundation in Chapter 3 which seeks to establish this linkage.

3 Theoretical Foundations

The most noticeable defect in both historical studies and current research arises mainly from a paucity of plural levels of support. Thus histories of union's partisan politics are largely aggregate, descriptive, and speculative, lethargic in their search for empirical data on individual levels.[1] On the other hand, voting behavior research in general and union voting studies in particular have been ahistorical and asystemic. One serious limitation of both these attempts is their atheoretical orientation. This lack is especially important because atheoretical statements at best describe, they never *explain*.

Our aim in this chapter is to develop a model of labor union voting behavior with theoretical foundations in empirical theories, speculative thoughts, and historical observations, and with empirical relevance to our data. Our purpose, again, is to explain fully a given political phenomenon.

Theoretical Context of the Problem

The central theoretical question of this study is, "How do members of labor unions and their families vote, and how do we explain the way they vote?" This question requires that we analyze the relationship between labor unions and their members with regard to the political world. Voting behavior viewed as a category of dependent variables includes a number of attitudinal and other behavioral factors that occupy the interim stages of the political decision-making process: political participation, sense of efficacy, involvement, issue orientation, party identification. Specifically, the question requires four levels of response.

First we have to ask precisely what is meant by labor union in this paper. In other words, what norms and expectations of political behavior does the union transmit to its members? The field abounds with historical and descriptive material that traces the evolution of the American labor unions' political position today. We allude to a set of generalizations arising from these historical perspectives for this part of our inquiry.[2]

Second, after we have established political norms peculiar to the labor unions and delineated their pattern of variation, both in intensity and character, from time to time and place to place, we narrow our focus to the manner in which members adhere to group norms, in order to specify conditions under which members' conformity is expected and strengthened. For this, we scrutinize factors peculiar to the group as well as characteristics of the individual as a member of society. We assume that regularities in the pattern of interaction between these two sets of characteristics will clarify the internal relationship between the individual and his group.

Again, we have seen a myriad of findings concerning this relationship; we reexamine most of them using our national data. Then we order our empirical findings and classify them according to a normative reference group theory.

As is usually true, the political behavior of some union members falls outside the usual group norm-to-individual behavior channel. The third and most important part of our investigation deals with this "deviant" political behavior to determine the conditions under which a member does not conform to the group norms. We view the forces behind nonconformity as disruptive variables that intervene between the group norm and a member's political behavior. This investigation involves perhaps the most complex set of inferences since there has not yet been a significant attempt to account for the sources and kinds of disruption.[3] We propose to arrange the outcome of this search according to the two related theories of the *comparative* reference group and relative deprivation as they apply to the political consequence of social mobility.

A theory is a "deductively connected set of laws."[4] For social science at this time, a theory may be a set of empirically testable and systematically related lawlike generalizations.[5] In this respect, what we have noted thus far is only a beginning, for a theory of labor union voting behavior requires two classes of effort.[6] First, to explain conformity and deviation, and hence probabilities of stability and change *within the group,* one needs to subcategorize statements within the larger theoretical question of the interaction between the group and the individual in the political arena. This categorization results largely from the narrowed focus on a given question and the explanatory schema most appropriate for it. Thus the variables within each category may be classified and ordered according to the laws pertaining to that category. After the regularities governing the conformity pattern and deviant tendencies are discovered, we still have to combine these laws to explain how members can respect group norms as well as defy them. To do this, we construct a *path* of decision making that considers both factors within the group setting and the shape of the general political map of which the particular group setting is a subcomponent.

Relevant Theories and Background Literature

The historical descriptive literature reveals the two most prominent characteristics of the American labor unions' partisan involvement. The most conspicuous of these has been a trend toward intense partisan involvement since the New Deal, particularly since the birth of the AFL-CIO until its de facto transformation as a party campaign apparatus peaked in the mid 1960s. The union's financing of Democratic campaigns is dramatic evidence of this trend, and their proliferation of campaign literature in recent times visually illustrates it.[7]

What is significant for our purpose is that the union did not limit its electoral mobilization campaign to union members; rather, as an internal Democratic organization, it shares the task of appealing to a much wider segment of the electorate than the unionized workers alone. The upshot of this expanded constituency is the broadened purview of their issue concern —including the so-called social issues. Greenstone's study of the AFL-CIO's lobbying in the Eighty-Ninth Congress showed the union's overwhelming support for aid to education, medicare, reapportionment, repeal of the 4 percent investment credit, and civil rights "not because they necessarily benefited the lower class but because their beneficiaries primarily voted Democratic or might be induced to do so." [8] It may be safe, therefore, to assume that the union has group norms that have been established in both the minds of the union leaders and, to varying degrees, the union members.[9] Among them are

1. Inculcation of political activism, rejecting the old-line laissez-faire business doctrine, and active pursuit of political means of achieving economic ends.
2. Emphasis on participation and involvement that follows from this activism.
3. Importance of job issues and social concerns.
4. Endorsement of the Democratic party as the political means for realizing the group's goals.

What links these and other organizational norms to the resulting political behavior of the members is a body of literature now identified as reference group theory.[10] According to Merton, "reference group theory aims to systematize the determinants and consequences of those processes of evaluation and self-appraisal in which the individual takes the values or standards of other individuals and groups as a comparative frame of reference." [11] The theory has been considerably refined and elaborated since its introduction by Hyman in 1942 [12] and has figured in many writings.[13] This is not the place to review the history of the theory, but it may be useful to sort out the concepts that directly bear on our inquiry.

The most important conceptual clarification of the functions of reference groups was made by Harold H. Kelley in his seminal article, "Two Functions of Reference Groups." [14] The first function, the normative reference group, sets and enforces standards for the member and rewards or pun-

Figure 3   Model of group political influence

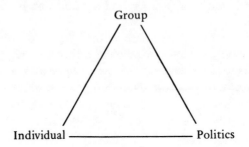

Figure 4   Group forces and disruptions

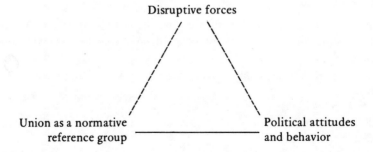

ishes conformity or nonconformity. The second, the comparative reference group, serves as a standard against which the individual can evaluate himself and others. These two functions are often served by the same group, and

... should prove to be merely special cases of more general theories about the *sources* and *nature* of standards which, in turn, should ultimately derive from fundamental theories of motivation and perception. The normative functions of reference groups may be expected to become part of a general theory of goal-setting and motivation which will also include other social determinants of standards (such as important individuals having the power to reward or punish), nonsocial factors in motivation, and the processes of self-motivation whereby social influences become internalized and operate through self-delivery of reward and punishment. The comparison functions of reference groups will be part of a general theory of perception and judgment such as is presently represented by the psychological theories of frames of reference. Comparison groups are, after all, only one of many kinds of comparison points within referential frameworks.[15]

Thus when an inquiry concentrates on the normative function of a reference group, the following points may be of primary importance:

1. The nature of the motivational relationship between the person and his reference group.
2. The importance of membership to the person.
3. Consequences of different kinds and degrees of motives of conformity.
4. Differentiated norms and standards associated with different positions within the group.
5. Factors facilitating the person's internalization of the group norms.[16]

Most studies of the union members' political behavior have borrowed heavily from this schema in investigating the political consequences, usually voting behavior, of the members' group affiliations.[17] Their main concern, therefore, is the group "distinctiveness" in consequential terms and possibly an analysis of its underlying factors. Philip Converse, for example, conceptualizes the relationship between the member and the union (reflected in the person's political behavior) in a triad "model of political influence situation." [18] He identifies three components of the model—the individual, the political world, and the group—and he treats each of the three in conceptually separate terms (Figure 3).

The path connecting the individual to the group is largely the person's identification with group norms and, hence, the degree of valence and cohesiveness of the group.[19] The direct relationship between the individual and politics, however, is defined in terms that bypass the consequence of

the person's group affiliation. These include short-term elements of politics
—candidate image, campaign perception—as well as such social and psychological attributes as economic class and party identification. Finally, the
dimension that comprises the group and the political world represents the
person's perceived affinity between the group and the political world.[20] In
our case, those variables gauging the member's view of legitimacy as well
as the nature of union's partisan involvement contribute to this category.[21]

The political behavior of a union member, then, is a function of the
member's identification with the union norms, the valence of the union to
the members, the perceived proximity and legitimacy of the union's relationship to politics, and finally influential factors that are neither generated
by nor influence the individual-to-group relationship *within* the group setting. These last factors are crucial; essentially, they make the model dynamic. The model allows us to explore the functional linkage between the
triad and the dependent political behavior as the three relationships of
the triad *jointly* mold the contents of the behavior. We defer the specifics
to later in this chapter.

What we have sketched thus far is a bivariate situation in which the
channel of the relationship connects the union as a normative reference
group to the member's political attitudes and behavior.[22] (See Figure 4.)
We have charted the sources of variation *insofar as* the norm transmission
pattern and its ultimate footprint on the members' political behavior are
concerned. Our focus has, therefore, consistently remained on the way in
which the group as a body of independent variables moves the individual
members in a manner congruent with its values.

What about the forces that disrupt—either erode or widen—the path
from the normative reference group to its members? Here we ask how we
may explain the roots of variance in political behavior that are not explained by group forces.

One way to introduce such a disruptive element is to examine more
closely the goals sought by labor unions. To the extent that economic ends
are the strongest motivation for joining a union (that is, selecting the normative reference group), we may expect an optimal degree of modification
in the individual-to-group relationship and its consequent impact on his
political behavior if we alter his economic background.

As working people rise to new levels of income and education; as they enjoy
greater security and more leisure; as ever greater numbers occupy technical,
skilled, and responsible positions; as they increasingly become home owners,
suburbanites, stockholders ... and as all assume more respected places in
society, important shifts are bound to occur in their political orientation.[23]

On a speculative level, there exists a large body of literature on social mobility. From the Greek philosophers to Karl Marx and from Max Weber to Talcott Parsons, this topic has captured the imagination of many theoreticians.[24] Only recently, however, have some political sociologists attempted to formalize a theory of social mobility.[25] We will focus on the political consequence of social mobility, which not only bears directly on our own theoretical focus, but also unfolds the other dimensions of the theory of social mobility as well.

One of the first scholars to attempt a conceptual clarification and theoretical structure of the problem was Seymour Martin Lipset, who suggested some political consequences of mobility. Tracing the unequal distribution of the privileged status to a "consequence of the conflict and tensions resulting from the contradictions inherent in the need for both aristocracy and equality" [26] in an industrial society, he explicitly assumes that the system forces a large sector of the population to accept a lower conception of its own worth relative to others.[27] This, in turn, leads Lipset to the analytic model that he uses to explore the political consequences—the model based on the notion of status discrepancy (or status inconsistency).

It is entirely conceivable that the political consequences of class deprivation might be different depending on what dimension of class is challenged ... when the occupational and consumption aspects of stratification are salient, the ideological debate and the political measures will be concerned with the issue of job security, redistribution of property, and income ... when the social class dimension is challenged or confused, the ideological debate will contain endless discussions of traditional values of ascription, often with elements of irrationality and scape-goating.[28]

However, when social mobility results in an imbalance in these two dimensions of class, the pattern of its political consequences appears quite diverse and eludes any attempt to generalize. Both kinds of imbalance or inconsistency are accompanied by two diametrically opposed political outcomes, testimony to the theoretical inadequacies of Lipset's formalization.[29] In a later ex post facto interpretation the findings on the American samples are set in a context of status striving and rejection.[30] Kenneth H. Thompson summarizes it well:

Here Lipset and Zetterberg suggest that the relatively greater tendency to take a left-wing orientation among the upward mobiles in Europe in contrast with the United States can be accounted for by factors forcing the upwardly mobile Europeans to retain links to the class of origin to a greater extent than upwardly mobile Americans.[31]

In other words, the status rejection and frustration that accompanies social mobility in Europe is presumed to be minimal in America, which, in turn, explains the conservative political consequences of American upward social mobility.[32] Some further studies have revealed varying conditions and outcomes. Bo Anderson's findings, for example, emphasize prior political socialization, viewing the relationship between political ideology and social mobility as largely spurious.[33] Still, Joseph Lopreato tests the impacts of two competing variables, consumption styles and status rejection, on the political dimension and finds the former far more powerful as a predictor.[34]

Pronounced disagreements are present in some descriptive studies as well.[35] The descriptive data offered by Lipset and Zetterberg identified conservatism as the most significant outcome of upward social mobility; more intriguing is their discovery that the socially mobile are more likely to be conservative than the middle class in this country.[36] Another study found a similar level of conservatism among both.[37] On the other hand, a few studies report conflicting results—from outright liberal attitudes to a milder conservatism that gradually grows toward the level of conservatism held by the middle class as the upwardly mobile grow older.[38]

Methodological diversities and inadequacies[39] coupled with the multidimensional nature of the problem's causal complexities are blamed for this contradiction.[40] The subject has recently become prominent; several views of the question have been proffered,[41] and, perhaps more significant, a few attempts have been made at integrating these crisscrossing approaches into a theoretically integrated structure.[42]

All these studies essentially view their "problem" as a dichotomy: either a move toward or away from the values and norms of the *destination* of mobility, the middle class.[43] This raises two problems that have serious implications for this book. The first comes from the proclivity in the model to deemphasize, if not exclude, variables associated with the class of *origin*. To deemphasize them amounts to a deliberate bias toward factors generated from the process of mobility which emphasize the appeal of the middle class.

The second difficulty, an indirect derivative of the first, arises from the absence of an opportunity to pose a causal question about the upwardly mobile whose partisan attitude and behavior remain unchanged or unmodified. Many studies have explored the change *toward conservatism;* very few, however, attempted to explain ideological persistence. The first instance of outright oversight and the associated neglect of causal inquiry is a logical outcome of the initial research question of the studies—why the Democratic partisan attitude persists *despite* upward mobility. Phrasing the theoretical question in this way excludes from the research design the factors related to social mobility which may ultimately prove to be more congenial to inertia than evocative of change.

To examine the seeds of change, therefore, is to investigate social mobility, while identification of resisting forces is equated with a search for processes *unrelated to mobility*. This is why early childhood socialization is often proffered as an antidote to change. By itself, this is not wrong, except when it stands as an *alternative* to social mobility to explain its political consequences.[44] As it turns out, both childhood socialization and social mobility contain forces for retaining as well as the potential for discarding the status quo. A more fruitful question would focus on the characteristics of social mobility conducive to change under certain situational conditions and the elements embedded in social mobility that sustain and strengthen the traditional tendencies in a specified setting.

In the following pages, we propose that persistent partisan attitudes are more than adjuncts to social ascendancy; instead, we shall demonstrate that persistence is a logical correlate of mobility as much as the outcome of modified partisan attitudes (Independents) and changed loyalty (the Republican allegiance). The difference in our model is its ability to specify conditions under which one outcome logically precedes the other at a given time. To construct this portion of the model, we appeal to literature on two intimately related theories—the comparative reference group and relative deprivation.

We shall proceed as follows. First, we summarize different levels of the theories that contribute to the theoretical underpinnings of the model of union voting behavior and return briefly to the dynamics of the theory of the normative reference group. Figure 5 displays sources of our theoretical foundations. After we chart the contributions made by these two theories to the linkages between the influence channel of the normative reference group and the external disruptions, we then identify some of the European and American schools of philosophical thought that converge with the predictive statements of our model. (See Figure 5.)

When we departed from the discussion of the normative reference group earlier, we did not specify how the three relational dimensions jointly influence the dependent political behavior. The problem, in essence, concerns two questions:

1. What is the background map of influence for each of the three dimensions and how are they related to each other?
2. How do we define the causal status of each of the three dimensions as we consider their confluence for the political behavior?

Figure 5   Theoretical foundations of union member voting behavior

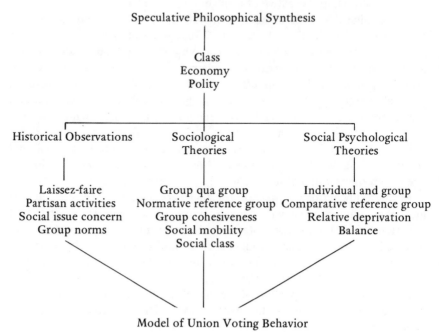

To start, we may view the group norms of the American labor unions as a set of *given* elements—linearly changing but not fluctuating in direction. There is reason to believe that labor's party alignment avoids a radical shifting of norms and has remained reasonably consistent over the last two decades or so.[45]

To raise questions on the underlying dimensions of the group variables (identification, legitimacy) is tantamount to unfolding the process of selecting a normative reference group. Although the literature in this field is scant compared with the selection of comparative reference groups, we can ask some specific questions[46] relating to a combined view of the social psychological literature. Both group dynamics studies and other social psychological studies agree that the normative group selection is a three-stage process: prior conditions, needs, and group identification.[47] While an individual's identification (or "sentiment") with group norms is presumed to be a function of needs that impelled his joining the group,[48] these needs are considered intervening factors between prior conditions and the group attraction.[49] The prior conditions in turn embrace two elements—interaction and norm consensus. This three-stage view of normative group selection explains a group's cohesiveness, since a high level of group cohesiveness can often be accounted for by interaction, norm consensus, and member needs.[50]

However, to the extent that the traits of a group *qua* group do not fully explain variation in group identification, we must look toward the individual background to explain individual variation *within a given group.* Two variables are age and education. Education consistently proves to be either a close correlate of identification or a factor closely related to forces that temper group identification. Since education increases the person's cognitive capacity and ability to relate to the world, it is reasonable to assume that educational level is directly related to the person's ability to evaluate the group and its standards. Indirectly, education is often a correlate of political interest, participation, and involvement;[51] and so those who are more active in union activities are more likely to be more intensely committed to its group objectives.

Age accounts for individual variation in identification in a complex way; in addition, age as a variable proves to be highly useful for explaining the causal ordering of group identification and partisan attitudes. This ordering is fundamental for our analysis. How do we know that group identification influences partisan attitudes? How do we know that partisan attitudes do not influence the individual's decision to join the union? We shall treat together age as a dimension of group identification and age as a critical variable ordering the causal status of partisan attitudes in relation to group identification.

Age is positively correlated with identification, but only to the extent that age is related to the length of union membership.[52] In fact, when the length of union membership is controlled, there appears a slightly negative relationship. Age also represents the *stage* in life when a person joined the union. As expected, the younger a person is when he joins the union, the greater his identification after a given period of time. This is intuitively pleasing, since age becomes a proxy for the degree of political and social orientation *before* joining the union. If we combine age as an indirect measure of union membership with the time of union entry, the proportion of life occupied by union membership is a powerful indicator of variation in identification.[53]

If length of membership increases identification, then this revelation favors the causal precedence of identification over partisan attitudes, in the sense that the identification is inculcated after entering the group. Perhaps more decisive in defining the causal status of partisan attitudes in relation to group identification is the very nature of labor unions. In ascribed secondary groups such as religious and ethnic communities, e.g., Blacks and Jews, the causal status of partisan attitudes unmistakably follows that of group identification. In groups that are essentially voluntary as well as politically active, however, it is not unreasonable to expect selection to be primarily due to partisan or ideological conviction.[54] Labor unions occupy a position somewhere in the middle of this continuum, since membership in a union is, by and large, involuntary, and the motive underlying the selection is largely economic. Whatever definitive partisan orientation develops may then usually be viewed as a function of group identification.[55]

The member's feeling of the legitimacy of the union's political involvement and his awareness of the nature of the group's partisanship can also aid in determining the causal order of the group variables. Under our decision that the member's identification with union objectives shapes his partisan attitudes, we can enumerate combinations of causal orders among the five variables—cognition of partisanship, feeling of legitimacy, identification, length of union membership, and partisan attitudes. We can then empirically test these combinations.

At this time, we propose that if the factors underlying the group variables external to the group are arranged in this sequence, and if this arrangement of external variables is connected to the elements within the group setting which we causally ordered in an empirically verifiable manner, we would have a fairly definitive sector of our total model identifying the channel of the norm transmission.

So far we have illustrated the disruptive forces operating on norm transmission with a theoretical reconstruction of social mobility and its political implications, and we have further suggested two interrelated theories for explaining the manner in which these disruptions occur. We now turn to the theories of the comparative reference group and relative deprivation.

We are concerned with the nature of the relationship among class, status, and political behavior *as this relationship interacts with the forces of the normative reference group*. What happens to the normative group forces when the generally patterned relationship among certain socioeconomic factors is introduced as an added dimension of influence? [56]

We start with two similar but analytically distinct definitions of socioeconomic elements. First, these factors are important to us only insofar as changes in them change political attitudes or behavior. Second, we shall examine the impact of socioeconomic determinants as a class of fixed variables. Thus our concern is limited to any discernible relationship, peculiar to unions, of socioeconomic variables to political attitudes and behavior. We deal with the latter first since the former is a simple theoretical variant.

One basic assumption we must make about comparison in politics is that political attitudes and behavior explained through the influence channel of a comparative reference group are essentially much more *rational* than either those formed through the normative reference group or those that result from early cathectic childhood socialization, for example.[57] To return to Kelley's distinction:

A study of *comparison* reference groups will involve different questions having largely to do with perceptual and judgmental processes. The following are some examples: What kind of stimulus does the comparison group present to the individual? Does it provide a highly structured and definite comparison point or is it an ambiguous stimulus capable of a variety of interpretations? What are the consequences of these different cases? In self-evaluations, what factors affect the size of the discrepancy the person perceives to exist between himself and the group norms? What are the effects of extremely high or low standards or comparison points? What is the nature of the scale along which comparisons are made? [58]

Self-evaluation is ubiquitous among humans (although the degree of one's involvement in it may vary), and information on the selection of standards for evaluation can specify conditions for a disgruntled or complacent state of mind. Only accepting the contention that the choice of comparisons is wholly random weakens the role of the union as a comparative reference group.[59] This contention, however, appears dubious.[60] Instead, it is more reasonable to view the process sometimes as a motivated process, whose intensity and nature varies from individual to individual.[61]

Figure 6   Causal sequence for satisfaction–dissatisfaction

| Selective of comparative reference group | ⟶ | Comparison | ⟶ | Relative deprivation- dissatisfaction | ⟶ | Cognitive balance of behavior |

Figure 7 Structure of dissonant and consonant comparisons (From Martin Patchen, "A Conceptual Framework and Some Empirical Data Regarding Comparisons of Social Rewards," in Herbert H. Hyman and Eleanor Singer, eds. *Readings in Reference Group Theory and Research* (New York: The Free Press, 1968), p. 167.

My earnings
――――――――――――   Compared to
His (their) earnings

My position on dimensions related to earnings
――――――――――――――――――
His (their) position on dimensions related to earnings

Figure 8   Intragroup and intergroup deprivation. From W. G. Runciman, *Relative Deprivation and Social Justice* (Berkeley, Calif: University of California Press, 1966), p. 33.)

Relatively deprived because of own position as member of group

Relatively deprived because of group's position in society		Satisfied	Dissatisfied
	Satisfied	A	B
	Dissatisfied	C	D

Figure 9   Types of relative deprivation in union income levels

Union Income Level

Types of relative deprivation from figure 8		High	Low
	A	I	II
	B	III	IV
	C	V	VI
	D	VII	VIII

On one hand an individual may choose a standard simply because it is *close* to his level of ability.[62] More specifically, in terms of evaluation standards closeness is an equivalent of *relevance,* while in terms of groups closeness is often a concomitant of a membership group. In both cases, referent power is a determinant of "closeness." [63] In terms of the motive's complexity, this level represents a simple desire to appraise oneself,[64] but union members may sometimes choose a standard deliberately, either "to make comparisons which are dissonant in favor of the other person" [65] or to experience a general rise in one's value.[66] Thus a person who compares himself with higher standards makes an upward comparison.[67]

Whatever the motive, either dissatisfaction or satisfaction can result. These states of mind are the central analytic focus for a relative deprivation theorist. A general statement of the theory, at least as used by its forerunners, is almost common sense.[68] One of the pitfalls of a "nontheory" is its infallibility, which frequently defies detection, especially when cloaked in post hoc analysis. Such was the chief weakness of the initial theory of relative deprivation; it could readily be utilized for an ex post facto interpretation and most importantly "to cover any conceivable outcome." [69]

One of the most important tasks is to postulate a chain of causality leading to a feeling of satisfaction or dissatisfaction. In our theoretical context, we may place the concept of relative deprivation somewhere in the interim position (Figure 6).[70] Perhaps the most significant contribution to the *theory* of relative deprivation was made by Martin Patchen, who further tightened the conditional specifications for generation of satisfaction or dissatisfaction.[71] His now familiar formula contains primary and secondary dimensions of comparison (Figure 7).

A perceived consonant comparison takes place when the "comparer perceives one side of this relation . . . as congruent with, or appropriate to, the other side of the relation. . . ." Similarly, "a perceived dissonant comparison is defined as one in which the comparer perceives the ratio on one side of the relation as incongruent with, or inappropriate to, the ratio on the other side of the relation." [72]

For a union member, the primary dimension may be his wage and the secondary dimension may be his noneconomic or social welfare.

Davis attempted to differentiate an in-group–out-group basis of deprivation.[73] Because the consequences are far-reaching, Runciman's extension of this attempt deserves our attention (Figure 8).

First, in a union we may expect comparisons among union members to be indistinguishable from comparisons within the working class in general, although standards may vary within the working class. A union member is no more likely to think of a union member's wage level than a professor is to compare his income with the salary of other AAUP members. More relevant would be standards for "manual workers," "skilled workers," or "professors" in general.[74]

Secondly, if we dichotomize the union member's income category into a level objectively higher than or equal to the group mean and a level objectively lower than the average, the cells in Figure 8 may find equivalents in the union income levels as shown in Figure 9.

Several considerations immediately emerge from Figure 9. We can eliminate cells I and II because they represent the gratified. The likelihood of a combination of between-group dissatisfaction and within-group satisfaction (V and VI) increases proportionately with the income level (hence V mostly). This is true because a higher income level reduces the chance of feeling deprivation relative to fellow members. Second, intergroup deprivations are perceived more frequently and more acutely when members know the standards of external groups and when the level that a class attains is characterized by mobility and achievement orientation.[75]

At the same time the most relevant source of relative deprivation among the high-income group within a union is *not* likely to be the income itself so much as the use of that income—that is, the life-style of a particular *social status* with which the union member has begun to compare himself. In Patchen's formula, the point of emphasis in the source (dissonance) of dissatisfaction among the high-income group tends to be the secondary dimension. This noneconomic or social dimension stresses the importance of opportunities for *future* social ascendancy. Therefore, the dissonance arising from perceived status dissimilarity varies inversely with the perceived possibility (aspiration) of assimilation[76] and actual claim to the position (expectation).[77]

By contrast, most of the low-income group within a union are likely to be located in the cells corresponding to the relative deprivation within a group (III, IV, VII, VIII), and the incidence of the low-income group in this category is much higher than the high-income group (hence III and VII). It is difficult to expect union members with a high income to feel deprived relative to other union members; the frequency will certainly drop as the income level rises. There is reason, however, to believe that this same low-income category will occupy much of VIII rather than IV. Unlike intergroup dissatisfactions, intragroup comparisons that are unfavorable (or dissonant) to the comparer are made for reasons that cannot often be attributed to sources other than the individual.[78] Yet, in a way, the claim to exemption from the self-responsibility is the only way of resolving the dissonance aside from a permanent acquiescence. As a result, conspiratorial theories or their variants (such as we–they or citizen–bureaucrat) often ensue when protest is based on relative deprivation and the deprived attribute the responsibility to others.[79]

Unlike high-income members, low-income members are likely to be dissatisfied because of a dissonance rooted in the perceived income imbalance. In terms of Patchen's equation, dissatisfaction stems from the primary dimension. While many unskilled workers may concede, for example, that they occupy a lower social status, they may be reluctant to agree that income difference is a fair representation of their low status. In other words, their feeling may very well be that they are poorer than they are less prestigious.

Thus far we have treated the concept of class in a fixed way. In this sense we are concerned with union members at *a given income level at a given time* and we compare them with others in another income category *at that time,* holding social characteristics constant. Social mobility and its political consequences can be treated as logical variants of the concept of class as a fixed variable with some additional features unique to mobility.

Much has been written about expectation and aspiration,[80] and, while the distinction between them is clear enough, their application to social mobility requires caution. If mobility denotes change in reference standards and consequent change from consonance to dissonance (and vice versa), both expectation and aspiration are related to the continuum of satisfaction–dissatisfaction in ways that reveal the nature of these feelings. For example, we are led to believe that the quantitative discrepancy between expectation and reward is crucial because it is not as easily tolerated as the gap between aspiration and reward. This is, we believe, only partially true and more applicable to the low-income group.

Aspiration increases as one's reward and expectations increase, but critically important here is the gap between aspiration and expectation. As one moves up the ladder of economic class and looks toward the nonmember comparative reference group, one's aspiration to traits of the nonmember group (e.g., middle class and its educational level) tends to become fairly stable,[81] if only because it rarely exceeds the perceived level of social status for the nonmember group. This is true even when the expectation level of realizing certain aspirations realistically continues to increase. As the expectation level approaches this more-or-less static aspiration level, a set of intervening factors minimizes any further ascendancy of expectations, that is, they maximize the feeling of status rejection.[82]

At this point, the aspirations of the upwardly mobile appear less distant, but are now nearly impossible to approach because of the unattainability of certain social characteristics (e.g., college education) attendant on the status sought. When this happens, the *net extent* of the gap between reward and aspiration is no longer so important. What is crucial is the *nature* of the perceived discrepancy between the fixed level of aspiration and expectation which tend to, but in reality are blocked from rising any further —almost in a permanent way. To become a middle class "technocrat," for example, presumes a level of education that to the union's upwardly mobile appears all but unreachable at their stage in life. In addition, the situation is likely to seem dismal to the upwardly mobile union member even for the next generation unless fundamental and long-range social remedies overcome most of the cumulative, class-specific disadvantages.[83]

This contrasts sharply with the expectations and aspirations of the low-income class who have stayed in the same position (the low-class stables) or have risen to that position (i.e., upwardly mobile to lower level), since their reference is a largely economic reward with relatively *open* possibilities for ascendancy. Even when the reward is not economic, their present class position is not close enough to the social status to discern and feel the pain of a permanently blocked expectation.

Once dissonant comparison takes place and dissatisfaction occurs—not always as a result of dissonance[84]—the remaining linkage to the behavior component must be established. Two possibilities arise: either nonaction or action. In the former case, social psychology of attitude formation and balance theory tell us that a cognitive or affective shift has taken place to resolve the dissonance.[85] Eulau found that inaction occurred frequently when the comparative referent power was meager, as in the case of the nonmember group.[86] Another factor held responsible for variation in the connection to the behavior component is the intensity of dissonance. Dissonance increases when deprivation is relative to *both* intragroup and intergroup standards (cell D, Figure 8), when class awareness is more acute, and when expectation increases at a faster rate than the reward because of emphasis on tangible instead of symbolic rewards.[87]

What labor unions do as normative reference groups is provide the facilitating factors that (1) give rise to dissonant comparison, (2) help translate it into dissatisfaction (i.e., relative deprivation), and (3) push the dissatisfied into action. We have historical reason to hypothesize that union members are more class conscious, more effective in ascribing failures to external sources (e.g., employers), more concerned with tangible goals,[88] and more powerful in raising a higher rate of expectation than reward can placate.

The behavior of union forces that pave the way for the sense of relative deprivation in pronounced ways often plays a neutral role in partisan terms. Thus the group forces conducive to dissatisfaction may not automatically invite or retain Democratic partisan attitude. All we know is that a union member is likely to feel more acutely dissatisfied and that the nature of the adopted evaluative standards differs as we move from one economic class to another and as we treat class as a fixed economic level or as part of the mobility process.

The clue to the directionality of political partisanship as related to the continuum of satisfaction–dissatisfaction lies in (1) union group variables, i.e., identification, length of membership; (2) the source of relative deprivation, i.e., the focused evaluative standards—economic values among the low-income group and social issues among the high-income group; and (3) the manner in which the union members *cognize* different political parties and their characteristic philosophy *in connection with* these standards central to different groups within the union.

The last two clues have two immediate implications for the American electoral process. First, for a given election, any change in the existing partisan division in the union members will be, *ceteris parabis,* a function of change in their cognition of the parties' roles with regard to economic and social issues. Second, over the long term, change in partisan division is determined by the change in the proportions of union members with low and high incomes. If the long-term trend is toward an increasing number of members with high income, and if the Democratic party is consistently associated with favorable social issues, then we can predict that unions will be increasingly able to mobilize Democratic voters among their members.

Demographic data indeed reveal a slow and gradual trend toward raising workers' income above the subsistence level.[89] This trend therefore favors *increasing salience of social issues* for union members. It is this current change in issue character for which the synthesized school of political and economic philosophy provides an explanation on a different level.[90] A brief description of this synthesis is in order.

A Marxian economic interpretation of the relationship between class consciousness and politics as the basis for working class involvement in politics has been partially vitiated for modern industrialized society in general and American politics in particular for several reasons. The increasing autonomy of the modern polity appears to require a multidimensional approach.[91] Moreover, the extent of political autonomy seems pervasive:

... this autonomy extended in the course of political development from the state to political parties. Paradoxical as it may seem, our analysis suggests that in national politics this same autonomy now extends to overtly economic union organizations or at least to their political specialists and top officials. For example, as factional leaders in the Democratic party, union officials joined in the discretionary decision to raise some issues, for example, Medicare, but gave less emphasis to others, like the problem of migrant labor. In each case, these priorities in part reflected political calculations of partisan advantage.[92]

Characteristics of the transition from the early European era of proletariat–bourgeoisie conflict to that of the modern confrontation between "economic authority" and "economic nonauthority" have undermined the strength of property and capital as an explanatory variable.[93] Among these characteristics are (1) the emphasis on *rationalization* as the primary source of social conflict and change to which the concept of authority bears direct relevance;[94] (2) the so-called decomposition of capital and the decomposition of labor which introduce the dimension of authority;[95] (3) the move from "mechanical solidarity" of labor to its "organic solidarity" as a result of the decomposition[96] and growing dependence on government to play the guardian role;[97] and (4) a consequent shift of labor's attention to a set of "noneconomic" issues—i.e., social or "consumer" issues—in the 1960s.[98]

This brief review of the European and American schools of speculation on the relationship among class, economy, and polity exposes a convergence among three levels: the philosophical accounts, historical observations, and empirical theories. The first describes factors underlying the change from the proletariat to the postproletariat period and predicts that future labor politics will be based largely on the consequences of instrumental rationalization. The result is a growing concern over social issues. In most general terms, these philosophical traditions enrich the "context of discovery." The second, the historical description, traces the process of labor's organizational infusion into the Democratic party as a campaign apparatus and predicts its new concern for a broadened constituency. The result is an increasing emphasis on social questions. Finally, empirical theories not only pinpoint the sector of labor in which this social awareness is gaining political prominence, but also offers a social psychological explanation of it to aid the researcher's attempt to specify and elaborate.

One final caveat remains. This discussion of empirical theories has centered largely around economic factors that disrupt group norm transmission. However, a complete portrait of the union member's political universe includes social and political variables that do not directly affect the economic basis of unions but which compete with the group forces of unions. Multiple normative membership is one such competition; nonunion group values present a cross pressure. For example, a long-time union member who enjoys a relatively higher income may face conflicting values from the local Baptist Church to which he belongs.

Early childhood socialization, especially cathectic socialization, often weakens or strengthens influences of a secondary reference group. A union member who has grown up in a strong Republican family may react to the union's political norms in an effete way. Including these and other non-union forces that challenge or complement union forces yields the model of union voting behavior represented in Figure 10.

A boundary for an explanatory model is not naturally closed or fixed; its size and shape vary with what one is explaining and with the extent to which one defines the relevance of the variables. Our central concerns are (1) the process and nature of norm transmission within a union and (2) the factors intimately related to the very rationale of the union's existence that either weaken or enhance norm transmission. The only other determinants of political attitudes and behavior that are important are those related to political socialization and multiple group membership, because they influence partisan attitude formation and voting behavior.

Some Hypotheses

The following *broad* hypotheses about labor union members' voting behavior in American elections are inferred from this discussion of our theoretical model. We will first test their general validity with the data from the presidential elections of 1952, 1956, 1960, and 1964. Then to test their applicability to a particular time frame, we will use the data from the presidential elections of 1968 and 1972 to examine key hypotheses. Finally, we will use insights culled from direct and indirect observations of the 1976 presidential election to project future labor union voting behavior.[99]

I. Union members are more politically involved than other American voters.
   A. Union members express more interest and participate more often in the political process than others.
   B. Union members have a greater sense of political efficacy than others.
   C. These hypotheses hold for different socioeconomic levels.
II. A greater proportion of union members identify with and vote for Democratic candidates than do other voters.
   A. This hypothesis is true across different socioeconomic levels.
III. Socioeconomic attributes of union members *positively* influence their Democratic partisanship.
   A. Socioeconomic attributes of other voters *negatively* affect their Democratic partisanship.

Figure 10   Model of union members' voting behavior

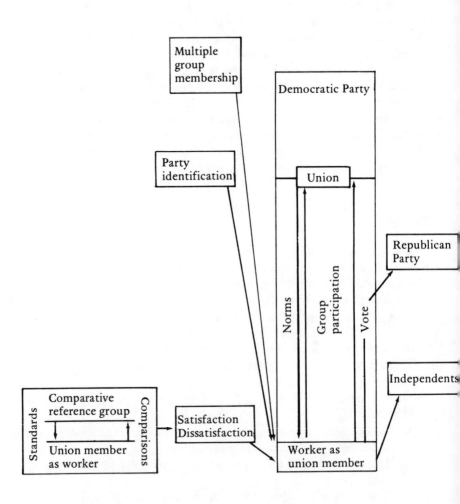

Union member as comparer   Union member as voter

IV. Union members' awareness of and identification with the union's political goals strengthen their Democratic partisanship.

    A. Socioeconomic attributes of union members are positively related to their relationship with the union.

    B. The proportion of a worker's life as a union member positively affects his Democratic partisanship.

V. Union members are more class conscious than others.

VI. Union members emphasize tangible economic and social goals more than others.

VII. Union members are better informed than others of their class and status relative to others in the society.

VIII. The class level of a union member tends to determine the comparison standard.

    A. Union members with a high income are likely to feel deprived relative to those outside the union.

    B. Union members with a low income are likely to feel deprived relative to those within and outside the union.

IX. Union members ascribe the reason for their class and status deprivation to others.

    A. Union members blame others for their deprivation more often than others if their income is low.

X. A smaller proportion of union members who are on a class level lower than the group average vote Democratic than do those union members whose class level is equal to or higher than the group average.

XI. A greater proportion of union members are upwardly mobile.

    A. Union members expect more economic and social rewards than do others.

    B. Union members' expectations of rewards increase at a faster rate with their upward mobility than that of others.

XII. Union members experience a more intense feeling of relative deprivation than others.

    A. Union members who are upwardly mobile are more dissatisfied than those who are the class stables.

    B. Union members whose upward mobility approaches the middle class tend to be more dissatisfied than those who rise toward the level below the middle class.[100]

XIII. Union members who are upwardly mobile toward the middle class are more conscious of social issues than any other election issues.

    A. Union members who rise toward a level lower than the middle

class are conscious of job security and other economic issues
more than any other election issues.

XIV. A greater proportion of upwardly mobile union members who approach the middle class vote Democratic than do the middle class
stables in the union.[101]

  A. A smaller proportion of upwardly mobile union members who
  rise toward a level lower than the middle class vote Democratic
  than do the low class stables in the union.[102]

Summary

Our theoretical model is assembled from plural levels of thoughts, descriptions, and theories—philosophical, historical, and empirical. Each
level provides the theoretical linkage in our model that is critical in explaining labor union members' voting behavior. Thus the philosophical
school of thought stimulates and structures discovery about the relationship among class, economy, and the modern polity. The historical description traces and describes the present political goals of American labor
unions. Both philosophy and history predict that the American workers
are becoming more concerned with social or consumer issues. Empirical
theories show how union members receive and translate these group objectives, and the political outcomes they predict on the style of the member's reception. We now test these linkages in subsequent chapters.

4   The Labor Union as a Normative Reference Group

Bemoaning a paucity of literature on vote mobilization by American labor unions, Harry M. Scoble writes:

Labor unions have carried out registration drives and get-out-the-vote drives in both primary and general elections and have done everything else that a political party does, including provision of free baby-sitting service on election day. At the level of description, facts abound; but at the level of analysis, knowledge remains fragmentary, shadowy, and highly unsystematic.[1]

By "description" Scoble means the methods employed by unions to mobilize votes; but "analysis" refers to impact analysis. His complaint is directed at the absence of data that use the correct baseline for measuring the union's political impact. Thus an estimation of union votes that is compared with the votes of the general public, *and not other organized workers,* essentially fails to account for the political impact of unions independent of other factors.[2]

Analyzing the question of the union's political impact requires a theoretical rationale for a study of labor union voting behavior. In terms of our theoretical model, the question concentrates on the political process by which unions influence their members, that is, the mode of group norm transmission. This, however, is only a partial answer, for the union's vote mobilization must be measured in terms of its impact on the system as well. In other words, one must investigate whether the votes of union members—how many are delivered and how—*matter* at all in the final analysis. We defer this question to Chapter 6 and deal here only with the internal mechanism of the union's political norm transmission. We propose to do this by (1) identifying the theoretical locus of the union as a group in the maze of political decision making by an individual member, (2) establishing distinctiveness of union votes, and (3) tracing the interaction of union influences on their members.

Union Influence on the Voting Decision

Exactly where does a union enter an individual's voting decision? The authors of *The American Voter* rely on the Gestalt theory and place the attitudinal field as the final mediator of all behavioral determinants.

The effect of all factors leading to behavior is finally expressed in the direction and intensity of the forces of a psychological field, in which the individual's attitudes toward the elements of politics have a central place. The elements of national politics—the presidential candidates, questions of group interest, the issues of domestic and foreign policy, the performance of the parties in the

Figure 11 Dual mediation model. From Arthur S. Goldberg, "Discerning a Causal Pattern among Data on Voting Behavior," *American Political Science Review* 60 (1966), p. 919. The members represent the standardized beta weights. The SRC data come from the 1956 election.

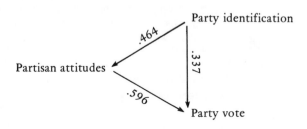

Figure 12 The influence relationship among partisan attitudes, party identification and vote.

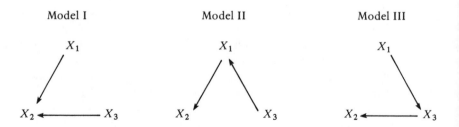

(X_1 =Partisan attitudes, X_2 =Party vote, X_3 =Party identification)

Table 6 Causal models for partisan attitudes, party identification, and party vote

Model	Prediction	Equation		Predicted value	Actual value	Degree of fit
I	(.176)	(.594)	=	.177	.318	.141
II	(.176)	(.318)	=	.560	.594	.034
III	(.318)	(.594)	=	.189	.176	.013

conduct of government—are not simply perceived by the individual; they are evaluated as well. Orientations to these objects, seen by the voter as positive or negative, comprise a system of partisan attitudes that is of primary importance for the voting act.[3]

In this model, attitudinal field is a dependent variable of two antecedent factors: relatively inert affective characteristics such as party loyalties, and cognitive (or evaluative) forces that can often explain short-term fluctuations in partisan division of vote.[4] Arthur S. Goldberg empirically tests the model and concludes that his evidence "is sufficient to give one qualms about regarding attitudes, as operationalized by *The American Voter,* as the final mediator." [5] Goldberg's model establishes the impact of party identification "not caught in the screen which those researchers drew across the funnel of causality." [6] (See Figure 11.)

Note the intensity as well as the direction of influence in this model. Two explanations can be offered for the apparently unusual influence of partisan attitudes on the vote. First, if, as Angus Campbell et al. theorize, partisan attitudes[7] closely reflect short-term factors more or less unique to a given election such as issues, campaign, and candidate image, then one can argue that the Eisenhower candidacy of 1956 conveniently explains away the independent influence of partisan attitudes *for that particular year.* Our merged data for the election years 1952–1964, which represent a network of normal relationships, display strikingly different connections.

Model III (Figure 12) shows the best fit (Table 6) in which the influence of partisan attitudes on behavior (vote) appears spurious.[8] Note, however, that the fit of Model III excels that of Model II only by a slight margin (.021), and an alternative theoretical interpretation on the basis of Model II (the cps model) may not seriously violate the statistical evidence.

The second point about the Goldberg model concerns the nature of partisan attitude as operationalized by the cps. The absence of any ordinal dimension within the variable defies any significant ordering of the items in it.[9] As a result, using the Pearsonian correlation coefficient here is less justified than in the case of the party identification variable, which is at least ordinal, and the vote variable, which can be often dichotomous and hence does not violate an interval assumption. The problem is not whether one can use a given parametric measure so much as how to interpret the results.

If we can concede both the indeterminateness of the cps model as a general theoretical device[10] and the limitations of the Goldberg schema, then weighing relative advantages of *either* model in a dichotomous man-

Table 7   Change in party identification of union and nonunion members
1952–1964 (In percentages)

Party identi- fication	1952		1956		1960		1964	
	Union	Non- union	Union	Non- union	Union	Non- union	Union	Non- union
Strong Democrat	25.3 N=121	21.2 N=271	26.1 N=122	19.8 N=241	31.8 N=93	20.9 N=174	37.9 N=141	23.? N=27?
Weak Democrat	28.4 N=136	23.2 N=297	25.7 N=120	23.1 N=281	26.4 N=71	24.4 N=203	26.1 N=97	24.? N=28?
Inde- pendent	24.0 N=115	27.1 N=347	27.0 N=126	23.4 N=285	24.7 N=72	20.6 N=172	22.6 N=34	23.? N=26?
Weak Republican	12.3 N=59	13.7 N=175	12.4 N=58	15.7 N=191	10.3 N=30	15.7 N=131	9.1 N=34	15.? N=7.
Strong Republican	10.0 N=48	14.9 N=191	8.8 N=41	18.1 N=220	6.8 N=20	18.4 N=153	4.3 N=16	13.? N=15·
Totals	100% N=479	100.1% N=1281	100% N=467	100.1% N=1218	100% N=292	100% N=833	100% N=372	100.1% N=116?

ner is less important than offering a clear conceptual representation of where a specific determinant belongs and what it is assumed to explain. Thus it is of little consequence to argue about the path of union influence in terms of the primacy of partisan attitudes or party identification. What is important is first to discern the area in which unions exercise political influence on the member's choice and the pervasiveness of the influence. An idiosyncratic schema of analysis need not seriously limit our conceptualization. After all, party identification also changes, and if we can demonstrate that union norms are closely tied to both cognitive and affective change, the labels should not prove a hindrance (Table 7). The political influence of the union is significant in all categories of party identification (Table 8). Especially noteworthy is the extent of the union's political impact on the weak identifiers (with the exception of Democratic voters in the "Weak Republican" category[11]) and the independents. If the deep psychological commitment of these voters to partisanship is relatively vulnerable to change, then union influence on them results from a cognitive shift. This, we believe, is important since in American electoral politics, save in a critical election, short-term factors are the chief determinants of the outcome. In other words, Key's responsible electorate cluster in the weak identifiers and independents[12] (Table 9).

The underlying reasons for the expressed attitudes are perhaps more revealing. Clearly 46 percent of union members cited group interest as the basis for their positive attitudes toward the Democratic party, compared with only 30 percent of nonunion members. Two additional reasons for union members' attitudes that rank closely behind the first are specific domestic issues (e.g., "good conditions" under the party) and the party's philosophy of government management. In addition, approximately 10 percent more union than nonunion members perceive a policy difference between the two parties on various issues (Table 10). Union members' concern with issues rather than party references appears consistently and much more vividly than that of nonunion members across *all socioeconomic levels*.[13]

In the parlance of voting behavior literature, the influence of union norms seems to take two routes—party identification and partisan attitudes. In the former case, the union's grip solidifies and helps retain the psychological commitment, especially when the voter is unsure of his loyalty. In addition, it encourages defection among those loyal to the Republican party, especially when their Republican party identification is less unconditional. In the latter instance, the attitudinal dimensions favorable to the Democratic party or Democratic candidates exhibit rational

Table 8   Union influence on the relationship between party identification
and party vote

Party Vote	Party Identification				
	Strong Democrat	Weak Democrat	Independent	Republican	Republican
Democratic	+5.6	+17.2	+10.5	+4.4	−1.8
Republican	−2.7	−11.8	− 7.4	−3.8	−1.4

Note: Cell entries represent the percentage deviation of the Democratic vote of union members from the Democratic vote percentage of nonunion members. Positive figures mean the margins by which union members exceed nonunion members in a given partisanship category.

Table 9   Percentage of union and nonunion members with positive attitudes
toward the Democratic Party and Democratic candidates

Attitude	Union	Nonunion
Like Party	67.65	59.57
Like Candidates	63.20	54.30

Note: Cell entries represent percentage of different totals due to residual categories. Total union N's are 1221 and 941 respectively; total nonunion N's are 3022 and 2332.

Table 10   Union and nonunion members' areas of perception of Democratic
Party differences on issues (In percentages)

Perceived areas of difference	Union		Nonunion	
Inflation, Cost of Living	9.7	(N=46)	16.5	(N=187)
Income, Wage	16.8	(N=80)	15.5	(N=176)
Employment	24.6	(N=117)	10.4	(N=118)
Taxes and government spending	13.0	(N=62)	21.0	(N=238)
Prosperity, Depression	17.6	(N=84)	20.9	(N=237)
War or peace	1.7	(N=8)	1.9	(N=21)
Farm policy	0.8	(N=4)	6.4	(N=73)
Group references	15.8	(N=75)	7.3	(N=83)
Totals	100%	(N=476)	99.9%	(N=1133)

calculations on the part of union members, particularly with reference to union goals as they relate to partisan division.

Union Members and Political Participation

Union members are interested in and participate to a greater extent in politics than others, the overall margin averaging consistently about 4 to 6 percent.[14] Slightly greater differences between union and nonunion members emerge in lower occupational categories (Table 11). This greater contrast is expected since it is for workers in low-achievement classes that the union's political impact can be optimal. This is true if only because the impact is optimal where the latitude of mobilization can be maximal.

This statistic is much more significant than it may appear, for at least two reasons. That unions can influence those who remain open to external pulls reveals the effectiveness of the transmission of group norms. Second, our finding has important ramifications for the labor union vote, since union members tend to fall into the low socioeconomic levels. For example, 75 percent of the members earn less than $8000 per year, and more than 70 percent of these earn less than $4500.[15] Educational levels dramatize this relationship (Table 12). Nine out of ten union members have no more than a high school education.

Our general expectation of greater political activity among union members appears to have been fulfilled. To the extent that we can attribute it to the impact of unions' political norms, we have reason to believe that norm transmission in unions is indeed lively.

Distinctiveness of Union Votes

Keeping in mind Scoble's earlier statement, we may now ask, "How do union votes differ from nonunion votes?" We assume that group norms and pressures generate a union vote pattern that is clearly distinguishable from the rest of the electorate in all comparable socioeconomic categories.

As Scoble complained, no authoritative source today scrutinizes union votes in ways that can benefit a social psychological inquiry. The most often cited studies thus far are V. O. Key's estimate,[16] the Gallup report,[17] and the CPS study.[18] Key's reconstruction of the voting pattern of the general electorate from 1936 to 1960 makes inferences from the data collected by research organizations such as the American Institute of

Table 11 Participation differences between union and nonunion members in
lower occupational categories

	Unskilled	Semiskilled or skilled	White collar
Always voted	+6.4	+8.0	+3.1
Very much interested	+8.3	+2.9	+2.8

Note: Cell entries represent percentage by which union members exceed nonunion members
in the participation categories.

Table 12 Educational levels of union and nonunion members (In percentages)

Educational Levels[a]	Union		Nonunion	
No education	0.84	(N=12)	1.06	(N=42)
Grade School	30.34	(N=432)	27.80	(N=1092)
High School	58.71	(N=836)	46.89	(N=1842)
College	10.11	(N=144)	24.24	(N=952)
Total	100%	(N=1424)	99.99%	(N=3928)

[a]Levels are not necessarily equivalents of completed levels. For example, *some* high school
education is also included in the third level.

Table 13 Voting pattern of union members and manual worker families
1936–1960 (In percentages)

	Union families	Manual worker families
1936	20	26
1940	28	34
1944	28	38
1948	27	34
1952	39	45
1956	43	50
1960	35	40

Source: George Gallup, "How Labor Votes," *Annals of the American Academy of Political
and Social Science* 274 (1951), pp. 118–124; the more recent data is from the Gallup report
as cited by V. O. Key, *Public Opinion and American Democracy* (New York: Knopf, 1968),
p. 523. No sample size was given.

Public Opinion (the Gallup poll), the National Opinion Research Center, the Roper poll, and the CPS studies. The nature of the consolidated data used for Key's analysis has never been defined in a way that permits systematic examination of the soundness of his statistical operations.[19]

In addition, Key's data on the labor vote prove extraneous to the votes of union members.[20] His data on the voting behavior of the working class are precisely that and no more, so that even a query about the labor "bloc" vote cannot be answered. Some investigators may have been misled by a section in Key's work on the pattern of presidential preference, 1944–1948, in relation to the distribution of responses to a question about governmental control of unions.[21] This of course says nothing about the union members' voting pattern.[22]

The second of these frequently used sources is a surprisingly simplistic and abbreviated body of data from George Gallup[23] (Table 13). Two limitations are obvious. First is the possibility of a comparative analysis:

As usual, the academic social scientists must have some reservation concerning the precision of comparative analyses by the Gallup organization; that is, the data reported in the text constitute a comparison of "union families" with "all manual-worker families," and there is no indication that the latter category is *exclusive* of the former. I suspect that it is not and that, for the reasons given in the text and drawn from CPS data, it unnecessarily deflates the extent of Democratic-orientation of unionists.[24]

The second limitation of the Gallup data is the extent to which one can compare votes of union and nonunion members. When only families of manual workers are used as a basis for comparison, one cannot extend the comparison to other occupations such as skilled and white-collar members. Further, the Gallup data cannot be used to investigate vote differences as a function of union influence present in other sociological categories such as income and education.

By far the most useful evidence comes from the CPS study which recognizes the very problem:

... we must contrast behaviors of group members not simply with those of the remainder of the population, but with the restricted part of that population that shares the peculiar life situations of group members. We want to isolate a *"control"* group of non-members that matches the *"test"* group of members on all important aspects of life situation save the fact of membership.[25]

The authors introduce a control mechanism that bypasses the problem of sample size, unlike in the case of the precision or distribution control and which, at the same time, provides a control procedure.[26]

No doubt, this method produces a control group[27] and supplies evalua-

Table 14   Union and nonunion votes (In percentages)

Votes	Union		Nonunion	
Democratic	53.3	(N=761)	36.3	(N=1432)
Republican	31.6	(N=451)	46.3	(N=1827)
Total	84.9%	(N=1427)	82.6%	(N=3943)

Note: Nonvoters and other residual responses are excluded.

Table 15   Distinctiveness of union votes and union party identification in four socioeconomic categories

Occupation	PV[a]	PI[b]	Income	PV	PI
Unskilled	+16.1	+5.2	Less than $3000	+12.7	+8.3
Skilled or			$3000–4999	+17.1	−5.9
Semiskilled	+18.8	+8.9	$5000–7999	+12.9	−13.5
White Collar	+14.4	+13.5	$8000–9999	+17.5	+15.1
			$10,000 or more	+29.3	+21.0

Age	PV	PI	Education	PV	PI
Less than 25	+12.4	+6.7	None	+31.0	+36.0
25–34	+10.4	+8.2	Grade School	+16.0	+10.1
35–44	+19.2	+13.7	High School	+15.3	+8.7
45–54	+22.3	+13.7	Colleges	+19.0	+20.6
55–64	+20.5	+15.4			
65 or over	+12.0	+2.8			

Note: Cell entries represent the difference between the Democratic percentage of union Democratic votes of union Democratic Party identification and the nonunion Democratic votes of Democratic Party identification in each category. A positive figure means the percentage margin by which union Democratic votes (or identification) exceeds nonunion Democratic votes (or identification).
[a]Party votes
[b]Party identification

tive standards for judging union votes and their distinctiveness along several social dimensions. The problem is the limited utility of such data beyond theoretical use. Proving group influence and hence group distinctiveness is one thing; whether the same data and operations used to prove the theory also lend themselves to practical *interpretations* is a different question. That the CPS control method cannot be used to make inferences specific to particular groups and individuals is its major limitation for our purpose. We need to know not only *whether* union's votes are distinctive, but also how much and with regard to what category.

Our data reveal the *general* distinctiveness of the union vote and union partisan loyalties as expected (Table 14); further, when four socioeconomic characteristics are held constant, the group distinctiveness of the union vote seems to persist on nearly all levels (Table 15).

We acknowledge the theoretical contention that the gap between partisan vote and party identification is a function of such short-term forces as campaign effects, candidate appeal, and issue salience. In view of this, our data (which reveal consistently greater differences between union and nonunion party *votes* than differences between union and nonunion party *identification*) suggest the manner in which union's political norms are transmitted. Obviously, the extent to which temporary change in partisan attitude introduces the possibility for a permanent shift in partisan loyalty depends on several factors: (1) length of union membership and hence incidence of party vote inconsistent with party identification, (2) the intensity of new attitudinal forces, and (3) the strength of the original party identification. Obviously the union influence is most directly relevant to the first two. Where the member's party identification conflicts with union norms, the union continues to disrupt the translation of effective party loyalty to party vote. Where party identification agrees with union demand, the union intensifies the affective commitment to cement the tie. The success or failure of union intervention depends partly on the initial strength of the affective tie. In extreme cases, the union can permanently convert one's party allegiance, but this apparently requires repeated disruptions and challenges and hence takes some time.

The intensity of new attitudinal forces is another determinant of the effectiveness of union norms as a group force. Here one must consider the member's ability to recognize union partisanship, the strength of his identification with union goals, his perception of the legitimacy of the union's political involvement, and the strength of emitted standards.[28]

Our expectation about the differences between the AFL and the CIO is largely met; the data show that more CIO members identify with the

Table 16   Party identification of different union members (In percentages)

Party Identification	CIO		Independents		AFL	
Strong Democrat	35.1	(N=99)	31.6	(N=31)	29.6	(N=186)
Weak Democrat	28.0	(N=79)	27.6	(N=27)	24.8	(N=156)
Independents	22.3	(N=63)	25.5	(N=25)	25.8	(N=162)
Weak Republican	9.6	(N=27)	10.2	(N=10)	11.6	(N=73)
Strong Republican	5.0	(N=4)	5.1	(N=5)	8.3	(N=52)
Totals	100%	(N=282)	100%	(N=98)	101%	(N=629)

Figure 13   Relationship between union and nonunion votes and occupation. Expressed in another way, the relationship between union membership and votes differs from category to category in occupation. Unskilled: Gamma=.315; Semiskilled or skilled: Gamma=.358; White collar: Gamma=.210.

Democratic percentage of
occupational categories

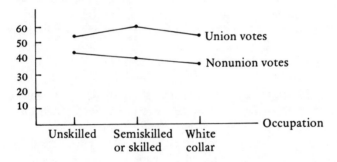

Democratic party (Table 16). Historically, the AFL's role in American politics is consistent with this finding.

One other feature of union voting must be mentioned. The class characteristics of two-party vote division have been clear since the New Deal,[29] but when the union vote is considered, this relationship is partially reversed. For example, the reversal occurs in the first two occupations (Figure 13) and especially in the last income category (Figure 14). This is explained by the very nature of socioeconomic categories. Members of higher-status socioeconomic categories share a common denominator other than the primary characteristic defining their level—that is, "the higher class persons are more likely to participate in politics than lower class persons;"[30] and a voter's income,[31] occupation,[32] and education are positively correlated with his political participation. It readily follows that union members at higher socioeconomic levels are more likely to be aware of and actively campaign for the union's political objectives. Aside from being more active and aware, high-class members in a union may relate their achievement to the union's political goals, political access, and political activity (Figure 15).

The slight decline in Democratic percentage for the middle-income and high occupational categories is probably due to the kind of unions to which these workers belong. Some 40 percent of all AFL members represent nearly 63 percent of the middle-income category ($5000–$7999); similarly, almost 70 percent of white-collar union workers belong to the AFL. AFL members have historically been less enthusiastic toward the Democratic party than CIO workers. The high-income categories ($8000 or more) may be less indicative of the kind of union to which a worker belongs than his status within the unions and, hence, his relationship to the group and its norms.

The Worker's Relationship to His Union

The relationship between sociological background variables and the worker's political behavior may be reversed once the group context of the union is considered. The class factors that have proved friendly to Republican partisanship have a way of redefining the worker's position within his union and hence his partisanship as well. We can now break group influence into several relationships emerging from the triad model (group, individual, and politics) and empirically order the causal sequence of these internal forces.

Figure 16 shows variables representing three dimensions within the

Figure 14   Relationship between union and nonunion votes and income

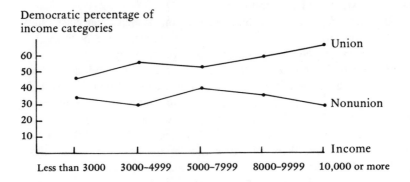

Figure 15   Relationship between union and nonunion participation and occupation

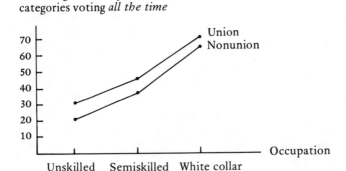

Figure 16   Group forces and partisanship

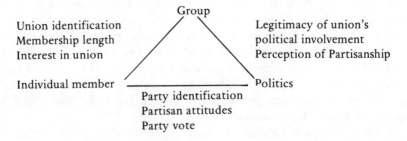

interaction map of the group forces.[33] The extent to which the member identifies with and expresses interest in the union's political goals and the length of his membership describe his relationship with the group. The extent to which he correctly identifies the union's partisanship and considers the union's political involvement legitimate represents his view of the group's connection to politics. Finally, the usual variables—party identification, party vote, and partisan attitude—link the individual to politics. The individual (Table 17) or *joint* impact (Table 18) of these variables have already been empirically established elsewhere.

In addition, these intraunion forces have been investigated as a function of the individual's background. As we pointed out in Chapter 3, length of union membership as a proportion of one's life is positively correlated with union identification. Converse, for example, found that the relationship between length of membership and union identification becomes pronounced when age is controlled for. Thus the length of union membership is not so crucial as the length of union membership *combined* with the member's age at the time he joined the union (Table 19).

Converse also found that education is a strong influence. He noted a "sharp variation in the clarity with which standards are reported to be perceived, as a function of both education and length of membership." [34]

To sum up, we have here four interacting categories of variables (Table 20). To discern the correct order for these variables, we select one "representative" of each set by employing the canonical correlation technique and identify the paths of sequential influence that best fit our data.[35]

The canonical correlation technique lets us match two sets of variables at a time to generate the six possible combinations. From each combination we can single out the variable in each set that is most strongly correlated to the *common denominator* (canonical variate) of that set *as it is related to the common denominator of the matched set*. We designate the six combinations by the letters A through F with the appropriately numbered sets and variables (see Table 20); the operations show the results in Table 21.

Three variables—age, length of union membership, and member's identification of union partisanship—consistently "represent" their own groups. According to our earlier theoretical formulations, we will simply regard party vote as the final dependent variable. The possible causal paths among the four variables are shown in Figure 17. If we assume one vanishing path at a time, the prediction equation and the actual values produce the measure of fit shown in Table 22.

These results give us a disjunctive model (Figure 18) in which ability to identify union partisanship is relatively free of both the extragroup

Table 17 Sense of union identification in relation to level of political involvement
(In percentages)

Political Involvement	Least Identified 1	2	3	Most Identified 4
High 4	17	14	26	34
3	19	29	24	23
2	36	33	26	31
Low 1	28	24	24	12
Total	100% (N=83)	100% (N=126)	100% (N=109)	100% (N=110)

Source: V.O. Key, *Public Opinion and American Democracy* (New York: Knopf, 1968),
p. 507. The data are from the 1956 election.

Table 18 Presidential vote across four secondary membership groups by strength
of group identification and belief in legitimacy of group political activity
(In percentages)

Belief in legitimacy of group political activity	Group Identification			
	High	Medium	Low	Total
Strong	72 (N=126)	64 (N=95)	55 (N=98)	65 (N=319)
Medium	62 (N=52)	55 (N=55)	45 (N=56)	53 (N=163)
Weak	67 (N=27)	45 (N=60)	33 (N=127)	41 (N=214)
Total	69% (N=205)	56% (N=210)	43% (N=281)	———

Source: Philip E. Converse and Angus Campbell, "Political Standards in Secondary Groups,"
in Herbert H. Hyman and Eleanor Singer, eds., *Readings in Reference Group Theory and
Research* (New York: The Free Press, 1968), p. 488.
Note: Each cell entry represents the Democratic percentage of the two-party vote for the
appropriate combination of group identification and sense of legitimacy. The "total" column shows the simple relationship between legitimacy and vote, with no control on identification. The "total row" shows the simple relationship between identification and the vote,
without control on legitimacy.

Table 19   Union identification, age, and length of union membership

Variables	
1. Union Identification	$12.3^r = +.33$
2. Length of Membership	$13.2^r = -.09$
3. Age	$23.1^r = +.36$

Source: Philip E. Converse, "Group Influence in Voting" (unpublished Ph.D. dissertation, University of Michigan, 1958), p. 120.

Table 20   Classification of intra- and extragroup variables

Set no.	SRC var. no.	External background variables	Internal group-to-individual variables	Internal group-to-politics variables	Individual-to-politics variables
I	1	x			
	2	x			
II	3		x		
	4		x		
	5		x		
III	6			x	
	7			x	
	8			x	
IV	9				x
	10*				x

Note: SRC variables are 1. age, 2. education, 3. union identification, 4. length of membership, 5. interest in union, 6. legitimacy of union, 7. legitimacy of electoral involvement, 8. identification of union's partisan goals, 9. party identification, and 10. party vote.
*Partisan attitude variables not included due to an absence of single-item representation.

Table 21   Representative variables for intra- and extragroup forces

Variables		Combinations					
		A (I+II)*	B (I+III)	C (I+IV)	D (II+III)	E (II+IV)	F (III+IV)
Set I	1	.60	.99	.88			
	2	−.79	.69	.74			
Set II	3	−.52			.17	−.23	
	4	.89			.98	.92	
	5	.03			.08	.05	
Set III	6		.41		.69		.52
	7		−.11		.57		.17
	8		.99		.72		.72
Set IV	9			.53		.85	.78
	10			.99		.52	.63

Note: Cell entries are canonical coefficients of the variables as related to canonical variate of the set. Canonical coefficients represent relative contribution of variables to the respective canonical variates (similar to standardized regression weights).
*Eigenvalues and canonical correlations (in parentheses) for the canonical correlates of the six combinations are Combination I, .303 (.550); II, .654 (.810); III, .398 (.631); IV, .451 (652); V, .389 (.623); VI, .785 (.886).

Table 22   Simon-Blalock testing of paths among intra- and extragroup variables as they are related to party vote

Vanished paths	Prediction equation	Actual value	Degree of fit
1	(.023)(.070)=.002	.532	.530
2	(.023)(.255)=.005	.266	.261
3	(.532)(.070)=.037	.023	.014
4	(.532)(.023)=.012	.070	.058
5	(.023)(.266)=.006	.255	.249

variables and the intragroup force. Moreover, the member's ability to identify his union's partisan direction is strongly correlated both with party vote and party identification ($r = .389$).

Age as a proxy for the proportion of life spent as a union member is, as expected, related to length of union membership. As Converse pointed out (Table 19), length of union membership is in turn correlated to identification with and interest in union objectives. Since the eigenvalue of combination V (relationship between the individual-to-group variables and the party vote, party identification, and partisan attitudes) is relatively weak, we can use the group identification variables and note the outcome.[36]

One additional comment on the variable representing the ability to identify union partisanship: Introducing the union identification variable does not seriously alter any existing linkages. Clearly, union partisanship must remain an exogenous variable within the given model. What we need, therefore, is a variable that explains a degree of variance in union partisanship identification—a variable that accounts for a variance in the cognitive skill. We find that education is the most closely related element ($r = .310$) and therefore introduce it into the model independently of the other group forces (Figure 19).

The model that reveals the confluence of union identification (as a function of the length of membership) and educational attainment on the member's ability to identify union partisanship is indeed informative to students of political socialization. For the process of political socialization from childhood to adulthood constantly involves competition and co-operation between the affective and cognitive components of attitudes. To be sure, one can have a sustained and intensified affection through a selective process of cognition in such a way that the latter reinforces the former. But given the general characteristics of the working class—the low level of their affective *commitment* to partisan politics and the effete nature of their cognitive tools of reinforcement—union norms as group forces are *cumulative* antidotes for anti-Democratic sentiments. At the same time, the union supplies the ammunition necessary to maintain and strengthen the level of Democratic support that a member already has.

Summary

The union's partisan influence appears across all sociological and occupational categories. The union's ability to encourage political participation and Democratic support appears greatest among the lower socioeconomic

Figure 17 Causal paths among extra- and intragroup forces as they are related to the party vote

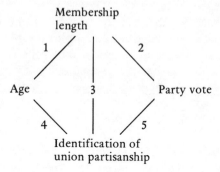

Figure 18 Revised causal paths among extra- and intragroup forces as they are related to the party vote

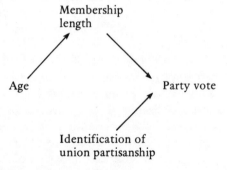

Figure 19 Revised model of causality among the intra- and extragroup forces

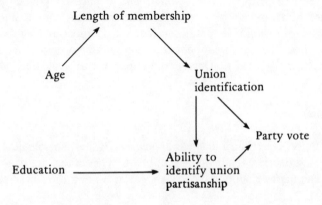

groups. Among these members an optimal degree of political apostasy occurs, and the forces necessary to intensify involvement and loyalty make the most visible contributions. To the extent that these *strengthen* and possibly *convert* the affective elements of political partisanship, union's normative role is indeed powerful.

On the other hand, when union norms are transmitted through partisan attitudes (as a rational component), the union again proves to be an impressive molder of attitudes friendly to the Democratic party. The union's conspicuous role in modifying and often reversing the relationship between wealth and politics suggests its peculiar ability to mobilize and benefit from those economic motives not purely pecuniary.

Thus by seizing on such secondary correlates of the class levels as participation and issue awareness, the labor union erodes hostile orientations and impresses members with the relevance of union norms to their welfare.

However one views the sequential ordering of party identification, partisan attitudes, and party vote, the union intervenes with impressive pervasiveness. The union's two-pronged influence through party identification and partisan attitudes has been recharted in terms of the relationship among constraints within the union and also in terms of the commerce between them and some of the external background elements. In Chapters 5 and 6, we shall elaborate the manner in which the union affects different classes of its members.

5 Political Consequences of Occupational Mobility of Union Members

The association between class and politics is weaker in the United States than in other Anglo-American countries; nevertheless, class has been a basis of voting, particularly since the New Deal.

Our data make it evident that a number of the major population categories have a persistent inclination toward one or the other of the two parties. The major theme of this group orientation in voting is social class. The prestige groups—educational, economic—are the most dependable sources of Republican support, while the laborers, Negroes, unemployed, and other low-income and low-education groups are the strongest sources of the Democratic vote.[1]

Some have even ascribed ideological differences to the two parties insofar as the class division of the electoral outcome is concerned. According to this ideological characterization, Republicans are more willing to accept "the justice of the present distribution of worldly goods between classes and regions," while Democrats "welcome government intervention to alter it." [2]

There seems to be general agreement that this class division of votes has been declining significantly and that the decline originates from the nation's *prosperity*.

The most striking feature of the polarization trend in the recent past has been the steady and rapid depolarization between 1948 and 1956. This decline occurred in a post-war period when the nation was enjoying a striking ascent to prosperity and a consequent release from the pressing economic concerns that had characterized the Depression.[3]

However, Robert R. Alford recently reexamined different bodies of data and concluded that "no evidence of either a decline of class voting, or any substantial change in the pattern of class-voting among major United States regions or religious groups has been found." [4] Despite persistent diversity of American politics, he notes a continuing pattern of class voting and its uniformity, so that occupational status, income, and other socioeconomic attributes distinguish the support of the two major parties more clearly now than in any other period since the Civil War.[5]

What concerned Alford explicitly was an empirical surface phenomenon —*whether* class voting has in fact declined. Implicitly, however, the theoretical underpinning of this question deals with more profound assumptions about the economic basis of politics. The central question is, "Does affluence alter partisanship?" In this chapter, we shall attempt to answer this question *directly* and *descriptively* as it relates to labor union voting behavior.

Working-Class Suburb

As early as two decades ago, the so-called new middle class composed
largely of the formerly poor attracted attention with their migration into
the suburbs. Concerning the political impact of one such instance of the
new ascendancy, Samuel Lubell wrote in 1951:

Outwardly at least there seemed nothing unusual about this Cleveland street.
Each two-story frame dwelling had its lawn in the front and garage in the
rear. If stained-glass windows and scrolled, oaken doors in some houses hinted
at a lost elegance, the lady cigar trees shading the sidewalks and the 'No
Through Trucks' sign at the corner stamped the street as still fair-to-do, middle
class. Driving by one would hardly give these houses a second glance. Yet it
was here that Thomas E. Dewey lost his chance at the Presidency.

To have beaten Truman, Dewey should have swept streets like this one,
with homes ranging in value between $15,000 and $20,000. Actually, he
managed only to break even. Of the three precincts converging upon the West
Boulevard Church, Truman carried one by eight votes, while Dewey squeezed
through in the other two by seven apiece. Perhaps nowhere else in the whole
country was the vote so close.

In the 1920's this area was overwhelmingly Republican. The fact that it
became a break-even zone in the raging political war is one of the more
portentous developments of the Roosevelt Revolution.

... In view of the usual sharp division in voting along economic lines, one
might expect people to turn Republican as they mount to better income
heights. There has indeed been much of that, particularly in the last few
inflation-haunted years. But in large part, as the poor and underprivileged
prospered and climbed they remained loyal to the Democratic party. The new
middle class, which developed in the 1940's, seems as Democratic by custom
as the other middle class elements are instinctively Republican.[6]

Of the Lubellian school of money and politics in general there is a
great number and variety here and abroad, as we noted in the previous
chapter. Among them, a study of auto workers in suburbia by Bennett
M. Berger and a survey of UAW members in Detroit by Arthur Kornhauser
confirm Lubell's conviction *for the union members* as well.

Whether the trend is for working people to assimilate a "middle class"
conception of their position in society or an alternative that stresses distinctive and divergent goals remains a crucial question. Our study of auto workers
contributes rather striking evidence that it is possible for wage earners to experience vast social and economic gains and yet remain steadfastly union oriented in their political views. This may well be the most significant of our
findings.[7]

On the other side, theories and speculations abound.[8] William H. Whyte's observation may serve as a prototype:

Figures rather clearly show that people from big urban Democratic wards tend to become more Republican and, if anything, more conservative than those whose outlook they are unconsciously adopting. . . .

Whatever the cause, it is true that something does seem to happen to Democrats when they get to suburbia. Despite the constant influx of Democrats the size of the Republican vote remains fairly constant from suburb to suburb.[9]

In this chapter, we pose the same question for union members: "Does affluence alter political attitudes and behavior of unionized workers?" Our chief task is to describe the political consequences of the union member's social mobility; we defer causal analysis to Chapter 6. In examining the so-called thesis of embourgeoisement and its applicability to union members, we deal first with the methodological discrepancies found in both schools—those confirming and rejecting the thesis—in order to demonstrate the ways in which divergent measurement procedures account for the inconsistent results. Next we devise a procedure for operationalizing the concepts of social mobility and change in political behavior to analyze our national data on union voting behavior.

Finally, we briefly review the economic concept of affluence, because we believe that examining the theoretical relevance of the definition of and variance in the independent variable can supply evidence for the causal discussion in Chapter 6.

Social Mobility and Political Behavior: Measurement Problems

The social science literature on social mobility and its political consequences contains a variety of inconsistencies in the measurement process—inconsistencies in the concept being measured and the variable used to represent it. Three inconsistencies appear:

1. No measurement of either the independent variable (social mobility) or the dependent variable (political behavior).
2. Measurement of fixed class levels at a given time as associated with measurement of political behavior at the same time.
3. Measurement of the independent variable operationalized as a "movement" but not the dependent variable.

Failure to measure either social mobility or its political consequences is prevalent among those who have studied the so-called politics of affluence. For example, Robert E. Lane in "The Politics of Consensus in an Age of Affluence" [10] "measures" the economic state of Americans using five indicators of economic progress; his sole purpose is to *assume away* any doubts about the fact that Americans live in an affluent age.[11] Convinced that the recent times—especially since 1950—have been characterized by the individual's affluence, he then proceeds to investigate, with the CPS data, the "politics and civics in an age of affluence" in the areas of trust, optimism, alienation, and political partisanship.

When investigating the political phenomena that he posits as dependent on economic factors, he makes both an implicit and explicit assumption about *individual affluence*. Thus when he tests his hypothesis that "in an Age of Affluence, (1) people slowly lose (or relax) their class awareness, (2) the link between social class and ideology changes . . . ," he employs the two-dimensional cross-tabulation method to demonstrate the relationship that he hypothesizes.[12] In doing so, he explicitly assumes that *aggregate* national affluence, as measured by his five indicators, not only characterizes the occupational categories today but applies *uniformly* to different classes according to a previous proportion of income distribution per class. If the social classes for which he tests the hypotheses had been defined by traditional income levels, Lane's assumption about the correspondence of the national economic level to class levels and individuals within them might have been less *explicit*. When Lane neglected to explain what is meant by manual workers in terms of income levels (or, more appropriately, affluence levels), he was in fact making assumptions that involve two stages of inference—first, the affluence of individuals earning different levels of income and, second, a certain proportion of these income earners belonging to a given occupational category.

Next, Lane's assumptions about the other population groups are less explicit because these groups are not defined primarily by economic factors. Hence when he proceeds to verify his hypothesis for religious groups and races, he implicitly assumes that these groups somehow remained beneficiaries of the national prosperity *at the rate and in the manner set prior to the age of affluence*.[13] Further, he assumes that not only groups but also individuals within the group receive their previous share of benefits from the national prosperity at identical rates. But all these assumptions must be at least quantified. As we shall see in this chapter, we must question even his original conviction about the aggregate level of economic affluence.

A number of studies used as their operationalized independent and dependent variables fixed levels of income or occupation and the respondent's declaration of partisanship at a given time.[14] After presenting tabulated data on UAW members in Detroit that shows a relationship between socio-economic factors and voting behavior in 1952, Kornhauser et al. note:

If we take only semi-skilled and unskilled white workers the results are actually in the direction of greater Stevenson support in the higher income districts.... These findings throw into question the view that as working people move into better districts they tend to become "middle class" and accordingly vote Re-publican.[15]

Many previous references describe a relationship between two variables at a given time and compare it with the relationship revealed earlier in history;[16] studies of social mobility in European countries also adopt this strategy. John H. Goldthorpe et al. and others first established a statistical association of income and "possessions," including house and car, with different occupational categories; then they explored the relationship be-tween these socioeconomic factors and partisan affiliation to conclude that

... the role of affluence in working-class politics, even as a necessary condi-tion of non-Labor voting, has still to be proven. A worker's prosperity, or lack of it, is only one element entering into the formation of his class and political awareness; and, when compared with the experiences and influences to which he is daily exposed at his place of work, in his local community, and within his own family circle, the effect of such purely material factors as level of income and possessions may well be a relatively minor one.[17]

In our case, this would be tantamount to using the association between socioeconomic factors and union voting behavior in each of the four election years to demonstrate a trend in the percentage of Democratic and Republican votes in each category from year to year. Again, to describe the secular trend in the voting pattern of socioeconomic classes and to infer from it political consequences of social mobility is not a tenable procedure. It neither depicts the individual movement on the class di-mension, nor records the shifting political behavior as a result of it.

The third group of methodological pitfalls is illustrated by an article by Kenneth H. Thompson that seeks to reevaluate literature on social mobility and its political consequences. Using the SRC data from 1948 to 1966, Thompson observes political correlates of social mobility opera-tionalized in terms of "movement" between father's and respondent's oc-cupation.[18] While his operationalization of the independent variable, class change, allows for measurement of movement and change over time, simply looking for the respondent's partisanship at a given time as a function of this movement seriously weakens his case. Thompson acknowledges this problem when he notes: "While the independent variable, class change,

Table 23   Occupational mobility and party vote (In percentages)

Party vote[a] and party identification[b]	Stables		Upward mobility by one level		Upward mobility by two levels	
	Union	Nonunion	Union	Nonunion	Union	Nonunion
Democratic vote	58.4 (N=296)	36.5 (N=425)	57.4 (N=116)	39.4 (N=252)	44.8 (N=13)	42.3 (N=30)
Democratic identification	59.2 (N=336)	43.6 (N=579)	57.2 (N=130)	42.2 (N=302)	44.1 (N=10)	46.7 (N=35)
Republican vote	28.4 (N=144)	50.0 (N=582)	31.2 (N=63)	47.8 (N=306)	44.8 (N=13)	46.5 (N=33)
Republican identification	17.1 (N=96)	31.4 (N=416)	14.1 (N=32)	29.9 (N=213)	29.4 (N=10)	25.4 (N=19)
Total vote	86.8% (N=440)	86.5% (N=1107)	88.6% (N=179)	87.2% (N=558)	89.6% (N=26)	88.8% (N=63)
Total identification	76.3% (N=432)	75.0% (N=995)	71.3% (N=162)	72.1% (N=515)	73.5% (N=20)	72.1% (N=54)

[a]Nonvoters and other residual categories are excluded.
[b]All subcategories of one party identification are collapsed to form one category of party identification for each party.

in the relationship is treated in a manner which allows for analysis of change over time, the dependent political change, commonly is not." [19]

According to Thompson's approach, our own data generate the kind of relationship shown in Table 23. Note that the trend in union members' voting pattern is visibly counter to that of nonunion members as the mobility increases; the percentage of Democratic votes among union members steadily falls as they gain social mobility while it increases among nonunion members. The gap between Democratic party identification and Democratic party vote among nonunion members is present in all three categories of occupational mobility—the gap that disfavors the Democratic party despite the percentage increase in Democratic vote along the mobility dimension. Although the Democratic percentage of nonunion members does decline on the mobility dimension, there is not the same gap between Democratic party vote and Democratic party identification.

One inference we can draw is this: *Fewer Democratic identifiers and Democratic voters are found among occupationally mobile union voters.* Further, partisanship shifts very little among the mobile union Democratic identifiers. In other words, they continue to vote Democratic at all three levels of occupational mobility. On the other hand, there is an actual loss of Democratic identifiers among nonunion voters. It may not be an overstatement to attribute the union voters' retention of Democratic identification to union persuasiveness.

Another way of stating this is that Democratic union members are less able to move upward in occupation than to maintain their status, but this says very little about the impact of social mobility on the Democratic union identifier. Even the decrease in the number of Democratic union members on the mobility dimension can be explained by length of membership. It may be that social mobility has actually taken place before voters joined their union, and a large proportion of the upper levels of occupational categories is represented by new members who attained their class level before joining the union.[20]

However, Table 23 shows that even among union voters, the Republican party recruits from other categories—in this instance, Independents. This is especially true in categories characterized by upward social mobility. Thus the percentage gap between union Republican voters and union Republican identifiers increases from 11.3 percent in the stable category to 17.1 percent and 15.4 percent in the two mobility groups. However, the gap between union Republican party voters and union Republican party identifiers is consistently smaller than the gap among nonunion voters (18.6 percent, 17.8 percent, and 21.6 percent among the nonunion members).[21] Still there is little doubt that the Republican party profits a great

Figure 20 Occupational mobility and percentage of those changing to Democratic Party identification among union and nonunion members. (Union □, Nonunion ■)

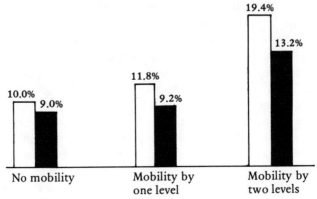

Figure 21 Occupational mobility and percentages of those changing to Republican Party identification among union and nonunion members. (Union □, Nonunion ■)

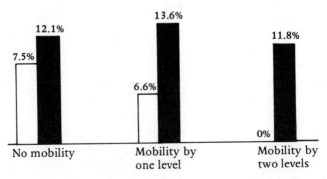

Table 24 Percentage difference between change to the Democratic and the Republican parties as a function of occupational mobility among union and nonunion members

	Occupational mobility		
	No mobility	Mobility by one level	Mobility by two levels
Union	+.5	+5.2	+19.4
Nonunion	−3.1	−4.4	+1.4

Note: Positive cell entries represent margin by which change to Democratic party identification exceeds change to Republican identification.

deal from both union and nonunion occupationally mobile Independents. Whether this greater attraction is *due to their mobility* and, more importantly, whether this indicates that mobility champions over union norms is not clear from Table 23. Nothing is known about their past voting habits or any deviation from it coincidental with the mobility; nor is there any way of determining which union Independents vote Republican in this instance, since no data on length of their membership, for example, is available.

We add one comment on the magnitude of mobile union Independents who vote Republican. Approximately one out of four union members are Independents (24.7 percent), and one out of three union Independents is occupationally mobile (35.4 percent). Thus if we assume that all mobile union Independents vote Republican, the net size of the Republican recruits from the union Independents is less than 9 percent of the total union vote.

Political Consequences of Occupational Mobility of Union Members

To measure the political impact of social mobility, we must be able to measure change or nonchange in voting habits and partisan allegiance of the individual union members. In other words, we have to operationalize the dependent variable, political change, in terms of a longitudinal movement at the same time that we operationalize the independent variable, class change, in terms of a class change over a period of time.

There are three categories of dependent variables: (1) those who have changed their partisan allegiance to the Democratic party, (2) those who have not changed in either direction, and (3) those who have switched their identification to the Republican party.[22] An ordinal dimension is believed to underly the values in this variable—increasingly favorable change to the Republican party as the values grow larger.

We mention three observations about the political consequences of social mobility. First, both union and nonunion members seem to move more toward the Democratic party as their social mobility increases, but they move at different rates; the rate at which union members change to the Democratic party rises much more rapidly than that of nonunion members (Figure 20). When we observe the change to Republican party identification, the difference is much sharper (Figure 21). If we consider the greater tendency of union members to switch their party identification to the Democratic party, then projecting these findings should considerably

Table 25 Partisan vote division among the unchanged party identifiers
(In percentages)

	Union		Nonunion	
Democratic vote	57.2	(N=618)	38.9	(N=1104)
Republican vote	27.3	(N=295)	43.2	(N=1226)
Total[a]	84.5%	(N=1081)	82.1%	(N=2841)

Note: Nonvoters and other residual categories excluded.
[a]Includes other residual categories.

Table 26 Political consequences of occupational mobility among semiskilled or
skilled union workers (In percentages)

Political consequences	No mobility		Mobility by one level	
Change to Democratic identification	11.3	(N=44)	7.3	(N=6)
No change	79.7	(N=310)	86.6	(N=71)
Change to Republican identification	9.0	(N=35)	6.1	(N=5)
Total	100%	(N=389)	100%	(N=82)

Note: No category for mobility by two levels because of occupational level.

Table 27 Political consequences of occupational mobility among nonunion
workers (In percentages)

Political consequences	No mobility		Mobility by one level	
Change to Democratic identification	9.5	(N=57)	13.7	(N=9)
No change	79.7	(N=476)	77.3	(N=51)
Change to Republican identification	10.7	(N=64)	9.1%	(N=6)
Total	99.9%	(N=599)	100.1%	(N=66)

Note: No mobility by two levels because of the occupational level.

inflate the difference between union and nonunion members in terms of party vote.

Second, the percentage difference between changes in party identification is not only much larger among union members than among nonunion members, but also *increases* as social mobility increases (Table 24).

Third, a greater proportion of union members than nonunion voters maintain their previous party identification. In the three categories of occupational mobility, the percentages of union members who have not changed their party identification are 80.5 percent (N = 426), 81.6 percent (N = 173), and 80.6 percent (N = 51). Among voters who retain their partisan loyalty as they gain occupational mobility, we find that more than twice as many union members vote Democratic as vote Republican (Table 25). Now if 57.2 percent of the union members who do not change vote Democratic, then the party vote division for socially mobile union members is approximately 70 percent to 20 percent in favor of the Democratic vote. This is a remarkable increase from the general division of approximately 55 percent to 35 percent. In other words, we can expect seven Democratic voters out of every nine socially mobile union members, while only five out of every eight union members *in general* vote Democratic. The experiences accompanying occupational mobility appear to impel the union member to favor the Democratic party.

In terms of the class level to which the union member ascends, we may classify the socially mobile into two different categories: one for union members who rise to the middle level (semiskilled or skilled) and one for union members who rise to the high level (white collar). The middle-level mobile and the high-level mobile reach their electoral decisions by opposite patterns. The percentages of middle-level mobile who change to the Democratic party drop with occupational mobility (Table 26). At the same time, the percentages of those who change to the Republican party also decrease. The only category that swells because of mobility is the one in which semiskilled or skilled union members have shown no partisan switch. All we can say is that the semiskilled or skilled union members who are occupationally mobile switch less often to the Democratic party than those who are not mobile. That this decrease also occurs in the Republican party indicates the general hesitancy of union members to change in either direction. In addition, accompanying occupational mobility is a greater proclivity on the part of these union workers to retain party identification. Most of the switchers are Independents, who account for 26.2 percent of semiskilled or skilled union members. Since most of the switchers (about 13 percent) are Independents, this reduces the total percentage of Independents to approximately 13 percent; these are the

Table 28 Occupational mobility and political consequences among union white-collar workers (In percentages)

Political consequences	No mobility		Mobility by one level		Mobility by two levels	
Change to Democratic identification	14.4	(N=10)	18.5	(N=24)	19.4	(N=6)
No change	73.9	(N=51)	78.5	(N=102)	80.6	(N=25)
Change to Republican identification	11.6	(N=8)	3.0	(N=4)	0	(N=0)
Total	99.9%	(N=69)	100% (N=130)		100% (N=31)	

Table 29 Occupational mobility and political consequences among nonunion white-collar voters (In percentages)

Political consequences	No mobility		Mobility by one level		Mobility by two levels	
Change to Democratic identification	9.0	(N=42)	8.7	(N=51)	13.2	(N=9)
No change	76.7	(N=359)	77.2	(N=453)	75.0	(N=51)
Change to Republican identification	14.3	(N=67)	14.1	(N=83)	11.8	(N=8)
Total	100%	(N=468)	100% (N=587)		100% (N=68)	

union members who may be open to a third-party movement. The comparable figures for semiskilled or skilled nonunion members show an opposite trend (Table 27). Apparently fewer factors keep semiskilled or skilled nonunion members from switching to the Democratic party.

White-collar union workers who are occupationally mobile show contrasting tendencies. The percentages of these workers who switch to the Democratic party increase sharply as mobility increases; the opposite holds true for those who switch to the Republican party—the percentages decrease as a result of mobility (Table 28). Further, the difference between white-collar workers who switch to the Democratic party and those who switch to the Republican party is much larger in each mobility category than it is for semiskilled or skilled union workers. For semiskilled or skilled workers, the differences are 2.3 percent in unmobile workers and 1.2 percent in mobile workers in favor of Democratic party identification, while the differences for white-collar union members are 2.8 percent, 15.5 percent, and 19.4 percent (mobility by two levels) in favor of the Democratic party. Similar trends among the nonunion white-collar votes emerge, but much less dramatically (Table 29).

Also important in the case of nonunion white-collar workers is the difference between those who switch and the direction of their switch: the difference is 5.3 percent among unmobile workers and 5.4 percent among those who have moved to the next higher level in favor of the Republican party. Among the highly mobile, the difference is 3.2 percent in favor of the Democratic party. All this, of course, is expected, given the relationship between class and politics *outside* the union. What is significant is that, even without the influence of union norms, mobility favors the Democratic party.

Applicable to these findings is our earlier generalization about the deviation of actual votes from party identification. In the case of union votes, this unmistakably favors the Democratic party. Therefore, it may be safe to infer that union members switch their votes to the Democratic party more than their net switch in party allegiance may indicate.

Are Workers Affluent Today?

We still have to causally analyze our findings on the political consequences of union members' occupational mobility, but we shall defer this analysis to Chapter 6. In this section we investigate the independent variable, that is, the affluence that results from occupational mobility.[23] To ask whether affluence accompanies economic status and occupational mobility is to ask about the *implied* independent variable.

When we hypothesize certain political consequences of social mobility, we are implying that social mobility has a psychological correlate closely related to the hypothesized outcome. Thus a good microtheory of social mobility and its behavioral consequences would spell out this linkage between mobility and political behavior, since the theoretical contribution would most likely be identifying and explicating this intermediate psychological element. This is not to deny that a *direct* investigation of mobility and its political consequences contribute to the aggregate data about voting. This would be like linking the summer season (and nothing else) with frequency of criminal behavior. The usefulness of findings from such an investigation resides on a different level.

Most researchers dealing either explicitly or implicitly with social mobility simply assume that *affluence* is the result of, for example, higher income or "better living" today. We ask whether this assumption is legitimate. Robert E. Lane uses five measures of affluence and concludes that:

1. The United States ranked second (out of 122 countries) in GNP per capita (Kuwait was the first) in 1957.
2. The United States ranks about seventh in equality of income distribution.
3. The rate [of annual GNP increase] in the United States 1962–65 is about the same as in the Common Market countries.
4. The American welfare programs . . . compare favorably in coverage and especially in absolute level of support with contemporary European programs.
5. With the possible exception of Italy, no European or developed Commonwealth country has suffered a recession (after the postwar reconstruction period) with anything like the depth or duration of the depressions of the twenties and thirties. This is also true of the United States.[24]

We can make comments about Lane's method, keeping in mind that our primary objective is to measure *domestic* affluence, or the sense of well-being *felt* by individuals within the United States. First, we can dismiss the measures that define American affluence relative to *other nations* as theoretically irrelevant to *domestic* affluence.[25] Second, we can also dismiss as irrelevant his measure of GNP, because it says very little about the affluence of *individuals,* especially union members. The measure that pertains most directly to our study is income distribution, but only within domestic bounds. As it turns out, even this should not be the first step of measurement, for we must first establish a general income increase.

To do this, we can choose among several strategies of measuring per capita income levels.[26] The most valid measure for our purpose is the following:

Income level = (Net income) − (Deductions, e.g., tax, Social Security)
                 − (Adjustments for living standards)

The inequities of the individual federal income tax in the United States are well established.[27] In addition, we must recognize that:

The federal income tax is not of course the only tax; in fact, other taxes account for roughly 60 percent of total taxes paid. These taxes—sales taxes, taxes on real estate, the corporate profits tax, excise taxes, etc.—generally fall much more heavily on the poor than on the rich. The sales and excise taxes, for example, take a fixed percentage of what people spend; since poor people are forced to spend all of their incomes, while rich people save a good portion of their incomes, the poor wind up paying a higher proportion of their income in taxes. The corporate profits tax probably only raises the price at which the corporations sell their products, and therefore the cost of the tax is actually borne by the consumers; if so, the distributive impact would be similar to that of the sales tax. Real estate taxes, where they refer to rental apartments, are probably passed on to the tenants in the form of higher rents.[28]

Thus we have to adjust for changes in purchasing power as measured by the Consumer Price Index.[29] One example of the resulting gross and spendable earnings of workers appears in Table 30. As expected, the adjusted increase in spendable take-home pay of American workers is minimal.[30]

During the period covered take-home pay increased approximately eight to ten dollars per week. So now we must identify the meaning of this increase *relative to* others in society since the feeling of affluence is measured by relative affluence and the degree of improvement over time. If, as economists contend, income *distribution* reveals the relative shares of individuals, income earners, or groups of individuals, we are struck by both the "neglect of distributional issues" among political scientists and economists and by the lack of agreement among those who investigate income distribution in the United States.[31]

The most pertinent question in this paper concerns labor's relative share:[32]

... several explanations have been advanced to account for the trend, i.e., for the apparent increase but actual constancy of relative shares. First, the government sector has consistently gained in importance over the period. By accounting practice, all the government contribution to national product is regarded as compensation of employees. Hence an increase in the government sector augments both numerator (the national wage bill) and denominator (national income) by the same amount, thus increasing labor's relative share....

Table 30 Gross and spendable average weekly earnings of production or non-supervisory workers on private nonagricultural payrolls, in current and 1957–1959 dollars, 1960–1969

Total private

| | Gross average weekly earnings | | Spendable average weekly earnings[a] | | | |
| | | | Worker with no dependents | | Worker with 3 dependents | |
Year	Current dollars	1957–1959 dollars[b]	Current dollars	1957–1959 dollars[b]	Current dollars	1957–1959 dollars[b]
1960	$80.67	$78.24	$65.95	$63.62	$72.96	$70.77
1961	82.60	79.27	67.08	64.38	74.48	71.48
1962	85.91	81.55	69.56	66.00	76.99	73.05
1963	88.46	82.91	71.05	66.59	78.56	73.63
1964	91.33	84.49	75.04	69.42	82.57	76.38
1965	95.06	86.50	78.99	71.87	86.30	78.53
1966	98.82	87.37	81.29	71.87	88.66	78.39
1967	101.84	87.57	83.38	71.69	90.86	78.13
1968	107.73	88.89	86.71	71.54	95.28	78.61
1969	114.61	89.75	90.96	71.23	99.99	78.30

Manufacturing

| | Gross average weekly earnings | | Spendable average weekly earnings | | | |
| | | | Worker with no dependents | | Worker with 3 dependents | |
Year	Current dollars	1957–1959 dollars	Current dollars	1957–1959 dollars	Current dollars	1957–1959 dollars
1960	$89.72	$87.02	$72.57	$70.39	$80.11	$77.70
1961	92.34	88.62	74.60	71.59	82.18	78.87
1962	96.56	91.61	77.86	73.87	85.53	81.15
1963	99.63	93.37	79.82	74.81	87.58	82.08
1964	102.97	95.25	84.40	78.08	92.18	85.27
1965	107.53	97.84	89.08	81.06	96.78	88.06
1966	112.34	99.33	91.57	80.96	99.45	87.93
1967	114.90	98.80	93.28	80.21	101.26	87.07
1968	122.51	101.08	97.70	80.61	106.75	88.08
1969	129.51	101.42	101.90	79.80	111.44	87.27

[a]Spendable average weekly earnings are based on gross average weekly earnings less the estimated amount of the workers' federal social security and income tax liability. Since the amount of tax liability depends on the number of dependents supported by the worker as well as on the level of his gross income, spendable earnings have been computed for two types of income receivers: (1) workers with no dependents and (2) a married worker with three dependents.
[b]The earnings expressed in 1957–1959 dollars have been adjusted for changes in purchasing power as measured by the Bureau's Consumer Price Index.

A second explanation has been sought in the diminishing importance of agriculture, a sector in which the relative share of labor is not only low but also understated in terms of real income. . . .

Another potential explanation, an empirical test of which to our knowledge has never appeared in print, involves the change in depreciation allowances. The permissible rate of depreciation or of capital consumption allowance has definitely increased over the post-war period. Since this is one item "subtracted out" when value added is computed, increasing rates of depreciation make the denominator proportionately smaller than it would have been with constant depreciation rates. Hence this force tends to augment labor's relative share.[33]

Ferguson and Moroney ask whether these factors account for the increase in labor's share and conclude that "there was no appreciable change in labor's relative share. . . ." [34] Some say that the relative share of the average income earner has declined steadily.[35] One explanation for this decline is that:

Taxpayers who reported under $20,000 in net taxable income, the vast majority, got 87% of their income from wages and salaries and only 3% from capitalist sources. At higher income levels, the share of wages and salaries falls steadily and that of capitalist income rise. The 53,000 taxpayers with net incomes exceeding $100,000 received only 15% of their income from wages and salaries and 67% from dividends and capital gains.

Moreover, these IRS data are biased to minimize the relationship between class and income. About one-third of the capitalist income reported to the IRS was tax-exempt, and therefore excluded from net taxable income.[36]

Another explanation refutes the claim that government spending policies remedy the inequality in income distribution. Military spending, which accounts for nearly one-third of governmental spending, and programs such as foreign aid, space, police, interest on public debt, and highways, which amount to one-sixth of governmental spending, do not directly benefit workers; often, they disproportionately benefit wealthy corporate interests.[37] By comparison, traditional welfare spending—on schools, health, welfare, and recreation—accounts for "just over one-fourth of government spending, and it is by no means obvious that these programs are primarily beneficial to the poor." [38]

Individual income levels for workers in this country have not made great strides in the past. Incremental income appears minimal; moreover, the net increase in spendable income adjusted for living costs is at least partly offset by the persistent inequality in income distribution. Thus the minimal income increase during this period may have had a negative impact for the average worker. His income increase may be just a small share of the total income increase, and this may produce a painful gap between his rising expectations (at least what constitutes a comfortable, satisfactory level of life) and his income level.

Summary

Methodological inconsistencies appear in the measurements of social mobility and its political consequences. "Movement" was the chief concept lacking in either independent or dependent variables, or both. We believe that these inconsistencies contribute to the failure to separate the impact of social mobility from the impact of the traditional relationship between class and political behavior.

Our analysis incorporates movement over time in both variables, and our findings differ from past assumptions and findings. The union's impact appears pervasive; more mobile union than nonunion members retain their previous party allegiance, and, of those who switch, more mobile union than nonunion members change to Democratic identification. We projected that the actual differences in vote margin would be far greater in the light of our earlier discoveries.

Finally, an investigation of income levels and income distribution in the United States suggests that income inequality persists; this persistence leads us to believe that the theories of comparative reference group and relative deprivation and the concepts of social mobility and class consciousness are powerful explanatory devices. Even if we assume that part of the increase in net spendable income is "genuine," after compensating for the changes in costs of living and inequality in income distribution, can we say that *affluence* is necessarily a result of the increase? If the answer is yes, we also believe that such an increase (or mobility) at the same time generates and intensifies factors that detract from this affluence—that is, they engender a sense of relative deprivation. It is to this theoretical framework that we now turn in order to *explain* our research findings.

In Chapter 3, we postulated that among the factors affecting norm transmission within labor unions, as normative reference groups, are the properties affiliated with the theory of the comparative reference group. It is these elements—social class, social mobility, class consciousness, and a sense of relative deprivation—that we hypothesized to be causally related to the patterns of political behavior among union members. Thus we predicted a negative impact for union members who are upwardly mobile toward the group mean—that is, we predicted a weakening of the Democratic tie but not accompanying attraction to the Republican party. For members rising to the middle class, we predicted a persisting, if not intensified, loyalty to the Democratic party.

In Chapter 5, we noted that these political outcomes occur as predicted. Now we need to link union membership status and the two contrasting political consequences. We believe that this will explain why union members vote the way they do and, more specifically, *why they vote differently from each other*.

Union members on all levels are more occupationally mobile than the comparable group of nonunionized workers (Table 31). This is not difficult to understand in view of the role that the union plays in the job security and economic welfare of its members. It is common for a UAW member to be promoted to a higher occupational category shortly after his initiation and to receive periodic raises. It is not difficult to find a parallel of social mobility among unionized workers, but it is the speed and assured regularity of occupational mobility that set the expectations of union members.

We also hypothesized earlier that social mobility is one of the causal elements related to class consciousness.[1] Our data support this hypothesis (Table 32). Class consciousness increases steadily with social mobility; more important is that class consciousness increases sharply from "no mobility" to "mobility by one level." Similarly, lack of class consciousness declines most conspicuously from "no mobility" to "mobility by one level."

If union members are generally more occupationally mobile, and, if occupational mobility is positively related to class consciousness, our expectation about union members' heightened level of class consciousness should be met. This inference proves valid when we compare the level of class consciousness of union members with that of nonunion members in comparable occupational categories (Table 33). Note that class consciousness *increases* steadily with the class level of the union members. The rejection that becomes more acute as the union member ascends toward a relatively higher class and as he begins to compare himself with his non-labor "neighbors" is obviously the primary factor in the generation of class consciousness.[2]

Table 31   Occupational mobility of union and nonunion members
(In percentages)

Occupational mobility	Semiskilled or skilled		White collar	
	Union	Nonunion	Union	Nonunion
No mobility	82.6 (N=389)	90.0 (N=597)	31.5 (N=74)	41.7 (N=468)
Mobility by one level	17.4 (N=82)	10.0 (N=66)	55.3 (N=130)	52.3 (N=587)
Mobility by two levels			13.2 (N=31)	6.1 (N=68)
Total	100.1% (N=471)	100% (N=663)	100% (N=235)	100.1% (N=1123)

Table 32   Social mobility and class consciousness (In percentages)

Class consciousness	No mobility	Mobility by one level	Mobility by two levels
Conscious	91.7 (N=1869)	97.1 (N=922)	98.2 (N=108)
Not conscious	8.3 (N=170)	2.9 (N=28)	1.8 (N=2)
Total	100% (N=2039)	100% (N=950)	100% (N=110)

Table 33   Class consciousness of union and nonunion members (In percentages)

Class consciousness	Unskilled		Semiskilled or skilled		White collar	
	Union	Nonunion	Union	Nonunion	Union	Nonunion
Conscious	97.2 (N=175)	95.6 (N=392)	98.1 (N=612)	96.8 (N=806)	99.2 (N=253)	96.3 (N=1265)
Not conscious	2.8 (N=5)	4.4 (N=18)	1.9 (N=12)	3.2 (N=27)	.8 (N=2)	3.7 (N=48)
Total	100% (N=180)	100% (N=410)	100% (N=624)	100% (N=833)	100% (N=255)	100% (N=1313)

Another hypothesis that we offered earlier viewed satisfaction as a function of class consciousness.[3] The theory that linked class consciousness and satisfaction is the relative deprivation theory, but testing the theory is not possible with our data.[4] Therefore, a direct test of this hypothesis bypasses several intermediate stages of variables and connections. The result clearly demonstrates that class consciousness is a strong determinant of satisfaction and dissatisfaction (Table 34).

Dissatisfied respondents seem to reveal the impact of class consciousness. Even if we combine the first two categories to get a "generally satisfied" group, 59 percent of those who are class conscious and 62 percent of those who are not class conscious fall into this category. Again, if class consciousness determines satisfaction or dissatisfaction, and if union members are more class conscious than others, it follows that union members will express a greater degree of dissatisfaction and a lesser degree of satisfaction. Table 35 confirms this thesis.

Given our conclusion that union members are more intensely dissatisfied with the status quo because of their social mobility and class consciousness, we turned to three factors to predict their political choice: (1) union group variables, (2) the source of relative deprivation, and (3) members' impression of the two parties in connection with (2).[5] We treated the first of these in Chapter 4; in this chapter, we deal with the remaining two considerations.

Two sources of relative deprivation—or two standards of comparison—were included in Martin Patchen's formula of comparison; we hypothesized that for low-class mobile workers (those rising toward the group mean) the primary dimension of comparison was largely economic, while for the high-class mobile workers (those rising toward the middle class) the primary dimension was Patchen's secondary dimension—factors related to social status. This question of the sources of deprivation is an empirical question of the *primacy* of the character of issues. An ideal tabulation of data for this question would reveal the rank-ordered salience of issues for these two groups of workers; the CPS separated social issues from job-related issues. Table 36 shows the distribution of attitudes of different mobility groups within the union. The results show that low-class mobile members are considerably more preoccupied with job issues than the high-class mobile workers and indirectly confirm our hypothesis.[6] A contrasting picture of the nonunion members is disclosed in Table 37.

On the other hand, those who are most mobile show the greatest concern for issues not directly related to economic questions. For example, responses to a statement calling for government to take an active role in establishing equal opportunity for employment and housing for blacks

Table 34   Class consciousness and satisfaction (In percentages)

Satisfaction–dissatisfaction	Class conscious	Not conscious
Satisfied	18.3 (N=788)	22.6 (N=36)
More or less satisfied	40.3 (N=1734)	39.0 (N=62)
Dissatisfied	41.4 (N=1781)	38.4 (N=61)
Total	100% (N=4303)	100% (N=159)

Note: The item on satisfaction-dissatisfaction appears only in 1956, 1960, and 1964; the N's here come from only those three files.

Table 35   Satisfaction–dissatisfaction with the financial status quo on the part of union and nonunion members (In percentages)

Satisfaction–dissatisfaction	Unskilled		Semiskilled or skilled		White collar	
	Union	Nonunion	Union	Nonunion	Union	Nonunion
Satisfied	20.3 (N=24)	25.8 (N=77)	17.3 (N=73)	23.2 (N=136)	16.5 (N=30)	15.1 (N=145)
More or less satisfied	43.2 (N=51)	40.6 (N=121)	39.1 (N=165)	39.4 (N=231)	35.2 (N=64)	37.8 (N=363)
Dissatisfied	36.4 (N=43)	33.6 (N=100)	43.6 (N=184)	37.5 (N=220)	48.4 (N=88)	47.1 (N=452)
Total	99.9% (N=118)	100% (N=298)	100% (N=422)	100.1% (N=587)	100.1% (N=182)	100% (N=960)

Note: The N's represent data from only three files, 1956, 1960, and 1964.

Table 36 Social mobility and attitudes of union members toward jobs
(In percentages)

Government's role in jobs[a]	No mobility		Mobility by one level		Mobility by two levels	
Agree	62.1	(N=352)	56.6	(N=125)	45.5	(N=15)
Not sure, depends	10.1	(N=57)	11.3	(N=25)	21.2	(N=7)
Disagree	22.2	(N=126)	26.2	(N=58)	30.3	(N=10)
No opinion	5.6	(N=32)	5.9	(N=13)	3.0	(N=1)
Total	100%	(N=567)	100%	(N=221)	100%	(N=33)

[a]The question used for this purpose was, "The government in Washington ought to see to it that everybody who wants to work can find a job." The choice of this item was largely utilitarian, that is, those who agree show sensitivity not only to the job issue itself but also to the role of government, which may reveal some dimensions of their partisan impressions as well. On the other hand, we acknowledge that those who disagreed are not necessarily *insensitive* to the economic issue or do not necessarily view it as the primary issue.

Table 37 Social mobility and attitudes of nonunion members toward jobs
(In percentages)

Government's role in jobs[a]	No mobility		Mobility by one level		Mobility by two levels	
Agree	48.6	(N=638)	46.6	(N=330)	48.6	(N=36)
Not sure, depends	12.3	(N=161)	9.5	(N=330)	12.2	(N=9)
Disagree	32.0	(N=420)	36.9	(N=261)	33.8	(N=25)
No opinion	7.2	(N=95)	7.1	(N=50)	5.4	(N=4)
Total	100.1%	(N=1314)	100.1%	(N=708)	100%	(N=74)

[a]See note a on Table 36.

Table 38 Difference between the social issue concern of union and nonunion mobile (In percentages)

Treatment of blacks in employment and housing	No mobility	Mobility by one level	Mobility by two levels
For	+7.0	+1.1	+12.2
Against	−7.3	−3.3	−9.0

Note: Cell entries show percentage deviation of union members from nonunion members by either a positive or negative margin.

Table 39 Occupation and union members' attitudes toward federal black legislation (In percentages)

Attitudes[a]	Unskilled		Semiskilled or skilled		White collar	
For	74.8	(N=80)	64.1	(N=241)	55.9	(N=95)
Against	18.7	(N=20)	29.0	(N=109)	30.0	(N=31)
Total	93.5%	(N=100)	93.1%	(N=350)	84.9%	(N=126)

[a]Unsure category excluded.

Figure 22 Occupational mobility and union members' attitudes toward federal black legislation

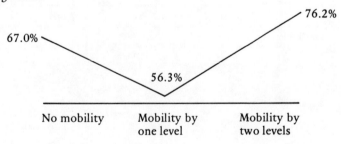

demonstrate that union members show a greater orientation to social issues than those who are not unionized (Table 38). Moreover, the difference appears largest in the case of the most mobile union members. As hypothesized, those with limited occupational mobility show the least favorable attitudes toward social issues, while the most mobile, both in union and nonunion (but especially union), express the greatest sympathy with social issues (Figure 22).

This relationship becomes completely obscured when straight fixed-class levels are used as the independent variable (Table 39). Similar findings apply to other noneconomic issues; the most mobile union members are the most sympathetic to federal involvement, and the modestly mobile members are the least concerned (Tables 40 and 41).

Issue and Party

A large majority of modestly mobile union members who believe in a strong governmental role in employment find neither the Democratic nor the Republican party close to their view. On the other hand, an overwhelming proportion of the most mobile union members who endorse federal involvement in noneconomic issues choose the Democratic party (Table 42).

The Responsible Electorate?

The most important assumption needed to link social mobility and the political behavior of union members concerns the degree of issue awareness among the general electorate. Some scholars have pointed out that voters' familiarity with political issues is strikingly low in America,[7] while the notion of the responsible electorate presents an opposite view of the American electorate.[8] On the basis of open-ended questions regarding the voter's issue concerns and his party preference on those issues in the elections of 1960 and 1964, one author concludes that "contrary to what has been found in the past, there is indeed considerable party relatedness of vote based on issues."[9]

Criticizing the traditional CPS method of using highly structured questions to measure issue awareness, RePass writes:

What is important to observe from this study is that by and large the voting public has at least a few substantive issues in mind at the time of an election, and the voters seem to be acting more responsibly than had previously been thought.... Furthermore, when we allow voters to define their own issue space, they are able to sort out the differences between parties with a fair degree of

Table 40 Occupational mobility and union members' attitudes toward federal medical aid (In percentages)

Federal medical aid	No mobility		Mobility by one level		Mobility by two levels	
Agree	68.1	(N=233)	62.0	(N=88)	72.7	(N=16)
Uncertain, depends	9.9	(N=34)	11.3	(N=16)	4.5	(N=1)
Disagree	21.9	(N=75)	26.8	(N=38)	22.8	(N=5)
Total	100%	(N=342)	100%	(N=142)	100%	(N=22)

Table 41 Occupational mobility and union members' attitudes toward federal school aid (In percentages)

Federal school aid	No mobility		Mobility by one level		Mobility by two levels	
Agree	66.0	(N=237)	58.5	(N=86)	70.0	(N=14)
Uncertain, depends	7.0	(N=25)	12.2	(N=18)	5.0	(N=1)
Disagree	27.0	(N=97)	29.3	(N=29.3)	25.0	(N=5)
Total	100%	(N=359)	100%	(N=147)	100%	(N=20)

Table 42 Partisan association of issues by union members (In percentages)

Perception of party in regard to issues	Modestly mobile union members supporting a federal role on the job issue		Most mobile union members supporting a federal role on noneconomic issues	
Democratic	22.4	(N=28)	85.0	(N=17)
Neutral	73.6	(N=92)	15.0	(N=3)
Republican	4.0	(N=5)	0.0	(N=0)
Total	100%	(N=125)	100%	(N=20)

accuracy. It would probably be going too far to say that the public has contextual knowledge upon which to base its decision. But we have shown that the public is in large measure concerned about specific issues, and that these cognitions have a considerable impact on electoral choice.[10]

Another study adhered to the CPS procedure and compared different levels of the public's issue perception in 1956 and 1968. It found that

... contemporary voters are far more likely to see a difference between the parties and to agree on the relative ideological positions of the parties. They more often believe that the parties are different, and that the Democrats are liberal and the Republicans conservative. The changes are not total or complete, and the data are limited, but they do indicate that the potential for responsible parties is slowly emerging.[11]

Pomper's explanation for the electorate's increased awareness of differences between the two parties on the issues is "directly political"; the political drama of the 1960s brought politics closer to home for most of the electorate. He also suggests that the 1964 election may have been the crucial event in the development of mass consciousness.[12]

From this review, we may derive two generalizations about issue awareness among the American electorate. First, as RePass points out, methodological limitations might have prevented researchers from identifying the issue of most concern to a given group of voters. Identifying it would have been possible had the survey provided a choice of issues and subsequently ranked the rest of the items with a measure of the electorate's understanding of them. Second, this primary area of concern may be increasing; hence the mass electorate may be broadening its area of concern. Issues that have traditionally been peripheral to the voter's primary interest may be gaining importance so that they, too, receive the same attention that the mass electorate once paid only to a narrowly defined issue category.

The Causal Order

Our analysis thus far makes the causal ordering of the variables fairly clear. Viewing union membership as an exogenous variable for our model here, we can draw a configuration as shown in Figure 23. Given seven variables, one could draw twenty-one relational paths.[13] We can test for all of them statistically by setting the standardized beta coefficients from the following structural equations equal to zero:

Figure 23   Relational configuration for union members and party vote

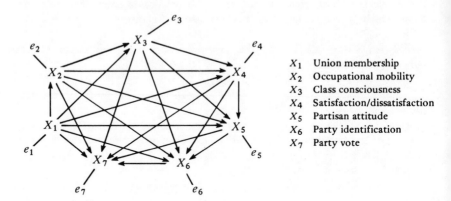

X_1 Union membership
X_2 Occupational mobility
X_3 Class consciousness
X_4 Satisfaction/dissatisfaction
X_5 Partisan attitude
X_6 Party identification
X_7 Party vote

Table 43   Vanishing partial correlation coefficients in the model

Variables	Partial correlation coefficients	Numerical values
X_1, X_5	$r_{51.234}$	0.015
X_1, X_6	$r_{61.2345}$	0.016
X_1, X_7	$r_{71.23456}$	−0.011
X_2, X_5	$r_{52.134}$	0.007
X_2, X_6	$r_{62.1345}$	0.009
X_2, X_7	$r_{72.13456}$	0.013
X_3, X_5	$r_{53.124}$	0.015
X_3, X_6	$r_{63.1245}X_3$	−0.022
X_3, X_7	$r_{73.12456}$	0.010
X_4, X_6	$r_{64.1235}$	0.025
X_4, X_7	$r_{74.12356}$	−0.006

Table 44   Vanishing partial correlation coefficients in the revised model

Variables	Partial correlation coefficients	Numerical values
X_1, X_3	$r_{31.2}$	0.024
X_1, X_4	$r_{41.23}$	0.019
X_2, X_4	$r_{42.13}$	0.021

$$X_1 = e_1$$
$$X_2 = b_{21}X_1 + e_2$$
$$X_3 = b_{31.2}X_1 + b_{32.1}X_2 + e_3$$
$$X_4 = b_{41.23}X_1 + b_{42.13}X_2 + b_{43.12}X_3 + e_4$$
$$X_5 = b_{51.234}X_1 + b_{52.134}X_2 + b_{53.124}X_3 + b_{54.123}X_4 + e_5$$
$$X_6 = b_{61.2345}X_1 + b_{62.1345}X_2 + b_{63.1245}X_3 + b_{64.1235}X_4 + b_{65.1234}X_5 + e_6$$
$$X_7 = b_{71.23456}X_1 + b_{72.13456}X_2 + b_{73.12456}X_3 + b_{74.12356}X_4$$
$$+ b_{75.12346}X_5 + b_{76.12345}X_6 + e_7$$

However, we can get the same result by setting partial correlations for the same set of variables equal to zero. Consider two structural equations:

$$X_1 = a_{10}X_0 + e_1 \qquad\qquad (1)$$
$$X_2 = a_{20}X_0 + e_1 \qquad\qquad (2)$$

Then multiplying equation (2) by X_1 gives

$$X_1X_2 = a_{20}X_0X_1 + a_{21}X_1^2 + X_1e_2$$
$$E(X_1X_2) = a_{20}E(X_0X_1) + a_{21}E(X_1^2) + E(X_1e_2)$$
$$r_{12} = a_{20}r_{01} + a_{21}$$
$$a_{21} = r_{12} - a_{20}r_{01}$$

Multiplying equation (2) by X_0 gives

$$X_0X_2 = a_{20}X_0^2 + a_{21}X_0X_1 + X_0e_2$$
$$E(X_0X_2) = a_{20}E(X_0^2) + a_{21}E(X_0X_1) + E(X_0e_2)$$
$$r_{02} = a_{20} + a_{21}r_{01}$$
$$a_{20} = r_{02} - a_{21}r_{01}$$
$$a_{21} = r_{12} - (r_{02} - a_{21}r_{01})r_{01}$$

Solving this last equation for a_{21} gives

$$a_{21} = \frac{r_{12} - r_{01}r_{02}}{1 - r_{01}^2}$$

The numerator of this expression is equal to that of the analogous partial correlation coefficient. Hence, when a_{21} vanishes, $r_{12} = r_{01}r_{02}$, or equivalently, $r_{12.0} = 0$. Therefore, in this model, a spurious relationship is suggested when $r_{12.0}$ is 0.

In Table 43 the partial correlation coefficients for the indicated sets of variables approach zero when other variables are controlled in a manner defined by the respective structural equations in Figure 23. A revised model, therefore, would include the relationships represented by Figure 24.

The partial correlation coefficients that vanish when we rewrite the structural equations are shown in Table 44.

Figure 24   Revised model of causal ordering between union membership and
party vote

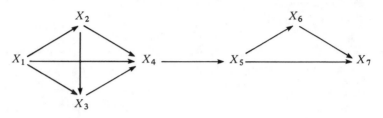

Figure 25   Second revised model of causal ordering between union membership
and party vote

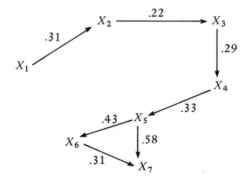

Figure 26   Final diagram of causality between union and voting

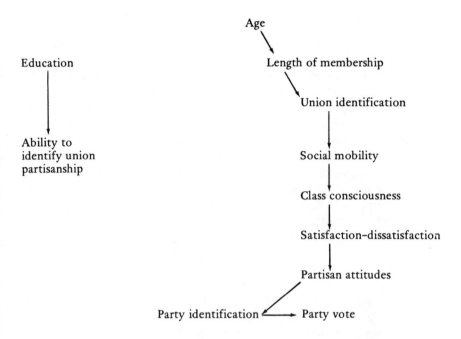

The revised model appears in Figure 25. The coefficients for paths in the model in Figure 25 are the estimates calculated from equations constructed on the basis of Wright's rule.[14] They represent the strength of the relationship that has been proven to exist by way of partial correlation analysis. The estimated coefficients differ from the simple standardized beta weights in that they consider error variance.

We can now construct a diagram of causal paths incorporating the additional components of union decision-making with which we dealt in Chapter 4 (Figure 26). The multiple regression analysis does not completely reveal the nature of the relationship; in addition, the connection between the continuum of satisfaction–dissatisfaction and partisan attitudes is mediated by the respondent's occupational level, since occupational level is a proxy for the *kind* of occupational mobility *for those who are mobile*. Again, the political consequence of upper occupational mobility is likely to be a Democratic vote while that of lower occupational mobility tends to be Independent politics.

Summary

In this chapter, we adopted two broad statistical approaches to examine the causal chains set forth in our theory. The results of the cross-tabulation method conform to our earlier expectations: (1) Union membership positively affects occupational mobility. (2) Occupational mobility intensifies class consciousness. (3) Class consciousness combats complacence. (4) All these influence political attitudes and behavior.

The causal modeling technique largely reaffirmed the postulated relationship and helped erect a formal network of a union member's decision-making process. Finally, considering our earlier findings on the internal makeup of group variables in the union setting, we constructed a complete diagram of causal ordering between union membership and political behavior.

7 The Impact of Labor Union Member Voting in Presidential Elections

Does the Labor Vote Count?

That organized labor has consistently voted Democratic since the New Deal is a truism; what is not clear is the size of the margin that separates labor unions from other sectors in society in the presidential elections and the extent to which this margin bears systemic importance. Berelson et al. found that the union vote in Elmira, New York, was 24 percent more Democratic than the vote in all other occupational categories.[1] Others found the average margin to be approximately 7 to 12 percent.[2] The CPS findings, which compare the labor vote with the control group, indicated that the size of margin was about 20 percent.[3] We have already discussed the *distinctiveness* of the union vote in Chapter 4. Now we have to study the remaining question of the impact of the union and the union vote on the *system* of American elections.

A decade ago Schattschneider posed the same question; his results appear in Table 45. Since "a substantial percentage of workers would have voted Democratic even if they had not belonged to unions," however, Schattschneider recalculated the labor vote in a typical presidential election, considering that an average of 74.7 percent of union members and 64 percent of nonunion members vote Democratic (Table 46).

Scoble points out three assumptions inherent in Schattschneider's argument that are incorrect: (1) 50 percent voting rate for organized labor; (2) no spread in voting rate between union and nonunion members; and (3) a party preferential differential of only 10 percent (the data available indicate about 16 percent). Accordingly, Scoble concludes that the net gain of the Democratic party as a result of union influence could be as much as 2,800,000, and that

... the *gross* impact of unionization may be estimated by alternatively hypothesizing what the Democratic vote would be if *all* 31,000,000 workers were unionized (over 16,000,000 votes) and what it would be if *none* of them were (just under 10,500,000 votes)—that is, the total variation for the relevant labor force could be as much as 5,848,700 votes at the present time and under projections of available data as to both turnout and Democratic-preference.[4]

In Table 47, we offer a slightly altered estimate of the union's net impact on presidential elections using data from four elections and Schattschneider' s procedure. We see that a substantial impact (3.5 million votes) is attributable to union influence. Our larger figure is due in part to three errors in Shattschneider's procedure and to the overestimation by both Schattschneider and Scoble of Democratic support among nonunion mem-

Table 45   Organized labor and presidential elections

Total membership of AFL-CIO	16,000,000
Since only about half of the membership votes in presidential elections, subtract	8,000,000
Votes actually cast by AFL-CIO members	8,000,000
Democratic share of the labor vote (70 percent of 8,000,000)	5,600,000
Republican share (30 percent of 8,000,000)	2,400,000
Subtract Republican share of the labor vote from the Democratic share to get net Democratic gain	3,200,000

Source: E. E. Schattschneider, *The Semi-Sovereign People: A Realist's View of Democracy in America* (New York: Holt, Rinehart and Winston, 1960), p. 50.

Table 46   Recalculation of labor vote in typical presidential election

Members AFL-CIO	16,000,000
Do not vote	8,000,000
Do vote	8,000,000
65 percent who would probably have voted Democratic even if not organized by labor unions, subtract	5,120,000
36 percent who would probably have voted Republican if labor had not been organized, subtract	2,880,000
Net Democratic advantage (if workers had not been organized)	2,240,000
Net gain for Democrats as shown in previous calculation concerning the vote of organized labor	3,200,000
Net gain for Democrats if labor had not been organized, subtract	2,240,000
Net gain for Democratic party attributable to unionization	960,000

Source: E. E. Schattschneider, *The Semi-Sovereign People: A Realist's View of Democracy in America* (New York: Holt, Rinehart and Winston, 1960), p. 51.

bers.[5] We estimate that the total figure in all three cases will decline if the "unionizable" portion of the nonunion electorate could be separated since it would increase the Democratic vote of the nonunion members and reduce the vote difference between union and nonunion members.

The average popular vote margin in presidential elections since the 1932 election has been approximately 7 million votes. Whatever the number of labor votes genuinely attributable to union influence, we can make two comments on the manner in which its impact is felt. First, the defection rate among union members appears to be much smaller than that among nonunion members;[6] this means that the bloc vote of labor unions is less vulnerable to short-term forces and thus provides the Democratic party more *dependable* support (Table 48).

Second, union members and their families constitute one-third of the total eligible voters in the United States, but in urban areas they are well over one-half of the potential voters.[7] Since the large urban industrial states that control large numbers of electoral votes are crucial in American presidential elections, the union vote carries a far greater weight for the ultimate outcome of a presidential election than its mere size may imply.

Labor Union Voting Behavior and Contemporary American Politics

Walter Dean Burnham, in his penetrating work *Critical Elections and the Mainstream of American Politics,* examined the evolution of the "system of 1896" and its impact on Pennsylvania politics. In his view, this system perfected the depoliticization of electoral politics and eliminated the links provided by political parties between voters and rulers.[8] He interprets the post-1929 reversal of this trend as only a transitory phenomenon; the "onward march of party decomposition" continues to manifest itself in split-ticket voting, reducing the number of party identifiers, particularly strong identifiers, and expanding the number of Independents. In addition, he holds that major changes in the rules of the game eased "the transition from a pre-industrial universe of competitive, highly organized mass politics to a depoliticized world marked by drastic shrinkage in participation." [9] He concludes:

The evidence lends some credence to the view that American electoral politics is undergoing a long-term transition into routines designed only to fill offices and symbolically affirm "the American way." There also seem to be tendencies for our political parties gradually to evaporate as broad and active intermediaries between the people and their rulers, even as they may well continue to maintain enough organizational strength to screen out the unacceptable or the

Table 47   Net impact of labor unions on the Democratic vote, 1952–1964

	Organized labor
Total number	15,000,000[a]
Voting rate	70%
Turnout	10,500,000
Democratic vote rate	62%[b]
Democratic vote	6,510,000
Republican vote	3,999,000[c]
Net Democratic gain	2,520,000
Democratic vote if not unionized	3,712,500[d]
Republican vote if not unionized	4,537,500[e]
Net Democratic gain if not unionized	825,000
Net Democratic gain attributable to unionization	3,345,000

[a]From Harry M. Scoble, "Organized Labor in Electoral Politics: Some Questions for the Discipline," *Western Political Quarterly*, 16 (1963), p. 674.
[b]Includes nonvoters who said they would have voted Democratic. This is to insure against double adjustment later when voting rate is considered.
[c]We assume dichotomous voting and no independents.
[d]Calculated on the basis of 55% turnout rate and 45% Democratic vote.
[e]Republican votes (total) actually exceed Democratic vote, 1952–1964:

	Democratic	Republican
1952	43,129,566	27,178,188
1956	34,226,731	34,108,157
1960	26,022,752	35,590,472
1964	27,314,992	33,936,234
Total	130,694,051	130,813,051

Therefore, we would expect nonunion Republican votes to exceed nonunion Democratic votes by a much greater margin.

Table 48   Democratic vote percentage of strong Democrats, weak Democrats, and Independents among union and nonunion members

Election	Strong Democrats		Weak Democrats		Independents	
	Union	Nonunion	Union	Nonunion	Union	Nonunion
1952	87.9	78.5	74.4	53.2	41.6	26.5
1956	71.4	66.0	55.1	39.2	26.4	17.3
1960	71.8	76.7	73.0	50.3	35.9	39.2
1964	85.0	75.2	69.1	57.3	64.9	42.2

radical at the nominating stage. It is certain that the significance of party as link between government and the governed has now come once again into serious question.[10]

We cannot deal with Burnham's evidence, since the shifts that he discusses occur in 1966, later than the period from which our data is drawn. But we submit that his reasons should be reviewed for at least one sector of the voting population:

Bathed in the warm glow of diffused affluence, vexed in spirit but enriched economically by our imperial military and space commitments, confronted by the gradually unfolding consequences of social change as vast as it is unplanned, what need have Americans of political parties? [11]

Our own evidence suggests that these same facts are the source of a strengthened tie, not eroded allegiance.[12] The threat to the Democratic party's hegemony over the working class does not originate in their affluence, partly because affluence is not where it is presumed to be and partly because affluence begets a demand for more tangibles. The real test of the Democratic party's hold on the unionized working class lies in its ability to maintain the relationship between its union members and the rest of its constituency, especially middle America.

Burnham is much more suggestive, and curiously so, when he cites David Apter's technological society as a possible leverage for a critical realignment—the conversion of the American social system from the traditional capitalist mixture of upper, middle, and working classes into a mixture of the technologically competent, the technologically obsolescent, and the technologically superfluous.[13] However, the technological basis of the American class system would strengthen rather than challenge the Democratic party for the time being. Whether this was true for the "Republican" elections of 1968 and 1972, and exactly what the Democratic victory in the 1976 presidential contest signifies for the labor component of the New Deal coalition are the topics for the remainder of this book.

8 Labor Union Voting Behavior, 1968–1976: A Further Test of the Theory

The theory of union voting behavior developed in this study treats the union in two different senses: as a normative reference group to explain the sources and modes of conformity, and as a comparative reference group to explain potential deviation. In addition, we have analyzed the systemic impact of union votes to insure the justifiability of our investigation. We then verified some of the hypotheses derived from the theory by testing them against the attributes of the American voter whose portrait was assembled from the presidential elections of 1952, 1956, 1960, and 1964. For our purpose, we considered this period a representative extension of the New Deal era. Since then, what has happened to American party politics has confused observers and divided analysts as much as it has churned the electorate.

Our theory survived the test of the earlier period. Now we have to test it against the American voter of the 1970s who, according to some, is a "changing American voter." In this chapter, we reexamine our propositions about the union voter; for this, we proceed as follows. First, we will delineate the idiosyncracies of this period—the 1960s and 1970s—in terms related to our theoretical concerns.

Second, we will present a comprehensive inventory and review of differing interpretations of this period, emphasizing some of the conflicting and mutually reinforcing points among them. We will show, for example, how confusing party identification with party vote often generates inconsistent statements about the American voter.

Third, we will use the data from the Center for Political Studies on the presidential elections of 1968 and 1972 to test the profile of the union voter derived from our theory. Specifically, for these elections we shall ask how the union voter was influenced by his group, how distinctive his votes were, and how his occupational mobility modified his partisan orientation. The portrait of the union voter that emerges from these analyses should provide us with at least a partial clue about the latest partisan coalitions.

Finally, this clue and the results of the American Institute for Public Opinion survey on the 1976 presidential election will be the basis for our projections about the future of American party politics. We shall show that our statements about contemporary American politics do not so much contradict interpretations of what is happening and what is to be expected as specify the conditions under which and the individuals for whom certain salient characteristics and trends hold true. Our findings will, we believe, clarify many generalizations about the 1970s and beyond.

Voter Characteristics of the 1960s and 1970s

It is said that the late 1960s and the early 1970s saw one of the most threatening developments in the character of the American electorate: the political apathy of Americans manifested by low voter turnout rates. Referring to the similarities between the 1920s and this period, Norman Nie et al. wrote:

In the earlier period [of the 1920s], our reconstruction locates a large number of nonvoters, mostly highly concentrated among those who later supported the Democratic party. Voting data from the twenties confirms our survey-based impressions of low participation: turnout in both presidential and congressional elections was substantially lower than in previous years and, by and large, lower than in subsequent years. The rate of non-voting in recent years is not as high as in the twenties, though turnout for both presidential and congressional contests have been somewhat lower in the sixties than it was in the fifties, and 1972 saw a substantial drop in presidential turnout.[1]

As we pointed out in Chapter 7, some observers view the current low level of participation as part of a long-term trend; Walter Dean Burnham, for example, sees it as having begun more or less with the "system of 1896" and continuing with the "march of party decomposition." [2] The 1976 election was no exception. "Despite media declarations on election night of a record turnout, turnout was the second lowest for modern presidential elections (55 percent of eligible voters, outdone only by 1948 with 52 percent)." [3] If we take the last two centuries as the period for comparison, no dispute is necessary. Participation by American voters has been significantly declining since the 1860s. Between 1860 and 1896, the estimated turnout of eligible voters in presidential elections fluctuated between 70 and 80 percent and exceeded 80 percent in 1860 and 1876.[4] Since 1896, however, the turnout rate has been lower; turnout was 43.5 percent in 1920, one of the two elections in which less than a majority of the eligible voters participated in the election.[5]

Our purpose is to observe the contours of recent American party politics as "defined" by the New Deal era and, in particular, to examine the secular trend of labor union voting behavior as a component of the New Deal coalition. More relevant to this study, therefore, is the rate of voter participation since the 1930s. If the period from 1932 to 1976 is our time frame, the 1960s and the 1970s in no way support the thesis of voter apathy (Table 49). We are dealing with a forty-year span but only twelve presidential contests. In five of these (1952, 1956, 1960, 1964, and 1968) the level of voting was visibly heightened; on the average, turnout was 61.3 percent, whereas the average for all the preceding elections, including

1932, was 55.1 percent. Not until 1972 did the voting rate decrease, by some 5 percent. Still the 1972 figure of 55.5 percent hardly represents a great decline from the pre-1952 New Deal era; if anything, the rate has increased slightly.

More important, a common explanation of the extraordinarily low level of voting during the 1920s, especially in the 1920 election, was that newly enfranchised women voters swelled the size of the total eligible electorate but failed to vote at the same rate as the male voting population. Something like this happened in the 1972 election. Some 11 million newly enfranchised young voters between eighteen and twenty increased the American electorate, but the dismally low participation rate for this group deflated the rate for the entire electorate. If we eliminate these young first-time voters from our tabulation, we find that 80.4 of 125.1 million eligible voters cast their votes—a stunning turnout of 64.3 percent for the 1972 election.[6] Obviously the elections of this period cannot be considered a distinctive category on the basis of voter turnout.

No less threatening to the future of American party politics is the current decline in mass partisanship. The commonly acknowledged three-tier version of a party—the party in the electorate, the party organization, and the party in the government—takes seriously the partisan loyalty of the mass electorate to the extent that wide-scale movements in the electorate are construed to have pervasive consequences for the party system as a whole.[7] Indeed, recent movements of this kind have excited many observers and analysts (Table 50). Gerald Pomper wrote:

The weakening of the bond of party is evident even among those who still consider themselves Democrats or Republicans. Loyalty is increasingly flabby, as weak partisans now outnumber those who strongly assert their party identification. Until 1964, strong and weak partisans were approximately equal in number; in 1972 the fainthearted predominated within the party ranks by better than a 3–2 margin. These trends apparently show the decay of partisan vigor.[8]

Joining the chorus of the aroused, Everett Carll Ladd, Jr., and Charles D. Hadley recently noted:

No facet of the current transformation assumes greater importance than the pronounced weakening of citizenry ties to political parties. Groups are relocating across party lines, to be sure, in response to new conflict structures. But equally impressive is the movement of voters away from firm partisan ties generally. We are becoming a nation of electoral transients.[9]

The statistics substantiate this concern; however, the description of this phenomenon as a decline in partisanship is, we believe, too general and too ambiguous to be useful. First, while the number of Independents

Table 49   Percent voting in presidential elections 1932–1976

Year	Percent voting
1932	52.4
1936	56.9
1940	58.9
1944	56.0
1948	51.1
1952	61.8
1956	59.3
1960	62.8
1964	61.9
1968	60.9
1972	55.5
1976	ca. 55.0[a]

Source: U.S. Bureau of Census, *Statistical Abstracts of the United States: 1976* (Washington, D. C., 1976), p. 364.
[a] Institute for Social Research, University of Michigan, *ISR Newsletter*, Winter 1977, p. 4.

Table 50   Party identification of American adults, 1937–1976 (In percentages)

	1937	1940	1944	1948	1952	1956	1960	1964	1968	1972
Strong Democrats					22	21	21	27	20	15
	48	41	41	46						
Weak Democrats					25	23	25	25	25	26
Independents	11	20	20	19.5	22	24	23	23	29	35
Weak Republicans					14	14	13	13	14	13
	33	38	39	30						
Strong Republicans					13	15	14	11	10	10

Source: The data for 1937–1948 are from the AIPO surveys: 1937, pp. 72, 104; 1940, pp. 208–209; 1944, pp. 328–329; 1948, pp. 429, 431–433; for the 1976 AIPO results, see the Gallup Opinion Index, Report, No. 137 (December 1976), p. 50. The data for 1952–1972 are from CPS (SRC). Although the earlier AIPO designs lacked the statistical rigor with which the CPS data are collected, "the data of the Gallup Poll (AIPO) are very similar even though the questions and categories are a little different." Frank Sorauf, *Party Politics in America*, third ed. (Boston: Little, Brown, and Co., 1976), p. 144, n. 2.

nearly doubled between the 1940 and the mid 1970s (40 percent), party decomposition represented by this figure may be party-specific. By 1976 the Democrats had recovered much of their strength; according to the distribution of partisan allegiance in October 1976 they had gained any-where from 3 percent to 6 percent over the average of all figures since 1937.[10] Against the average of all corresponding figures for 1952–1972, the Democratic total of 1976 increased by two to five points. In terms of the Michigan data alone, the 1976 total inched within 0.1 percent of the 52 percent in 1964, the highest Democratic figure ever since 1937. Further, the 1974 figure of 40 percent for Independents proved highly ephemeral; by 1976, its size had dwindled to a mere 29 percent.[11] In addition, even at the 1974 peak for Independents, "many of these people [were], in fact, nonimmunized citizens: they [were] young (nearly half of the Independents in 1974 were under thirty-five and had no sustained experience of support for one or the other party.)" [12]

That the proportion of Independents had been steadily increasing up to 1974, is, however, undeniable. Equally true is that the composition of the Independents has changed; they no longer resemble the stereotyped nonvoters lacking civic information and participatory zeal.[13] They now appear better educated and more politically conscious.

More significant is the fact that Independents' indifference to elections is not paralleled by apathy toward all politics. On five of six measures of more general involvement, the unaffiliated are more active, aware, or more confident than the real partisans, although they do evidence less subjective efficacy, the belief that "people like me have political power." However, even compared to the strong partisans, Independents are somewhat more likely to write letters to public officials and to vote on all public referenda—forms of political activity distinct from party competition.[14]

Their higher level of formal education is one of the themes most central to Ladd and Hadley:

A number of factors associated with the weakening of party organizations and of party regularity in the electorate are widely appreciated. The level of ex-posure to formal higher education has climbed markedly, and one main effect of this "higher education explosion" has been to extend dramatically the pro-portion of the population which feel no need for parties as active intermedi-aries in the voting decision.[15]

It seems, then, that the greatest partisan decline occurs almost solely in the Republican party. Plainly, the Republican party's 23 percent in 1976 is 8.7 percent less than the average of all previous figures since 1937 and 2.5 percent less than it was during the extended New Deal era, 1952–1972.

This fact ought to conceal the internal movement which, albeit not a clear break, certainly points to a weakening partisan tie with *both* parties. Unmistakably clear is the migration of party identifiers from the strong to the weak category as of 1972.[16]

Aside from its obvious meaning, the general dilution of partisan loyalty implies increasingly volatile voting behavior despite partisan identification. In other words, the weakened partisan voter is more vulnerable to such short-term factors as candidate appeal, issues, campaigns, and secondary group influences. This vulnerability creates a proclivity toward partisan apostasy[17] and at local levels encourages a nonpartisan habit of split-ticket voting.[18]

Two more characteristics distinguish contemporary American politics. Related to the wane of party politics is an increase in issue awareness among American voters. Issues were highly related to votes in the late 1960s,[19] and this concern has tended to increase from the 1950s to the 1960s.[20] Finally, for the period, the old theme of affluence and the accompanying thesis of embourgeoisement was revived. Thus: "A working class which is middle class and *conservative*. Yes, that is a distinctive feature of postindustrialism. And it follows, primarily, from the condition of affluence." [21]

Our review of the recent trend in party identification should weaken this argument, unless the retention of Democratic strength is due to the entrance of new voters (a highly untenable thesis) and unless the increase in Independents is due to Democratic workers' turning conservative middle-class citizens.

To sum up, the "convulsions" and the "changing fabric" of the American electorate during the 1960s and the 1970s were the results of a visible increase of Independents (though superficially receding by 1976), a steady decline of Republican loyalists, and generally weakened party ties among both parties that make them more vulnerable and more volatile. In addition, the same period may have seen growing voter sensitivity to and awareness of issues and the increasing relevance of these issues in determining his final vote.

Interpretations and Forecasts

Given these developments, an electoral realignment seems an imminent possibility. Whether such a realignment occurs or not, the concept of realignment provides us with a criterion for summarizing and classifying interpretations of what is happening and what can be expected beyond 1976.

The definition of party realignment originally developed by V. O. Key included three elements: (1) a high level of electoral involvement, (2) "a sharp alternation of the pre-existing cleavage within the electorate," and (3) the persistence of the newly realigned electorate for several succeeding elections.[22] While Key originally measured in terms of actual votes cast in local elections, he later modified this method when he tested the idea with a figure showing a long-term trend in the population—partisan registration in Boston.[23] Nevertheless, throughout his work, Key tested the notions of realignment and critical election with the vote results. In addition, as to exactly what constitutes a durable, persistent alignment, Key wrote, "How long such a trend should persist to fall within the definition may be left inexact, but a movement that extends over a half century is a more pervasive indication of the existence of the phenomenon in mind is one that lasts less than a decade." [24] Thus the major difference between the Michigan scheme and Key's classification of elections based on realignment is that the Michigan scheme uses the underlying distribution of party identification and Key resorts to vote statistics.[25]

The difference between these two typologies is crucial since obfuscation of (or oblivion to) the difference between party vote and party identification as classificatory criteria introduces unnecessary confusion both within and about various interpretations of our current political experiences.[26] We shall return to this question later, but now we can discuss and evaluate various versions of what has happened.

To begin, we can divide the literature on this topic into two categories: analyses that detect movement and change in the American electorate, and those that see continuity cloaked in a transitory disturbance.[27] The first category includes at least four variants. The first acknowledges the broken continuity but sees no partisan realignment in the offing. A full-scale analysis by the Center for Political Analysis notes:

. . . there is no evidence which indicates that realignment in the classical sense of massive conversion from one party to the other has occurred or is occurring. It is also less than certain that the prevailing political conditions and the partisan defection of Democrats in the 1972 election imply the future ascendancy of the Republicans as the majority party. The normal vote data . . . definitely support the findings . . . which suggest the maintenance of the social bases of support for the two parties that have been evident through the past decades.

If realignment of the social bases of party support had occurred, we would find the disappearance of previous long-term relations between partisan divisions and demographic variables. Also, new long-term relations, such as the better educated becoming more Democratic and the relatively less well educated exhibiting greater Republican identification should become evident. But, in general, we find that voting in 1972 *accentuated* the traditional relationship between partisan differences and place of residence, religion and race; maintained the relationship with occupational class and *union affiliation;* and deviated from or blurred only slightly the relationship with education and regional differences.[28]

Nie et al. concur:

The scenarios for a new majority coalition are many: a new Republican majority based on the white middle class heartland coupled with an affluent but disaffected white working class; a new conservative majority of similar composition but not tied to the Republican party; a new liberal coalition of the affluent intelligentsia and the least well-off members of society; a "real" majority of middle Americans; a reconstruction of the New Deal coalition based on common economic interest. We believe that some of these groupings represent plausible coalitions. But they are likely to be temporary coalitions of voters around a particular candidate. They are less likely to form the basis of a new, stable party system.[29]

The reasons as they see it are many. The issues responsible for the decline of the party system—Vietnam, racial conflict, Watergate—were not sufficient foundations for a new party system. Nor have ensuing developments such as unemployment and inflation become realigning issues. The party positions on these issues had not crystallized, and the candidates faced the dilemma of choosing between a centrist position on the one hand, and the need to placate certain sectors in the electorate, especially the new voters, on the other. Further, the gap between candidates and parties that has appeared in recent elections may make a new political coalition more difficult; issues have been more closely connected to candidates than to parties.[30]

The second group of those who detect change not only see the broken continuity but clearly anticipate dissolution of the present party coalitions as we know them, although they confess no knowledge of the new coalition's form. Walter Dean Burnham's treatment of party decomposition has been discussed elsewhere.[31] Ladd and Handley follow suit, when they note:

By the 1970s, enough had changed to usher in a basic transformation of the American party system. Let us, then, bid fond farewell to the old New Deal coalitions. The system of which they were parts, along with the social era which nurtured it, having served us well, have slipped into history.[32]

They attribute change to higher education, new elite coalitions of intelligentsia within both parties, the rising level of affluence, the emergence of the electronic communication media, the intensified pace of Americans' mobility, and the growing importance of issues and the candidates' positions on them.[33] They differ from the first group in that they are more certain that the present party coalitions will disappear.

The third group treats the new party realignment more or less as a "given" and examines various possibilities for realignment. These range from Kevin Phillips' view of the new emerging Republican majority[34] to the prediction by Arthur Schlesinger, Jr., that the Democratic party will be rejuvenated into a new party.[35] Finally, some who anticipate the deterioration of the present party system leave its future to factors seen as crucial to the making of the next party system. Richard Scammon and Ben J. Wattenberg observe:

Three ideas of contemporary psephology have been enunciated and elaborated on. The first concerns the new potency of the Social Issue when and if it is brought to a referendum level. The second concerns the middle-minded, unyoung, unpoor, unblack nature of the electorate. The third concerns the one essential political strategy: the drive toward the center. The implementation of these three ideas, we believe, will be critical factors in the Presidential elections of the 1970's.[36]

Paul Abramson joins this group. Noting the declining connection between social class and party choice, he suggests that generational change may be the route of the coming realignment.[37]

All these observations depend on the assumption that recent developments in the American political scene earmark a profound change; the disagreement centers on the direction of the movement henceforth. Some, however, believe that the continuity of the party system has been preserved through the late 1960s and the early 1970s. "This view foretells [the system's] continued vitality, and in particular the continued ascendancy of a coalition very much resembling that which FDR presided over." [38] James L. Sundquist acknowledges the importance of four issues since the 1940s—consumerism, Vietnam, law and order, and race—but concludes that they have not been powerful enough to invite realignment.[39] Another investigation focuses on the trend in party identification and concludes:

... analysis of changes in the socio-demographic bases of partisan identification over the last twenty years revealed that no new pattern of partisan alignment was readily observable. While there have been in recent years noticeable changes in the aggregate distribution of partisan identification in the United

Figure 27 Combined possibility of Democratic Party identification and party vote, 1968–1972. (No "Loss and Gain" category for party vote since it can be only one or the other.)

Democratic Party identification, 1968–1972

		Loss	No change	Gain	Loss and change
Democratic	Loss		D_1		D_2 (when loss=gain)
Party vote	No change				
1968–1972	Gain				

Figure 28 Combined possibility of Republican Party identification and party vote, 1968–1972 (No "Loss and Gain" category since it can be only one or the other.)

Republican Party identification, 1968–1972

		Loss	No change	Gain	Loss and gain
Republican	Loss				
Party vote	No change				
1968–1972	Gain	R_1			R_2 (when loss) gain)

Table 51 Comparison of party identification and party votes 1937–1964 and 1968–1976 (In percentages)

		Party identification	Party vote
Democratic party	1937–1964	45.75	51.95
	1968–1976	45.67	43.41
Democratic loss or gain for 1968–1976		no change	loss
Republican party	1937–1964	30.88	46.61
	1968–1976	23.33	50.67
Republican loss or gain for 1968–1976		loss	gain

Source: Calculated from the figures in Table 50

States, these changes did not reveal any specific pattern of change in the socio-demographic bases of partisan identification over the same period of time.[40]

Even defections among certain ranks of the Democrats seem to buttress this view. Based on a recent survey, John Stewart comments on the Democratic apostasy: ". . . these defections from the Democratic presidential column cannot hide an equally undisputed fact: the FDR coalition has not come apart at the seams." [41]

The most important conflicts and differences among these observations came from a simple confusion between two measurement criteria: party votes actually cast and the pattern of distribution of party identification over the same period. Some conflicts are inevitable because one author consistently uses party identification as the criterion while another consistently uses party votes.[42] Some difficulties arise because these two measures are interchanged in one analytic work,[43] or, still, because the referent used in the dialogue between analysts is not mutually consistent.[44] Considerable elegance results if we devise a fairly tight scheme of classification by reducing all the questions to some specific, ascertainable empirical issues. This can be accomplished as follows.

First we establish two sets of data: one for the period 1968–1976, and one for the earlier period from the 1930s to 1964. We compare the recent period with the earlier one in terms of party identification and party vote (Table 51). In examining the recent period, we can consider both components in order to display all possible pairs as shown in Figures 27 and 28. We can immediately eliminate all cells in Figure 27 except cells D_1 and D_2 on the basis of Table 51. Similarly, we can eliminate all cells from Figure 28 except R_1 and R_2. Now we can have four possible combinations of party identification and party vote (Figure 29).

While we have narrowed the entire array to four possibilities, note that S_1 and S_3 assume that the distribution of Democratic party identification is static. In other words, for S_1 and S_3 to be factual and representative of the period, no substantial movement of party identifiers within the Democratic coalition could have happened. We have reason to believe that this assumption is incorrect. Our recent data show, at least at one point, animated movement among the Democratic party identifiers of various unions.[45] In other words, we can assume that some losses and gains, however moderate, occurred among the subcategories of Democrats. Thus only two situations are left to consider: S_2 and S_4. These situations involve some commotion within and among components of the Democratic party which eventually cancelled each other but which lost Democratic presidential votes (8.54 percent) in comparison with the previous period, the 1930s to 1964. At

Figure 29 Possibilities of two-party division of party identification and party vote, 1968–1972

S_1: Same Democratic party identification, loss in democratic vote, and loss in Republican identification, gain in Republican vote.

S_2: Loss and gain cancel out in Democratic identification, loss in Democratic vote, and loss in Republican identification, gain in Republican vote

S_3: Same Democratic party identification, loss in Democratic vote, and loss outweighing gain in Republican identification, gain in Republican vote

S_4: Loss and gain cancel out in Democratic identification, loss in Democratic vote, and loss outweighing gain in Republican identification, gain in Republican vote

Table 52 Change in party identification of union and nonunion members 1968–1972 (In percentages)

	1968		1972	
	Union	Nonunion	Union	Nonunion
Strong Democrat	25.4	22.1	19.0	13.5
	(N=103)	(N=272)	(N=129)	(N=263)
Weak Democrat	27.8	25.5	27.0	25.7
	(N=113)	(N=314)	(N=183)	(N=500)
Independent	28.8	27.8	39.2	33.8
	(N=117)	(N=343)	(N=260)	(N=658)
Weak Republican	12.3	14.6	9.0	14.9
	(N=50)	(N=180)	(N=61)	(N=290)
Strong Republican	5.7	10.1	5.9	12.1
	(N=23)	(N=124)	(N=40)	(N=236)
Total	100%	100.1%	100.1%	100%
	(N=406)	(N=1233)	(N=679)	(N=1947)

the same time, in these situations the Republicans enjoy an increase (by 4.06 percent) but they suffer from either an uncompensated unilateral loss in the strength of party identification or more loss than gain.

The question we face for delineating the character of contemporary American politics, therefore, is greatly simplified. For example, what are the shape and nature of the upheavals within the Democratic party that generated no noticeable change in the distribution of party identification? Was a serious loss in one category offset by an equal gain in another? Who defected from the Democratic party to cause the loss in the total votes? Are these two sets of questions related? Similarly, were there no new recruits to the Republican party? Who are those who have left the party in such a great number (7.55 percent) since the mid 1960s? From whom did they reap such an impressive level of support recently? We can gain significant insights by posing the same set of questions for union members and their families.

Labor Union Voting Behavior: 1968–1972

We can use the data sets from the Center for Political Studies for the presidential elections of 1968 and 1972 to test selected aspects of the two principal parts of our theory of labor union voting behavior: the labor union as a normative reference group and the labor union as a comparative reference group.[46] To analyze the former, we shall examine the distinctiveness of union votes and some of the more important socioeconomic correlates, as we have done in Chapter 5. This query should show whether the theory is valid when tested by a different period and whether the Democratic party is indeed experiencing a major "disarray." To analyze labor unions as comparative reference groups, we shall examine the impact of mobility, class consciousness, satisfaction with the condition of life, and the like. Aside from testing our original theory, these analyses should show the implications, if any, of the changing contextual variables for the union voting behavior, for example, the consequence of the so-called affluence.

This section then will conclude with a synoptic view of the union voter in the late 1960s and the early 1970s that should provide us with some of the data necessary for a political projection beyond 1976.

Distinctiveness of union votes, 1968–1972 [47]   From Table 52 we can make several observations. The decline in union Democratic identification during the period 1952–1964 and the decline during the period 1968–1972 differed by 7.23 percent, the lowest level being 46 percent in 1972.

Figure 30 Income and percentage of Democratic votes among union and non-union voters, 1968

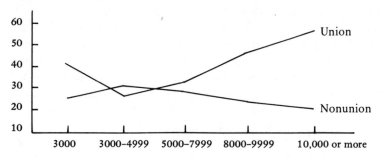

Figure 31 Income and percentage of Democratic votes among union and non-union voters, 1972

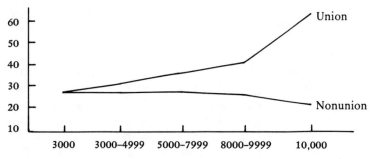

Table 53 Participation difference between union and nonunion members 1968–1972

	Unskilled	Semiskilled	White collar
Always voted	+9.5	+6.9	-3.6
Very much interested	+1.0	+0.8	-7.0

Note: Cell entries represent percentage figures by which union members exceed nonunion members. For example, in the voting category of voting, the figures for the union occupational groups are 49.4%, 47.4%, and 59.4%, and for the nonunion occupational groups, the figures are 38.7%, 40.5%, and 63.0%. For the "Very interested" category, the corresponding figures are 30.8%, 31.4%, and 35.4%, for the union voters, and 29.8%, 30.6%, and 42.4% for nonunion voters.

At the same time, however, Republican identification also declined by 2 percent. Curiously enough, this decline is due largely to the election of 1972, a Republican landslide victory. In that year, the union's Republican identification slipped to 14.9 percent, the second lowest level (second only to the Democratic landslide victory of 1964) in the entire period 1952–1972.

Two additional observations are worth mentioning here. With the exception of 1952, the proportion of union voters identified as weak Democrats was largest in 1968 and second largest in 1972. Further, the proportions of Independent union voters in 1968 and 1972 were the largest in this period, reaching an astonishing 39.2 percent in 1972. The message seems clear: union disenchantment with the Democratic party in 1968 and 1972 was not translated into identification with the Republican party. Rather, it was manifested in weakened or no support for both parties by union voters' joining the ranks of Independents. The conspicuous swell of Independents among the union voters makes it equally clear that disenchantment, at least in 1972, was even more pronounced among union voters than among the rest of the electorate; it was a passionate reaction but not an outright repudiation. What was happening with the union voter seems to exaggerate the tendencies of the general electorate.

Despite the recent surface erosion, union forces remain equally, if not more, impressive. The data generated for a table comparable to Table 5 in Chapter 4 suggest that deviation in the percentage of the Democratic vote is always positive for union voters while it is negative for nonunion voters. As expected, the deviation was maximal among the weak identifiers and greater than the earlier period. The distinctiveness of union votes and union party identification in selected socioeconomic categories, such as those used in Table 15, has been largely preserved. Especially significant is the retention of the gap between the Democratic proportion of both union and nonunion high-income voters (Figures 30 and 31). The importance of this retention becomes clear when we replicate the displays of Table 11 in Table 53 for the recent period. The negative figures for the white-collar category show that the difference in the Democratic proportion of union and nonunion voters remained stable when only the voting respondents were considered, but the two measures of participation show reversed data for union members in the white-collar category. This is consistent in all other measures of participation.

What this *implies* is that white-collar members and their families became considerably more apolitical. Notice, for example, that only 35.4 percent of the white-collar union members were "very interested," a result that contrasts greatly with our earlier finding. Thus we assume that white-

Table 54 Occupational mobility and change to the Democratic Party
1968–1972

	No mobility	Mobility by one level	Mobility by two levels
Union	50.4	63.6	69.2
Nonunion	50.0	50.5	51.7

Note: Cell entries represent the percentage of those who switched to the Democratic Party.

Table 55 Percentage difference between change to the Democratic and Republican parties as a function of occupational mobility among union and nonunion members, 1968–1972

	No mobility	Mobility by one level	Mobility by two levels
Union	0.8	27.2	38.4
Nonunion	0	1	3.4

Note: Cell entries represent the percentage margin by which change to the Democratic Party exceeds change to the Republican Party.

collar union members in particular did not defect outright but decreased participatory activities.[48]

Occupational mobility and union voting   We showed earlier that the Thompson approach of measuring movement only in the independent variable (i.e., mobility) was not consistent with our theory and that it therefore did not test the derived hypothesis relating to the political consequences of occupational mobility.[49] Hence, we also measure movement in the dependent variable (party switch) as in the earlier period. The results show that the proportion of those who change to the Democratic party increases as mobility increases (Table 54). Further, the percentage difference between those who switch to the Democratic party and those who switch to the Republican party appears far greater' than for the previous period, as shown in Table 24. This time the differences are positive even for nonunion members (Table 55).

Like the earlier period, the present period shows: (1) the effect of the union on mobility level (Table 31); (2) the effect of social mobility on class consciousness (slightly more this time) (Table 32); (3) the effect, albeit moderate, of union on class consciousness (Table 33); (4) the effect of class consciousness on satisfaction (Tables 34 and 35); (5) the effect of social mobility on union voters' attitudes toward job issues (Table 36); and (6) the effect of mobility on union voters' attitudes toward federal activism in social issues such as civil rights, medical aid, and school aid. Most important of these findings for our purpose are (5) and (6), especially the new findings that show heightened (and not lowered) endorsement for federal intervention in job and social issues.

Why, then, did union members' behavior fail to manifest itself in Democratic votes in the 1968 and 1972 elections? The answer seems to be that the final linkage is missing—that is, there was a missing connection between members' attributes and attitudes on the one hand, and their perception of the Democratic candidates on the two salient issues, on the other. A much smaller proportion of those who endorsed federal activism on jobs and social issues saw the necessary connection between these issues and the positions of Humphrey and McGovern. A great proportion of the Wallace votes, for example, appear to have come from those who saw in him a dollar-for-dollar return from the federal government, which he claimed was impeded because of "those folks in Washington," the "they" of the "we–they" dichotomy.

1976 and Beyond

All the inferences in the preceding section appear to be reinforced by the 1976 presidential election in which 63 percent of the union voters (against 36 percent of the nonunion voters), supported Jimmy Carter, second only to the nonwhites (85 percent). In a way, then, the labor union voting behavior was never fundamentally undermined in a relative sense. Referring to the period 1952–1972, Nie et al. noted:

Union members have . . . persisted in their Democratic voting. A Democratic candidate for the House of Representatives, for example, can on the average expect to obtain 60 to 70 percent of the union vote, and a Democratic presidential candidate, even if he does badly, will do less badly among union members than one would expect on the basis of national figures. This has not changed over time.[50]

The CPS analysts, as summarized in the earlier paper, reached a similar conclusion in their later article on the 1972 presidential election.[51]

Whatever loss there was among union Democratic identifiers, it seems clear that the spill largely favored Independents: "As of 1973, however, these votes had not moved to the Republican column, . . . only to independent status. In no region of the country, was there a significant gain for the GOP." [52] The reason for the weakened Democratic commitment among union voters is found in the missing linkage—the two most important issues for union members and their families and the perceived positions of Humphrey and McGovern. The only catch is that the concern about federal relief in noneconomic areas seems to be gaining importance among union members, especially as they gain economic ascendancy (or as they think they do). *Economic issues still occupy the most important position,* even though social concerns are narrowing the gap, and the evidence suggests its continued ascendancy in the future:

. . . the relatively lower correlation between the economic issues and the liberal–conservative scale suggests a decreased emphasis on economic differences and a greater concern with the social, cultural and perhaps humanitarian values underlying political conflict and cleavages.[53]

Stewart, in this connection, notes the difference between the so-called public disapproval of governmental overactivity as an abstract folk ideology and the public's pragmatic endorsement of specific social agenda:

Not surprisingly, when the issue is cast in general ideological terms, there *is* significant public support for the contention that there is too much government spending. In the special January survey, 66 per cent of the public agreed that "we should hold the line on federal spending by cutting back on certain government programs—even those that many people think are important." But when the issue is presented in terms of specific social programs, the same high level of public support for government spending that existed in 1964 is again expressed—Nixonian rhetoric notwithstanding.[54]

That the public sees the centrality of government's role in problem solving seems clear, whether that attitude reflects postindustrial citizen socialization or an intellectual preference. The Roper poll on this very subject is revealing: six in ten favor a big federal effort to solve problems caused by race and poverty; the same proportion of the public wants major action to establish "more controls to protect the consumer." In addition, four-fifths favor a major government effort to slow inflation, and the same proportion wants a big move against crime and drugs.[55] These findings should not be blurred and their importance should not be underestimated simply because they might be conditioned responses to generalized government "vs" citizen questions. Nor should their significance be denied because of the public's vehement rejection of *inefficient* problem solving, since the inefficiency is invariably viewed as yet another instance of "them" being served and "us" being left out.

To posit political conservatism as a consequence of the so-called affluence of the 1960s and the 1970s is to misread the process of social mobility and the wants and demands that it excites—the process that generates not complacence but more demands, though those demands are being qualitatively altered. Our theory incorporating the notion of relative deprivation predicted precisely this phenomenon, for union members in particular and the electorate in general, and our present data bear it out. Further, the *fact* of affluence in recent times was challenged, at least in the sense in which it was meant to be used for the argument of embourgeoisement. The takehome pay of an average worker increased minimally between 1960 and 1969 (approximately $7.50 in spendable average weekly earnings); in addition, the shape of income distribution in the United States pointed to more, not less, inequality. These conditions seem true of more recent times as well.[56] Despite the negligible increase in takehome pay, bloated gross income figures create hopeful illusions for the average worker. The skewed income distribution exacerbates the pain of relative deprivation. Even for those for whom "affluence" is a reality, the gap between aspiration and expectation can never be bridged with the improved income status alone.[57] For many of these workers, government represents the last and only source of hope.

As issue awareness grows, perhaps in more pronounced ways for union voters, and as their social concerns become as important as traditional economic concerns, behavioral cues will be found less and less in the abstract psychological foundation of party identification that sells an amorphous idea on a wholesale basis, and more and more in a set of concrete, tangible issues and a candidate's positions on them. The short period 1964–1972 witnessed two astounding landslide elections (1964, 1972) despite the absence of "valence" issues or an extraordinarily charismatic candidate. This, in turn, was attributed to the "changing fabric of the American electorate" in the time of the "changing dynamics" of American society.[58] Conspicuous on the recent political scene is the growing tendency of the American voter to bypass, though not painlessly, partisan loyalty and to examine directly the issues and the candidates.[59] Whether this is consistent with anyone's model of rationality seems of little relevance here.[60]

Without a crystalline personal representation of social and/or economic issues during this period, many union voters opted for a suspended wait-and-see strategy, lingering in the relatively less painful region of Independents. For many of them Jimmy Carter was a vast improvement in this regard. The CPS and Gallup alike reported a traditional Democratic resurgence, but it fell far short of a decisive move back to the Democratic coalition by union members. Fifteen percent of them saw no difference between the two candidates, and this suggests a conditional to reluctant support.[61] While Carter was elected *because* he was an outsider to Washington politics, that status alone did not convince union voters of either his efficiency or substance beyond what the slim margin of his victory would indicate. Until most of them are convinced, it is not likely that their portion of the shaken coalition will resettle. One of the determinants of how fast and where the union voters and, indeed, the majority of the American electorate will settle can be found among the social issues that are steadily gaining ground against the traditional economic concerns. For, as we have seen, the voting behavior of union members and their families dramatizes and foretells the proclivities of many others.

Notes

Chapter 1

1. This, of course, coincided with the general transformation of social science as a whole from a discipline largely dominated by historical, organizational, and normative approaches to that of an empirical, quantitative, and analytic emphasis. See, for example, Robert Dahl, "The Behavioral Approach in Political Science: Epitaph for a Monument to a Successful Protest," in Nelson W. Polsby, et al., eds., *Politics and Social Life* (Boston: Houghton Mifflin, 1963), pp. 15–25; Austin Ranney, ed., *Essays on the Behavioral Study of Politics* (Urbana: University of Illinois Press, 1962), especially E. M. Kirkpatrick, "The Impact of the Behavioral Approach on Traditional Political Science," pp. 1–30; William Albig, "Two Decades of Opinion Study: 1936–1956," *Public Opinion Quarterly* 21 (1957), pp. 14–22; L. D. White, ed., *The State of the Social Science* (Chicago: University of Chicago Press, 1956).
2. Peter H. Rossi, "Trends in Voting Behavior Research: 1933–1963," in Edward Dreyer and Walter Rosenbaum, eds., *Political Opinion and Electoral Behavior: Essays and Studies* (Belmont, California: Wadsworth, 1966), pp. 67–78. For individual evaluations, see Peter Rossi, "Four Landmarks in Voting Research," in Eugene Burdick and Arthur Brodbeck, eds., *American Voting Behavior* (Glencoe, Ill.: The Free Press, 1959), pp. 5–54; Angus Campbell, "Recent Development in Survey Studies of Political Behavior," in Ranney, *Behavioral Study of Politics*, pp. 31–46.
3. See, for example, H. F. Gosnell, *Machine Politics: Chicago Style* (Chicago, University of Chicago Press, 1937), which applies the technique of factor analysis to the election outcome of the 1928 presidential election in Chicago.
4. For the pitfalls of using "ecological correlations," see W. S. Robinson, "Ecological Correlations and the Behavior of Individuals," *American Sociological Review* 15 (1950), pp. 351–357, in which the author gives some concrete examples in social science research. For further comments on the same problem, see L. A. Goodman, "Ecological Regressions and the Behavior of Individuals," *American Sociological Review* 18 (1953), pp. 663–664; P. F. Lazarsfeld and A. H. Barton, "Quantitative Measurement in the Social Sciences," in D. Lerner and H. D. Lasswell, eds., *The Policy Sciences* (Stanford: Stanford University Press, 1951), pp. 189–192; L. A. Goodman, "Some Alternatives to Ecological Correlations," *American Journal of Sociology* 44 (1959), pp. 610–625; and for an excellent discussion of the problem as it specifically influences voting behavior studies, see Austin Ranney, "The Utility and Limitations of Aggregate Data in the Study of Electoral Behavior," in Ranney, *Behavioral Study of Politics*, pp. 91–102.
5. V. O. Key, *Southern Politics* (New York: Knopf, 1949); Gosnell, *Machine Politics*; H. F. Gosnell, *Getting Out the Vote* (Chicago: University of Chicago Press; 1927); Louis Bean, *Ballot Behavior* (Washington, D.C.: American Council on Public Affairs, 1946); Louis Bean, *How to Predict Elections* (New York: Knopf, 1948); Stuart Rice, *Quantitative Methods in Politics* (New York: Knopf, 1928).
6. One author focuses, for example, on a body of data on the geographical pattern of voting and the extent to which it confirms some of the prominent historical observations on Southern politics. Key, *Southern Politics*.
7. Here, our reference is to the sociological group characteristics as well as other

"surface" traits such as sex, age, and race, which are essentially accessible variables in the census sources.

8. In other words, "the units of analysis are political entities...." Peter Rossi, "Trends in Voting Behavior" in Dreyer and Rosenbaum, *Political Opinion*, p. 69.

9. For example, Stuart Rice, *Farmers and Workers in American Politics* (New York: Columbia University Press, 1924).

10. For example, income characteristics of partisanship which are among the strongest correlates of the post–New Deal politics.

11. This is not to suggest that the trend of analyzing the political meaning of voting behavior is a logical consequence of such studies; rather, the argument here is to identify the point of interest held by contemporary researchers that was more or less *natural* given the historical background and the incipient state of the behavioral approach. In other words, individual acts of voting did not constitute the ultimate interest of these analysts.

12. Perhaps the most prominent and active institution in voting behavior research, particularly in terms of cooperative projects and data repositories, has been the Survey Research Center of the University of Michigan. The Center also engineers the Inter-University Consortium for Political Research which is engaged in training programs for social scientists. Also, the Bureau of Applied Social Research of Columbia University; the International Data Library and Reference Service, University of California, Berkeley; the Louis Harris Political Data Center, University of North Carolina; the National Opinion Research Center, University of Chicago; the Roper Public Opinion Research Center, Williams College; the Yale Political Data Program, and others. Some of the representative products of this period include: Paul Lazarsfeld, et al., *The People's Choice*, 2d ed. (New York: Columbia University Press, 1948), which studies the 1940 presidential election in Erie County, Ohio; Bernard Berelson et al., *Voting* (Chicago: University of Chicago Press, 1954), which investigates the 1948 national contest in Elmira, New York; Angus Campbell and Robert Kahn, *The People Elect a President* (Ann Arbor, Michigan: Survey Research Center, University of Michigan, 1952), which reports the results of a small-scale study of the 1948 election; Angus Campbell et al., *The Voter Decides* (Evanston, Ill.: Row, Peterson, 1954), which was the first large-scale study of the 1952 election based on a nationwide sample survey; and Angus Campbell et al., *The American Voter*, which analyzes primarily the results of the 1952 and 1956 elections. These more recent works were not, however, without their early predecessors, e.g., C. E. Merriam and H. F. Gosnell, *Non-Voting* (Chicago: University of Chicago Press, 1924), but the kind of national analysis articulating the typical social psychological approaches did not materialize until the efforts by the Columbia and the Michigan groups began in earnest.

13. These are section rubrics taken from a chapter entitled, "The Dynamics of Voter Choice," in Emmette S. Redford et al., *Politics and Government in the United States*, 2d ed. (New York: Harcourt, Brace & World, 1968), pp. 227–263, especially pp. 232–241.

14. Chapter 4, "Voters in America," in Gerald M. Pomper, *Elections in America: Control and Influence in Democratic Politics* (New York: Dodd, Mead & Co., 1968), pp. 68–98.

15. Ibid., pp. 92–98.

16. The term comes from a book title by the same phrase, V. O. Key, *The Responsible Electorate: Rationality in Presidential Voting* (New York: Vintage Books, 1968). Here, Pomper quotes Key who found it "perverse and unorthodox" to argue "that [the voters] are not fools straight-jacketed by social determinants or moved by sub-conscious urges triggered by devilishly skillful propagandists," Pomper, *Elections in America*, p. 80.
17. Pomper, *Elections in America*, p. 80.
18. Ibid., p. 81.
19. Ibid., pp. 81–82.
20. Ibid., pp. 86–91.
21. Ibid., p. 92.
22. V. O. Key, "The Politically Relevant in Surveys," *Public Opinion Quarterly* 24 (1960), pp. 54–61; V. O. Key and Frank Munger, "Social Determinism and Electoral Decision: The Case of Indiana," in Burdick and Brodbeck, *American Voting Behavior*, pp. 281–299, as quoted in Walter D. Burnham, "The Changing Shape of the American Political Universe," *American Political Science Review* 65 (1965), p. 7. Aside from the above, see Bernard Crick, *The American Science of Politics: Its Origins and Conditions.* (Berkeley, Calif.: University of California Press, 1959); D. E. Butler, *The Study of Political Behavior* (New York: Humanities Press, 1959); Herbert J. Storing et al., eds., *Essays on the Scientific Study of Politics* (New York: Holt, Rinehart & Winston, 1962); and Lindsay Rogers, *The Pollsters: Public Opinion, Politics, and Democratic Leadership* (New York: Knopf, 1949). Some articles include Ralf Dahrendorf, "Symposia on Political Behavior," *American Sociological Review* 29 (1964), pp. 734–736; Christian Bay, "Politics and Pseudopolitics: A Critical Evaluation of Some Behavioral Literature," *American Political Science Review* 59 (1965), pp. 39–51.
23. Burnham, "Changing Shape," p. 7.
24. Walter D. Burnham, *Critical Elections and the Mainspring of American Politics* (New York: Norton, 1970), pp. x–xi.
25. Ibid., p. 8. Also, for a typical work, see V. O. Key, *Public Opinion and American Democracy* (New York: Knopf, 1961).
26. Angus Campbell et al., *Elections and the Political Order* (New York: Wiley, 1966), p. 159; also see, Donald E. Stokes and Gudmund R. Iversen, "On the Existence of Forces Restoring Party Competition," Campbell, *Elections*, pp. 180–211; For other evidences of this kind of convergence, see also: Philip E. Converse, "Continuity and Change in American Politics: Parties and Issues in the 1968 Election," *American Political Science Review* 63 (1969), pp. 1083–1105, especially pp. 1095–1101; for methodological accommodations of this trend, see O. Dudley Duncan and Beverly Davis, "An Alternative to Ecological Correlations," *American Sociological Review* 18 (1953), pp. 665–666; Hubert Blalock, *Causal Inference in Non-Experimental Research* (Chapel Hill, N.C.: University of North Carolina Press, 1965), ch. 4; Leo A. Goodman, "Some Alternatives to Ecological Correlation," *American Journal of Sociology* 64 (1959), pp. 610–625; O. Dudley Duncan, et al., *Statistical Geography* (Glencoe, Ill.: The Free Press, 1961), pp. 60–80; Gudmund R. Iversen, *Estimation of Cell Entries in Continuity Tables When Only Margins are Observed* (Ph.D. dissertation, Harvard University, 1969); Donald E. Stokes, "Ecological Regression as a

Game with Nature" (unpublished manuscript); and W. Phillips Shively, " 'Eco-logical' Inference: The Use of Aggregate Data to Study Individuals," *American Political Science Review* 63 (1969), pp. 1183–1196.

27. Harry M. Scoble," Organized Labor in Electoral Politics; Some Questions for the Discipline," *Western Political Quarterly* 61 (1963), pp. 666–685.

28. Donald C. Blaisdell, *American Democracy under Pressure* (New York: Ronald Press, 1957), p. 115.

29. Scoble, "Organized Labor," pp. 666–667, 671–675.

30. Ibid., p. 671 (emphasis mine).

31. Burnham, *Critical Elections,* p. ix.

32. The case in point is well illustrated by the conveniently minimal attention given to the historical setting in Campbell, *American Voter,* which occupies barely five pages in the volume of nearly 600 pages. The authors' postures have an apologetic note: "But anyone who works with extensive data on a social process as important as a presidential election must feel a responsibility to provide *some* historical description." p. 8 (italics added).

33. The Social Research Center investigators seem keenly aware of the utility of a theory at least. "If theory can guide historical descriptions, the historical context of most research on human behavior places clear limitations on the development of theory." Ibid., p. 9. However, there seems to be a good deal of confusion on the meaning of a theory, particularly in connection with empirical generalizations, hypotheses, and even "middle-range" theories. See Ibid., pp. 8–9 and, for the so-called funnel of causality, Ibid., pp. 24–32. Most of these attempts often resemble what might be termed an "explanation sketch." Carl G. Hempel, "Explanatory Incompleteness," in May Brodbeck, ed., *Readings in the Philosophy of Social Science* (New York: Macmillan, 1968), p. 410.

34. Martin Fishbein and Fred S. Coombs, "Modern Attitude Theory and the Explanation of Voting Choice," an unpublished paper delivered at the annual meeting of the American Political Science Association, Chicago, 1971.

35. The reason is admittedly clear: the primary concern of psychologically oriented survey researchers has been the inertia or "drag" represented by habitual party loyalty, and hence voting behavior in general. Converse et al., "Continuity and Change," p. 1099.

36. Key, for example, was "quite explicit in his desire to explain movement and change in the electorate" and hence more attentive to short-term forces as they affect the electoral outcomes. Ibid., p. 1096.

37. For example, Anthony Down, *An Economic Theory of Democracy* (New York: Harper & Row, 1957); William N. McPhee, *Formal Theories of Mass Behavior* (New York: The Free Press, 1963); and James Coleman, *Community Conflict* (Glencoe, Ill.: The Free Press, 1957).

38. For a succinct discussion of laws and their roles in scientific inquiry, see Carl G. Hempel, *Philosophy of Natural Science* (Englewood Cliffs, New Jersey: Prentice-Hall, 1966), ch. 5, pp. 67–82.

39. For criteria of scientific concept formation and theories, see Ibid., chs. 6 and 7, pp. 83–101.

40. The word "thought" is used deliberately to distinguish a class of descriptive and normative literature from explanatory schemata and theories.

41. See the section on studies of labor union voting behavior in ch. 2. In this study,

the term "labor union voting behavior" refers to the voting behavior of the members and their families unless otherwise noted.

42. For the sampling procedure and other aspects of the survey method used by the SRC, see Campbell et al., *Voter Decides,* pp. 3–4 and Appendices, pp. 188–235; memoranda describing the methods of study design, interviewing, coding, sampling, and analysis employed by the SRC, University of Michigan; for general discussions, see Samuel J. Eldersveld, "Theory and Method in Voting Behavior Research," *Journal of Politics* 13 (1951), pp. 70–87 and Seymour M. Lipset et al., "The Psychology of Voting: An Analysis of Political Behavior" in Gardner Lindsey, ed., *Handbook of Social Psychology,* Vol. 2 (Cambridge, Mass.: Addison-Wesley, 1954), pp. 1124–1175.

43. Angus Campbell, "A Classification of the Presidential Elections," in Campbell et al., *Elections and the Political Order,* pp. 63–77, especially pp. 69–74. (This is a revised version of the authors' earlier classification in Campbell et al., *American Voter,* pp. 531–538.)

44. For a discussion of the short-term forces, see Campbell et al., *American Voter,* chs. 3 and 8.

45. This, of course, applies only to the period following the New Deal era. Thus:

In view of all that we have said, how are we to characterize the two elections for which we have adequate survey data? The Eisenhower elections were clearly not maintaining elections. Neither were they realigning elections in the sense of a profound shift of the nation's party identifications having occurred in this period. Yet the question might well be raised of whether they were not the early elections of a realigning electoral era. We believe they were not, for reasons that a brief review of our findings may serve to make clear.

The most immediately relevant information that we can draw out of these studies is the fact that in both 1952 and 1956 the number of people who called themselves Democrats outnumbered those who identified themselves as Republicans, and this ratio showed no tendency to move in the Republican direction between the two years. What is more, the Republican Party did not recruit a heavy majority of young voters who were coming into the electorate, although these years did see the Democratic proportion of new voters reduced to something like half.

A second important item is the evidence that for the most part those Democrats and Independents who voted for Eisenhower at the time of his two elections preferred the man but not the party. This is dramatically demonstrated by the high proportion of ticket-splitting reported by these people. Three out of five in 1952 and three out of four in 1956 were not willing to support the Republican slate even though they voted for its presidential candidate. It is especially significant that this separation of the candidate from his party was greater in the second Eisenhower election than in the first. If we compare 1952 to 1932 it seems probable that the potential for shift created by the Democratic victory in 1932 was realized in 1936, whereas whatever readiness for shift was present in the electorate in 1952 seems to have largely faded out by 1956.

Ibid., p. 537.

46. Ibid., ch. 6.

47. V. O. Key, "A Theory of Critical Elections," *Journal of Politics* 17 (1955), pp. 3–18.

48. V. O. Key, *Politics, Parties and Pressure Groups,* 5th ed. (New York: Crowell, 1964), pp. 522–526.

49. Philip E. Converse et al., "Stability and Change in 1960: A Reinstating Election," in Campbell et al., *Elections and the Political Order,* pp. 78–95.

50. Of the three requirements for a landslide election, the 1964 election does not, of course, satisfy that of "lack of confidence," since it meant continuation of a Democratic administration.

51. Here, our chief defense is found in two directions: the need itself and the relative hazards of a small sample size. "The sample is too small if its results are not precise enough to make appreciable contributions to decisions." Leslie Kish, *Survey Sampling* (New York: Wiley, 1967), p. 25.

52. For the law, see Hubert Blalock, *Social Statistics* (New York: McGraw-Hill, 1960), p. 138; for the meaning of random sampling procedure, see Kish, *Survey Sampling,* pp. 26–30.

53. Kish, *Survey Sampling,* p. 25.

54. For a discussion of cluster and stratified sampling techniques, see Kish, *Survey Sampling,* chs. 3, 4, and 5.

Chapter 2

1. For the history of American labor before the twentieth century, see bibliography sections in John R. Commons et al., *History of Labor in the United States* (New York: Macmillan, 1936) and Joseph G. Raybeck, *A History of American Labor* (New York: Macmillan, 1961). Aside from the general works on the history, there are several separate monographs of bibliography on various aspects of the American labor movement. For our purpose, the study of the history is brought to the mid 1960s since our purpose is to derive a theory of labor union voting behavior that will be tested with the *general* data from 1952 to 1964. As pointed out in Chapter 1, however, we will have an occasion to test the applicability of the theory to the period that extends beyond the 1960s.

2. Raybeck, *American Labor,* pp. 192–194.

3. V. O. Key, *Politics, Parties and Pressure Groups,* 5th ed. (New York: Crowell, 1964), pp. 44–45.

4. Selig Perlman, *A Theory of the Labor Movement* (New York: Macmillan, 1928), pp. 162–163. For data relating to sociological implications of this topic today, see Richard Centers, *Psychology of Social Classes* (Princeton: Princeton University Press, 1949), p. 86.

5. Ibid., p. 164.

6. Louis Hartz, *The Liberal Tradition in America* (New York: Harcourt, Brace & World, 1955), chs. 1 and 2.

7. R. W. Dodge, "Some Aspects of the Political Behavior of Labor Union Members in the Detroit Metropolitan Area" (unpublished Ph.D. dissertation, University of Michigan, 1953), pp. 18ff.

8. Commons et al., *History of Labor,* p. 40.

9. J. David Greenstone, *Labor in American Politics* (New York: Knopf, 1969), p. 18.

10. Perlman, *Theory,* ch. 5.

11. Lewis L. Lorwin, *The American Federation of Labor* (Washington, D.C.: The Brookings Institution, 1933), p. 355. See also, Philip Taft, *The A. F. of L. in the Time of Gompers* (New York: Harper, 1957), pp. xvii–xviii. For detailed lists of antiunion activists, consult Leon Wolfe, *Lockout* (New York: Harper & Row, 1965), p. 18; Commons et al., *History of Labor,* p. 495; and Robert Littell, "Undercover Man," in Heber Blankenhorn, ed., *Public Opinion and Steel Strike* (New York: Harcourt, Brace & World, 1921).

12. Commons et al., *History of Labor,* p. 48.

13. Ibid., pp. 504–508.

14. Greenstone, *Labor in American Politics,* pp. 25–29.

15. Ibid., p. 25; Taft, *A. F. of L.,* pp. xiv and 179 especially for a vivid example; Michael Rogin, "Voluntarism as an Organizational Ideology in the American Federation of Labor: 1886–1932" (unpublished M.A. thesis, University of Chicago, 1959), p. 39. For an account of the Socialists' successful revenge against Gompers, see Lorwin, *American Federation of Labor,* pp. 30–31.

16. Key, *Politics,* p. 57.

17. Greenstone, *Labor in American Politics,* p. 26.

18. Rogin, "Voluntarism," p. 160; also see Grant McConnell, *Private Powers and American Democracy* (New York: Knopf, 1966), ch. 3.

19. Marc Karson, *American Labor Unions and Politics* (Carbondale, Ill.: Southern Illinois University Press, 1958), p. 305; Robert F. Hoxie, "President Gompers and the Labor Vote," *Journal of Political Economy* 16 (1908), p. 700.

20. Gerald N. Grob, *Workers and Utopia* (Evanston, Ill.: Northwestern University Press, 1961), ch. 8.

21. Taft, *A. F. of L.,* p. 289.

22. Ibid., pp. 389–391. See especially *The Reports of the First, Second, Third and Ninth Annual Conventions of the American Federation of Labor* cited in Ibid., pp. 300–301.

23. *Report of the Proceedings of the Twelfth Annual Convention of the American Federation of Labor* (1892), p. 13.

24. Juanita M. Kreps, "Developments in the Political and Legislative Policies of Organized Labor: 1920–1947" (unpublished Ph.D. dissertation, Duke University, 1947), p. 1.

25. Philip Taft, "Labor's Changing Political Life," *Journal of Political Economy* 45 (1937), pp. 637–638.

26. Karson, *American Labor Unions.*

27. Lorwin, *American Federation of Labor,* pp. 88–89.

28. Raybeck, *American Labor,* pp. 198–200 and 268–271.

29. Key, *Politics,* p. 58.

30. Milton Derber, "Growth and Expansion," in Milton Derber and Erwin Young, eds., *Labor and the New Deal* (Madison, Wis.: University of Wisconsin Press, 1957), pp. 1–44. For specific classes of union membership data, see Irving Bernstein, "The Growth of American Unions," *American Economic Review* 44 (1954), pp. 301–318 and "The Growth of American Unions, 1945–1960," *Labor History* 2 (1961), pp. 131–157. For information on individual unions, see

U.S. Bureau of Labor Statistics, *Directory of National and International Labor Unions in the United States.*

31. Hoxie, "President Gompers," p. 694.

32. Rogin, "Voluntarism," pp. 169 and 104; Lorwin, *American Federation of Labor,* pp. 88–89.

33. Lorwin, *American Federation of Labor,* p. 127.

34. Greenstone, *Labor in American Politics,* p. 31.

35. Karson, *American Labor Unions,* p. 55.

36. Greenstone, *Labor in American Politics,* p. 31.

37. *Charities and the Commons* 21 (1908), pp. 149–150; Samuel Gompers, "The Campaign and Labor's Future," *American Federationist* (Dec. 1908), p. 1065; and J. A. Cable, "Labor's Political Duty," *American Federationist* 15 (1908), p. 839.

38. Avril E. Harris, "Organized Labor in Party Politics: 1906–1932" (unpublished Ph.D. dissertation, University of Iowa, 1937), pp. 150 and 156.

39. Ibid., p. 380; T. Wilbain Goodman, "The Presidential Campaign of 1920" (unpublished Ph.D. dissertation, Ohio University, 1951), pp. 295, 396.

40. Lorwin, *American Federation of Labor,* pp. 210–211.

41. Ibid., pp. 406–407.

42. Ibid., p. 211.

43. Ibid., pp. 211–212.

44. Greenstone, *Labor in American Politics,* p. 28.

45. Lorwin, *American Federation of Labor,* p. 229.

46. Quoted by Rogin, "Voluntarism," p. 145 and *AFL Proceedings* (1926), p. 51.

47. Taft, *A.F. of L.,* pp. 479–480.

48. Ibid., p. 483; Vaughan D. Bornet, *Labor Politics in the Democratic Republic* (Washington, D.C.: Spartan Books, 1964), p. 299.

49. As quoted in Taft, *A. F. of L.,* p. 484.

50. *Report of Proceedings of the Forty-Fourth Annual Convention of the American Federation of Labor* (1924), p. 174; Taft relates an account of a vigorous opposition by two members of the Executive Council of the AFL, Taft, *A. F. of L.,* p. 485.

51. *Memories of Herbert Hoover, 1920–1933* (New York: Macmillan, 1952), p. 202.

52. V. O. Key, "A Theory of Critical Elections," in Donald G. Herzberg and Gerald M. Pomper, *American Party Politics: Essays and Readings* (New York: Holt, Rinehart & Winston, 1966), p. 426. Also a similar analysis was extended to Connecticut, Maine, New Hampshire, and Rhode Island. See Ibid., p. 427.

53. Ibid., p. 426.

54. Duncan MacRae and James A. Meldrum, "Critical Elections in Illinois," *American Political Science Review* 54 (1960), pp. 669–683. The aggregate data used came from the *Blue Book of the State of Illinois* (Springfield, biennial) and Secretary of State, Illinois (comp.), *Official Vote of the State of Illinois Cast at the General Election.* The United States sources are from Louis H. Bean, *How to Predict Elections* (Westport, Conn.: Greenwood Press, 1948); *Statistical Abstract of the United States* (1912); and *Congressional Quarterly Almanac* 8 (1952).

55. MacRae and Meldrum, "Critical Elections," p. 669.

56. Greenstone, *Labor in American Politics,* p. 37.

57. Derber, "Growth," p. 3. An estimate is made at 7.7 million in 1939 and 14.2 million in 1948 excluding Canadian members. Bernstein, "American Unions."

58. Later, the Congress of Industrial Organizations.

59. Charles P. Anson, "A History of Labor Movement in West Virginia" (unpublished Ph.D. dissertation, University of North Carolina, 1940).

60. Joel Seidman, *The Needle Trades* (New York: Farrar and Rinehart, 1943), pp. 189ff.

61. Derber, "Growth," p. 9; also Selig Perlman, "Labor and the New Deal in Historical Perspective," in Derber and Young, eds., *Labor and the New Deal*, p. 366.

62. W. Lloyd Warner and J. O. Low, *The Social System of the Modern Factory* (New Haven, Conn.: Yale University Press, 1947).

63. Derber, "Growth," pp. 18ff.

64. Key, *Politics*, p. 59.

65. Perlman, *Theory*, p. 169.

66. Arthur Schlesinger, Jr., *The Crisis of the Old Order* (Boston: Houghton Mifflin, 1957), p .3.

67. Ibid., chs. 24, 26; Bernard Karsh and Philip L. Garman, "The Impact of the Political Left," in Derber and Young, *Labor and the New Deal*, pp. 98–99; and Irving Bernstein, *The Lean Years* (Boston: Houghton Mifflin, 1960), ch. 13.

68. Karsh and Garman, "Political Left," pp. 96–97; Mary H. Vorse, *Labor's New Millions* (New York: Modern Age Books, 1938), pp. 64–65, 93; and Raymond Walsh, *CIO: Industrial Unionism in Action* (New York: Norton, 1937), pp. 60 and 123.

69. Murray Edelman, "New Deal Sensitivity to Labor Interests," Derber and Young, eds., *Labor and the New Deal*, p. 189.

70. Ibid., pp. 189–190.

71. Ibid. and Greenstone, *Labor in American Politics*, pp. 46–47.

72. Raybeck, *History of Labor*, ch. 25.

73. For example, George Berry of the Printing Pressmen. See Taft, *A. F. of L.*, p. 305 and Kreps, "Developments."

74. Arthur Schlesinger, Jr., *The Politics of Upheaval* (Boston: Houghton Mifflin, 1967), pp. 181–182.

75. Louise Overacker, "Labor's Political Contributions," *Political Science Quarterly* 14 (1939), p. 58.

76. This was briefly interrupted in 1940 when the AFL officially opted for neutrality and Lewis of the CIO was opposed to Roosevelt. Taft, *A. F. of L.*, p. 307.

77. Greenstone, *Labor in American Politics*, p. xiv.

78. Samuel Lubell, *The Future of American Politics* (New York: Harper & Row, 1965) p. 174.

79. "The percentage of union members rose from 12 percent in 1930 to 36 percent in 1945, while union membership soared from 3,400,000 to more than 14,300,000, an increase of 10,900,000 during American labor's period of lushest growth. The percentage of organized members fluctuated in the late 1940's and early 1950's, down and then up again but began slipping steadily after 1955, to 32 percent unionized in 1962, nearer 31 percent today." Edward T. Townsend, "Is There a Crisis in the American Trade-Union Movement? Yes." *Annals of the American Academy of Political and Social Science* 350 (1963), p. 3.

80. "Is There a Crisis in the Labor Movement? No," *Annals of the American Academy of Political and Social Science* 350 (1963) p. 15. For the trade unionists' views, see Solomon Barkin and Albert A. Blum, "Is There a Crisis in the American Trade-Union Movement?—The Trade Unionists' Views," *Annals of the American Academy of Political and Social Science* 350 (1963), pp. 16–24. The remainder of the same issue of the *Annals* is devoted to several articles on specific aspects of the problem.
81. Labor's support of Bryan, Wilson, and Roosevelt was never *official*.
82. Key, *Politics,* pp. 60–68; Hugh A. Bone, *American Politics and the Party System* (New York: McGraw-Hill, 1955), p. 114; New Jersey State CIO Council, *The Effectiveness of CIO-PAC in New Jersey in 1950* (Newark, 1951); Alexander Heard, *The Costs of Democracy* (Chapel Hill, N.C.: University of North Carolina Press, 1960), pp. 108 and 205; and John H. Fenton, "The Right-to-Work Vote in Ohio," *Midwest Journal of Political Science* 3 (1959), pp. 241–253.
83. The magnitude and method of labor's financial involvement is not easy to determine. "It is extremely difficult to obtain any reliable and comparable data that span more than two elections—as Alexander Heard, the author of the most exhaustive treatment of money in politics [*Costs of Democracy*], has carefully noted." Harry M. Scoble, "Organized Labor in the Electoral Process: Some Questions for the Discipline," *Western Political Quarterly* 16 (1963), p. 675. The questions that remain unresolved are: "How much, in fact, has organized labor committed its potential resources to electoral politics? How efficiently, in fact, has it exploited these committed resources? And what, in fact, have political scientists done by way of systematic analysis to answer these first two questions?" Ibid., p. 678.
84. We shall not deal here with either aggregate trend analysis such as the Gallup studies or with national data such as the SRC findings. We shall examine them in detail in Chapter 4.
85. For example, see the representative body of reference group theories in Herbert H. Hyman and Eleanor Singer, *Readings in Reference Group Theory and Research* (New York: The Free Press, 1968). See Chapter 3 for a detailed analysis.
86. Four types of UAW members resulted from this scale: Prolabor–Political, Prolabor–Apolitical, Nonlabor–Political, and Nonlabor–Apolitical. See Arthur Kornhauser et al., *When Labor Votes: A Study of Auto Workers* (New York: University Books, 1956), ch. 6.
87. Joel Seidman et al., "Political Consciousness in a Local Union," *Public Opinion Quarterly* 15 (1951), pp. 692–702. Also the participation study by Arnold M. Rose, *Union Solidarity* (Minneapolis, Minn.: University of Minnesota Press, 1952).
88. Jack Barbash, *Labor's Grass Roots* (New York: Harper & Brothers, 1961), p. 197.
89. Kornhauser et al., *When Labor Votes,* p. 67.
90. Harold L. Sheppard and Nicholas A. Masters, "Political Attitudes of Union Members: The Case of the Detroit Auto Workers," *American Political Science Review* 53 (1959), p. 447.
91. Sidney Lens, "Labor and the Election," *Yale Review* (Summer 1952), p. 577. Fay Calkins finds this to be true in her observation of the CIO-PAC in five

cases. One of the reasons she gives for the failure of the PAC in its campaign against Taft in 1950 was that the members simply did not accept the union politically. "The average Ohio CIO member was not so distressed about PAC's issues as to become extremely active in pushing them in 1950. He may have favored CIO legislative demands; he may have preferred Ferguson to Taft; but he still looked upon his union as an economic rather than a political weapon. He did not see the labor movement as a political crusade in which his personal interests were deeply involved." Fay Calkins, *The CIO and the Democratic Party* (Chicago: University of Chicago Press, 1952), p. 27.

92. ". . . the following elements in the UAW-CIO's view of the proper political orientation and behavior of its members consistently stand out: The good union members will . . . be familiar with some of the social welfare programs backed by the union, CIO and the Democratic Administration—especially housing, rent control and civil rights." Harold L. Wilensky, "The Labor Vote: A Local Union's Impact on the Political Conduct of its Members," *Social Forces* 35 (1956–1957), p. 113; Kornhauser et al., *When Labor Votes,* especially 211; and Norman Blume, "The Impact of a Local Union on Its Membership in a Local Election," *Western Political Quarterly* 23 (1970), pp. 138–150.

93. For a recent report, see Blume, "Impact of a Local Union," p. 150.

94. Kornhauser et al., *When Labor Votes,* ch. 3.

95. Seidman et al., "Political Consciousness," p. 30 and Irving Bernstein, "The Politics of the West Coast Teamsters and Truckers" in Jack Barbash, ed., *Unions and Union Leadership* (New York: Harper & Brothers, 1959), p. 294.

96. Jack Barbash, *The Practice of Unionism* (New York: Harper & Brothers, 1956), p. 258.

97. Calkins, *CIO,* p. 27.

98. Bernstein, "Politics of the Teamsters," p. 249.

99. Bernard Berelson et al., *Voting* (Chicago: University of Chicago Press, 1954), p. 40.

100. Joseph Rosenfarb, "Labor's Role in the Election," *Public Opinion Quarterly* 8 (1944), p. 384.

101. For one thing, the scope of the data used permitted a systematic description of variation in only one case, the SRC studies. Even here one would easily run into the difficulty of small cells when controlling for different variables.

Chapter 3

1. To clarify the scope and purpose of his work as a descriptive study, Greenstone wrote: "Labor's activity, of course, is not tantamount to effectiveness in winning elections. In fact, the assessment of such effectiveness requires extensive survey techniques beyond the scope of this research." J. David Greenstone, *Labor in American Politics* (New York: Knopf, 1969), p. 9.

2. For two prominent generalizations, see Greenstone, ch. 2, especially pp. 60–62.

3. The SRC's emphasis on continuity and stability of the American electoral scene is explained in terms of the primary dependent variable, party identification. On the other hand, the notion of the rational electorate explains party votes— or, more precisely, the deviation of actual votes from psychological identification—largely in terms of short-term forces such as candidates' appeal, issue

salience, campaign effects, and the like. What we suggest in this portion of our paper is that there may be another source of the SRC's stability-oriented analysis —their treatment of various secondary reference groups primarily in normative ways. In this way, the tendency is to emphasize the norm transmission rather than norm modification or norm rejection. See Philip E. Converse et al., "Continuity and Change in American Politics: Parties and Issues in the 1968 Election," *American Political Science Review* 63 (1969), pp. 1097–1100, and V. O. Key, *The Responsible Electorate: Rationality in Presidential Voting, 1936–1960.* (New York: Vintage Books, 1968), ch. 1.

4. May Brodbeck, "Models, Meanings, and Theories," in Llewellyn Gross, ed., *Symposium on Sociological Theory* (New York: Harper and Row, 1959), p. 378. See also a very succinct discussion of theory, laws, concepts, hypotheses, and explanations in Carl J. Hempel, *The Philosophy of Natural Science* (Englewood Cliffs, New Jersey: Prentice-Hall, 1966).

5. Richard S. Rudner, *Philosophy of Social Science* (Englewood Cliffs, New Jersey: Prentice-Hall, 1966), p. 10.

6. We endorse the particular view of theory as an explanatory schema that orders and connects empirical generalizations, or, for social science at this time, lawlike statements, into a coherent whole. There are, however, other definitions of theory, for example, as a descriptive device. See Ernest Nagel, *Structure of Science* (New York: Harcourt, Brace & World, 1961), p. 85.

7. Harry M. Scoble, "Organized Labor in Electoral Politics: Some Questions for the Discipline," *Western Political Quarterly* 16 (1963), pp. 669–671.

8. Greenstone, *Labor in American Politics,* p. 352.

9. What we mean here amounts to *consistency* of values and demands. In other words, we believe that the union politics of the 1960s have reached the level where the union leaders' values and norms have attained a measure of uniformity and consistency. The degree of the consistency, uniformity, and salience of the group norms are closely related to the members' cognition of and affection toward the group goal. See below for a discussion on this topic.

10. For an excellent source of readings in this field, consult Herbert H. Hyman and Eleanor Singer, eds., *Readings in Reference Group Theory and Research* (New York: The Free Press, 1968). See also some complementary sources in the group dynamics field that take a sociological approach: for example, Harold B. Gerard, "The Anchorage of Opinions in Face-to-Face Groups," *Human Relations* 7 (1954), pp. 314ff; and Elizabeth Bott, "The Concept of Class as a Reference Group," *Human Relations* 7 (1954), pp. 259–285.

11. Robert K. Merton and Alice Kitt Rossi, "Contributions to the Theory of Reference Group Behavior," in Hyman and Singer, eds., *Readings,* p. 35.

12. Herbert H. Hyman, "The Psychology of Status," *Archives of Psychology* 269 (1942), pp. 147–165. For a brief review of the history, see Hyman and Singer, eds., *Readings,* pp. 3–21.

13. For some of the examples, see the bibliography in Ibid., p. 7.

14. Hyman and Singer, eds., *Readings,* pp. 77–83.

15. Kelley, "Two Functions of Reference Groups," in Hyman and Singer, eds., *Readings,* p. 82.

16. For the facilitating role of the subgroups, see Norman Kaplan, "Reference Groups and Interest Group Theories of Voting," in Hyman and Singer, eds., *Readings,* pp. 461–472.

17. Angus Campbell et al., *The American Voter* (New York: Wiley, 1966), especially ch. 12.
18. Philip E. Converse and Angus Campbell, "Political Standards in Secondary Groups," Hyman and Singer, eds., *Readings*, pp. 473–489.
19. For an index of group identification, see Philip E. Converse, "Group Influence in Voting Behavior" (unpublished Ph.D dissertation, University of Michigan, 1958), pp. 173–178.
20. Leon Festinger, "The Role of Group Belongingness in Voting Situation," *Human Relations* 1 (1947), pp. 154–180.
21. Merton and Rossi, "Contributions," p. 76.
22. The two different concepts of partisan attitude or allegiance as a psychological concept and partisan voting as a behavioral element are theoretically differentiated in Chapter 4.
23. Arthur Kornhauser et al., *When Labor Votes: A Study of Auto Workers* (New York: University Books, 1956), p. 274.
24. Theodore Geiger, *Soziale Umschichtungen in einer dänischen Mittelstadt* (Aahrus Universitet, 1951). David Glass, ed., *Social Mobility in Britain* (London: Rutledge and Kegan Paul, 1954). S. M. Lipset and Reinhard Bendix, "Ideological Equalitarianism and Social Mobility in the United States," *Transactions of the Second Congress of Sociology, II* (London: International Sociological Association, 1954), pp. 33–54. Max Weber, *The Theory of Social and Economic Organization* (New York: Oxford University Press, 1947). Talcott Parsons, *Essays in Sociological Theory* (Glencoe, Illinois: The Free Press, 1954).
25. Seymour Martin Lipset and Hans L. Zetterberg, "A Theory of Social Mobility," in Seymour Martin Lipset and Reinhard Bendix, *Class, Status, and Power: Social Stratification in Comparative Perspective*, 2d ed. (New York: The Free Press, 1966), pp. 561–573. For a less systematic but provocative treatment of the topic, see Daniel Bell, ed., *The New American Right* (New York: Criterion Books, 1955) and Richard Hofstadter, *The Age of Reform* (New York: Knopf, 1955), pp. 131–172.
26. Lipset and Zetterberg, "Social Mobility," p. 570.
27. Thorstein Veblen, *The Theory of the Leisure Class* (New York: The Modern Library, 1934), pp. 30–32.
28. Lipset and Zetterberg, "Social Mobility," p. 571. Among some of the representative works on status inconsistency are Elton F. Jackson and Richard F. Curtis, "Conceptualization and Measurement in the Study of Social Stratification," in Hubert M. Blalock and Ann B. Blalock, eds., *Methodology in Social Research* (New York: McGraw-Hill, 1968), ch. 4; Eton F. Jackson, "Status Consistency and Symptoms of Stress," *American Sociological Review* 27 (1962), pp. 469–480; G. E. Lenski, "Status Crystallization: A Non-Vertical Dimension of Social Status," *American Sociological Review* 19 (1954), pp. 405–413; and Hubert M. Blalock, "Status Inconsistency, Social Mobility, Status Integration and Structural Effects," *American Sociological Review* 32 (1967), pp. 790–801.
29. In dealing with the studies that report these puzzling consequences—a political orientation to the left *and* a political orientation to the right—Lipset's theory offers no explanation of the conditions under which one is more likely to occur than the other. This is, of course, a testimony to the inadequacies of his theory. Lipset and Zetterberg, "Social Mobility," pp. 571–573. Some of the studies to which Lipset refers are Robert Michels, *Political Parties* (Glencoe, Ill.: The

Free Press, 1949), pp. 260–261; Lawrence A. Fuchs, "American Jews and the Presidential Votes," *American Political Science Review* 49 (1955), pp. 385–401; David Riesman and Nathan Glazer, "The Intellectuals and the Discontented Class," in Daniel Bell, ed., *New American Right*, pp. 66–67; W. L. Warner and J. O. Low, *The Social System of the Modern Factory* (New Haven, Conn.: Yale University Press, 1947); and Eleanor E. Maccoby et al., "Youth and Political Choice," *Public Opinion Quarterly* 18 (1954), p. 35.

30. Lipset and Zetterberg, "Social Mobility," p. 573.

31. "Upward Mobility and Political Orientation: A Reevaluation of the Evidence," *American Sociological Review* 36 (1971), p. 223.

32. Some recent examples of European social mobility and its political consequences include Bo Anderson, "Some Problems of Change in the Swedish Electorate," *Acta Sociologica* 6 (1963), pp. 241–255; Joseph Lopreato, "Upward Social Mobility and Political Orientation," *American Sociological Review* 32 (1967), pp. 586–592; W. G. Runciman, "Embourgeoisement, Self-Rated Class and Party Preference," *Sociological Review* 7 (1964), pp. 137–153; and John H. Goldthorpe et al., *The Affluent Worker: Political Attitudes and Behavior* (London: Cambridge University Press, 1968), ch. 3.

33. Anderson, "Problems of Change."

34. Lopreato, "Upward Social Mobility."

35. That is, in those studies the political consequences were noted and *described* rather than causally analyzed. These descriptions differed.

36. Lipset and Zetterberg, "Social Mobility," p. 573.

37. Maccoby et al., "Youth and Political Choice."

38. Fred Greenstein and Raymond Wolfinger, "The Suburbs and Shifting Party Loyalties," *Public Opinion Quarterly* 22 (1958), pp. 473–483, and Kenneth H. Thompson, "Upward Social Mobility and Political Orientation: A Reevaluating of the Evidence," *American Sociological Review* 36 (1971), pp. 223–235.

39. For a lengthy discussion of different measures of the independent variable (social mobility), see Lipset and Zetterberg, "Social Mobility," pp. 564–565; Kenneth H. Thompson extends his observations to the dependent variable as well, "Upward Social Mobility," pp. 232–233.

40. For analytic problems from a statistical point of view, see Blalock, "Status Inconsistency, Social Mobility," and Hubert M. Blalock, "Status Inconsistency and Interaction: Some Alternative Models," *American Journal of Sociology* 73 (1967), pp. 305–315.

41. Four categories of literature can be identified: the status inconsistency approach; consequence-oriented analysis; the so-called Gibbs–Martin status integration approach; and the structural or compositional effects approach. The representative works include Jackson and Curtis, "Conceptualization," O. D. Duncan, "Residential Areas and Differential Fertility," *Eugenics Quarterly* 11 (1964), pp. 82–99; O. D. Duncan, "Methodological Issues in the Analysis of Social Mobility," in Neil J. Smelser and Seymour Martin Lipset, eds., *Social Structure and Mobility in Economic Development* (Chicago: Aldine, 1966), pp. 90–95; P. M. Blau, "Structural Effects," *American Sociological Review* 25 (1960), pp. 178–193; Jack P. Gibbs and Walter T. Martin, *Status Integration and Suicide* (Eugene, Oregon: University of Oregon Press, 1964), chs. 2 and 3.

42. Walter T. Martin, "Socially Induced Stress: Some Converging Theories," *Pacific Sociological Review* 8 (1965), pp. 63–69.

43. For example, in those instances where these ideological elements have been defined as Republican votes.

44. Anderson offers "strong Swedish political socialization" as an explanation. Anderson, "Problems of Change," p. 248.

45. Here the direction is emphasized because the intensity has been steadily on the increase as we pointed out earlier.

46. Hyman and Singer, eds., *Readings,* pp. 14–15.

47. For example, Dorwin Cartwright and Alvin Zander, eds., *Group Dynamics: Research and Theory* (Evanston, Ill.: Row Peterson, 1953), and George C. Homans, *The Human Group* (New York: Harcourt-Brace, 1950).

48. Also included is the need of associating with others. See Kurt Back, "Influence through Social Communication," *Journal of Abnormal and Social Psychology* 46 (1951), pp. 9–23.

49. Robert K. Merton, "Continuities in the Theory of Reference Groups and Social Structure," in Robert K. Merton, *Social Theory and Social Structure* (New York: The Free Press, 1957), pp. 281–368.

50. Back, "Influence," and Converse, "Group Influence," pp. 108–109.

51. Stephen E. Bennett and William R. Klecka, "Social Status and Political Participation: A Multivariate Analysis of Predictive Power," *Midwest Journal of Political Science* 14 (1970), pp. 355–382.

52. For a similar discussion on party identification and age, see Campbell et al. *American Voter,* pp. 161–162.

53. Ibid., pp. 163–165.

54. Americans for Democratic Action, for example.

55. Interaction effect is taken into account.

56. Many social characteristics seem to be at least correlates of economic factors, although the exact causal ordering has not been established as yet. For an effort to sort out the exact amount of variance in dependent political behavior explained by each variable within this category, see Bennett and Klecka, "Social Status."

57. In terms of rationality, we would rank comparative behavior highest and party identification (as a result of early socialization) lowest. Political action based on norms of a group to which one belongs would rank somewhere in the middle. For a stimulating discussion of the politics of tangibles as the politics of rationality, see Murray Edelman, *The Symbolic Uses of Politics* (Urbana, Ill.: University of Illinois Press, 1967).

58. Kelley, "Two Functions," p. 82.

59. James A. Davis, "A Formal Interpretation of the Theory of Relative Deprivation," *Sociometry* 22 (1959), pp. 287–288.

60. Ibid., p. 282.

61. Martin Patchen, "A Conceptual Framework and Some Empirical Data Regarding Comparisons of Social Rewards," in Hyman and Singer, eds., *Readings,* pp. 172 and 184.

62. Leon Festinger, "A Theory of Social Comparison Process," in Hyman and Singer, eds., *Readings,* pp. 123–146; and Ralph H. Turner, "Reference Groups of Future-Oriented Men," *Social Forces* 34 (1955), pp. 130–136.

63. John R. P. French and Bertram Raven, "The Bases of Social Power," in Dorwin Cartright, ed., *Studies in Social Power* (Ann Arbor: University of Michigan Press, 1959), pp. 150–167. Also Festinger, "Social Comparison Process."

64. Patchen, "Conceptual Framework," p. 173.
65. Ibid.
66. Festinger, "Social Comparison Process," p. 125.
67. Ladd Wheeler, "Motivation as a Determinant of Upward Comparison," *Journal of Experimental Social Psychology* Supplement 1 (1966), pp. 27–31. Dorothy A. Thornton and A. John Arrowood, "Self-Evaluation, Self-Enhancement, and the Laws of Social Comparison," *Journal of Experimental Psychology* Supplement 1 (1966), p. 46.
68. This is not the place to review the history of relative deprivation theory. Suffice it to say that the first work that utilized the theory to explain the dissatisfied subjects was Samuel A. Stouffer et al., *The American Soldier* (Princeton, New Jersey: Princeton University Press, 1949).
69. Nathan Glazer, " 'The American Soldiers' as Science," *Commentary* 8 (1949), p. 493.
70. The word "concept" is *deliberately* used here.
71. Martin Patchen, *The Choice of Wage Comparisons* (Englewood Cliffs, New Jersey: Prentice-Hall, 1961).
72. Patchen, "Conceptual Framework," p. 169. This is similar to Festinger's notion of social comparison.
73. Davis, "Formal Interpretation," pp. 287–288.
74. W. G. Runciman, *Relative Deprivation and Social Justice* (Berkeley, California: University of California Press, 1966), ch. 9.
75. Wheeler, "Motivation"; Thompson, "Upward Social Mobility"; Patchen, *Choice,* p. 36.
76. For example, Kurt Lewin et al., "Level of Aspiration," in J. M. Hunt, *Personality and Behavior Disorders,* vol. I (New York: The Ronald Press Co., 1944), p. 341.
77. In other words, what one believes is due him.
78. Patchen, "Conceptual Framework."
79. Patchen reasoned that when a low income is combined with lack of responsibility, the sense of relative deprivation is sharp. This is, in essence, a restatement of the earlier principle that a combination of intergroup and intragroup deprivation generates an intense feeling of dissatisfaction. This is so because lack of responsibility refers to an "exploiter" from a source external to the group, and a low income is equivalent to intragroup deprivation.
80. See, for example, Peter Blau, *Exchange and Power in Social Life* (New York: Wiley, 1964), p. 145.
81. Some found educational aspirations are fairly similar across social classes. A. J. Jaffe and Walter Adams, "College Education for U.S. Youth: The Attitudes of Parents and Children," *American Journal of Economics and Sociology* 23 (1964), pp. 269–283.
82. Lopreato, "Upward Social Mobility."
83. Another possible source of relative deprivation occurs when comparing a perceived amount of work input with a perceived level of income: the result is an imbalance in the ratios of these components. Thus a union member may feel deprived because he may have to work more hours for an income level comparable to his next-door neighbor who is, for example, a computer programmer.
84. This point should be emphasized since dissonance with regard to a particular situation at a particular time can be superseded by an equal or greater degree

of consonance in a different situation at the same time or at a different point in time. Often this point in time can be a future reference. Thus one who feels that the possibility of immediately resolving the dissonance is good may be able to forego any significant degree of dissatisfaction.

85. See for an excellent summary and bibliography of the balance theory, Morton Deutsch and Robert M. Kraus, *Theories in Social Psychology* (New York: Basic Books, 1965), pp. 68–75.

86. Heinz Eulau, "Identification with Class and Political Role Behavior," in Hyman and Singer, eds., *Readings,* pp. 490–503.

87. Edelman, *Symbolic Uses,* ch. 1.

88. According to Edelman, the most distinguishing characteristic of American interest groups is their competition for tangible goals as opposed to the symbolic rewards sought by the mass. Ibid., chs. 1 and 2.

89. See Chapter 5 for details.

90. Greenstone refers to this as consumer politics; for this and other synthesis, we borrow heavily from Greenstone's restatement of the speculative schools. Greenstone, *Labor in American Politics,* pp. 387–408.

91. For an astute discussion on this topic, see Max Weber, "Politics as a Vocation" and "Class, Status, Party," in H. H. Gerth and C. Wright Mills, eds., *From Max Weber* (New York: Oxford University Press, 1959).

92. Greenstone, *Labor in American Politics,* p. 376.

93. A revision based on Ralf Dahrendorf, *Class, and Class Conflict in Industrial Society* (Stanford, California: Stanford University Press, 1959), p. 136.

94. Curiously enough, Marx paid a good deal of attention to this problem which serves as a new basis of class conflict. Karl Marx and Friedrich Engels, "Manifesto of the Communist Party," in Lewis S. Feuer, ed., *Basic Writings on Politics and Philosophy* (Garden City, New York: Doubleday, 1959), p. 254.

95. Dahrendorf, *Class Conflict,* p. 377.

96. Emile Durkheim, *The Division of Labor in Society* (New York: Free Press, 1960).

97. "As these interests become manifest, our formulation assumes that the bulk of each group is likely to seek governmental assistance. Thus their conflict is often not over whether the government should interfere in economic life but over which class government policies should favor." Greenstone, *Labor in American Politics,* p. 383.

98. For a list of economic and consumer issues, see Ibid., p. 392.

99. We cannot overemphasize the heuristic nature of this part, given the secondary nature of our analysis, certain violations, statistical assumptions, and methodological peculiarities as well as the property of the data sets themselves. For the elections of 1968 and 1972, however, certain concrete hypotheses can (and will) be tested for verification.

100. What we are saying here essentially amounts to balancing two sets of determinants against each other and speculating about the outcome. Each class has a group of factors unique to itself that give birth to and intensify the feeling of dissatisfaction. For the better-paid union members there are the elements of the "permanently" blocked expectation (hence, status rejection) and higher educational level (hence, a sharper feeling of deprivation), while for the low income category there is the low income itself, combined with the responsibility ascribed to others.

101. Again, to infer partisan and behavioral consequences from these two sets of conditions requires knowledge about the relevance of the Democratic party, as perceived by the high-income group, to social issues, and the relevance of the Democratic party, as perceived by low income members, to economic issues.

102. The upwardly mobile members who approach middle class will (as the intergroup deprived) see the need of union's continued Democratic partisan effort on social issues to close the intergroup gap. On the other hand, the upwardly mobile members who rise toward a level lower than middle class may still be subject to intragroup as well as intergroup deprivation. As a result, the responsibility may be ascribed both to the perceived *inefficacy* of the union in improving their lot and to the perceived *efficacy* of the external groups in intercepting their economic rewards. Therefore they may decide to vote independently for a third-party candidate. It is least likely that they will vote Republican because of the mass perception of the Republican party's historical role toward the low class in general. For the findings on the stability of the New Deal impressions of the Democratic Party, for example, as the party for the poor, emphatic of the federal regulation of business, see Donald Stokes et al., "Components of the Electoral Decision," *American Political Science Review* 52 (1958), p. 386.

Chapter 4

1. Harry M. Scoble, "Organized Labor in Electoral Politics: Some Questions for the Discipline," *Western Political Quarterly* 16 (1963), p. 671.
2. Jack Kroll, "Labor's Political Role," *Annals of the American Academy of Political and Social Science* 274 (1951), pp. 118–122; and Avery Leiserson, "Organized Labor as a Pressure Group," Ibid., pp. 108–117.
3. Angus Campbell et al., *The American Voter* (New York: Wiley, 1966), p. 66.
4. Ibid., ch. 4, pp. 64–88.
5. Arthur S. Goldberg, "Discerning a Causal Pattern among Data on Voting Behavior," *American Political Science Review* 60 (1966), p. 916.
6. Ibid.
7. Partisan attitudes here are represented by an index composed of eight variables, four party and four candidate questions. Two of each group of four seek to find the specific positive reason while the remaining two purport to disclose the underlying reasons for negative attitudes. For a detailed procedure followed to construct the index, see Donald Stokes et al., "Components of Electoral Decision," *American Political Science Review* 52 (1958), pp. 367–387.
8. This method of evaluating causal models deals with establishing causal orders through a recursive set of simultaneous structural equations. The sequential causal ordering is possible because these equations allow one to change values of a variable appearing at a particular point or immediately subsequent to it so that in the equations $x_1 = e_1$, $x_2 = b_{31}x_1 + e_2$, $x_3 = b_{31}x_1 + b_{32}x_2 + e_3$, $x_4 = b_{41}x_1 + b_{42}x_2 + b_{43}x_3 + e_4$, a change in e_1 will affect all x's, a change in e_2 will affect x_2, x_3, and x_4, but not x_1, and a change in e_4 will produce a change only in x_4. Changes in e_4, therefore, cannot affect relationships that are in previous equations but only influence subsequent variables and equations. Hubert M. Blalock, *Causal Inferences in Nonexperimental Research* (Chapel Hill, N.C.:

University of North Carolina Press, 1964), p. 59. For the Simon-Blalock method, see also Ibid., ch. 3, pp. 61–94; Herbert Simon, *Models of Man* (New York: Wiley, 1957), chs. 1 and 3, especially ch. 2, pp. 61–94; and Hubert M. Blalock and Ann B. Blalock, *Methodology in Social Research* (New York: McGraw-Hill, 1968), pp. 144–178.

9. The categories within each one of these eight items are strictly nominal. For example, an item that measures the voter's attitudes favorable to the Democratic party, is constructed as follows: "Is there anything in particular that you dislike about the Democratic Party?"

    1. People within party
    2. Issues and government management
    3. Government activity and government philosophy
    4. Specific domestic policies
    5. Foreign policy
    6. Group or self interest
    7. Party responses
    8. Others.

For the problem of violating levels of assumed measurement, see Blalock, *Causal Inferences,* pp. 32–35.

10. Goldberg, "Discerning," p. 915.

11. The small percentage deviations, both positive (Democratic) and negative (Republican), in the strong identifier categories are presumably a result of the attitudinal rigidity that minimizes the probability of change. Weak Republican category showing comparatively smaller deviations can be explained by the *direction* of change, i.e., the switch to the Democratic party.

12. V. O. Key, *The Responsible Electorate: Rationality in Presidential Voting, 1936–1960* (New York: Vintage Books, 1968), ch. 2, pp. 9–28.

13. One of the questions asked in connection with the election was, "What would you say is the most important reason why you would vote for the candidate?" The question elicited subjective open-ended responses which were later elaborately coded in a multicolumn, multiresponse format.

14. The participation index comprises several items ranging from simple participation by way of voting to door-to-door campaign participation. Each one of the items has dichotomous values so that construction of the index simply depends on summation of scores. Here, however, we take the strategy of investigating these items separately largely because of the uncertain status of the index in terms of its reliability and some discernible disparity in the pattern of responses to the items. See Donald R. Matthews and James Prothro, *Negroes and the New Southern Politics* (New York: Harcourt, Brace & World, 1966), pp. 524–525, and Stephen E. Bennett and William R. Klecka, "Social Status and Political Participation: A Multivariate Analysis of Predictive Power," *Midwest Journal of Political Science* 14 (1970), pp. 361–362.

15. If we keep in mind the average income standards for the period 1952–1964, the category label "low class" may be less appropriate for all workers earning less than $8000 during that period than it is today.

16. Key, *Responsible Electorate,* ch. 3, especially pp. 34–39.

17. George Gallup, "How Labor Votes," *Annals of the American Academy of Political and Social Science* 274 (1951), pp. 118–124.

18. Campbell et al., *American Voter,* ch. 12, pp. 295–332. Also see Angus Camp-

bell and Homer C. Cooper, *Group Differences in Attitudes and Votes* (Ann Arbor, Michigan: Institute for Social Research, University of Michigan, 1956).

19. Converse et al., "Continuity and Change in American Politics: Parties and Issues in the 1968 Election," *American Political Science Review* 63 (1969), pp. 1095–1100.

20. One scholar seems to miss this point when he interprets Key's evidence as the union vote from 1936 to 1948. J. David Greenstone, *Labor in American Politics* (New York: Knopf, 1969), p. 4.

21. Key, *Responsible Electorate,* p. 55.

22. This measurement of attitudes toward the governmental role in regulating unions may or may not be related to the union member's political attitudes.

23. For example, the data were used by two prominent scholars, V. O. Key in his *The Public Opinion and American Democracy* (New York: Knopf, 1961), p. 523, and Scoble, "Organized Labor," pp. 673–674.

24. Scoble, "Organized Labor," p. 673, note 31.

25. Campbell et al., *American Voter,* p. 304.

26. For a complete description of the control mechanism, see Philip E. Converse, "Group Influence in Voting Behavior" (unpublished Ph.D. dissertation, University of Michigan, 1958), pp. 178–190.

27. Converse explains the nature of the *group* in this way:

> The control for the union group was constructed first, and its characteristics differ slightly from those of the other three groups. Precision controls were applied, not only to region and urban–rural residence, but to occupation status as well. Other variables were distribution-controlled with only minimum attention paid to the problem of matching distributions *within* the precision control cells. In other words, when a tentative control group was found to have a surplus of individuals over 50 years of age, elderly people were "unloaded" not specifically from the precision-control cells in which the surplus was most marked, but freely from the total residual control group, This strategy was shifted in processing the last three groups. Here only two variables—region and residence type—were precision controlled, but the distributions of the remaining control variables were matched within the six cells which resulted. This matching was not perfect; discrepancies between test and control groups within precision cells would show a slightly larger average than those which emerge when total distributions are compared. However, the primary tactic was to correct control group distributions within the precision cells defined by region and residence, and among Catholics, Negroes, and Jews no marked within-cell distortion remains.

Ibid., pp. 179–180. The only problem here is that while this makes the calculation of "distinctiveness of the union votes" possible, one is hard put to find a proper practical label for the control group. Thus we still lack, as a specific control group, for example, workers who earn $5000 a year and who are not unionized.

28. The emitted standards were ranked in terms of their strength which is determined by the results of a content analysis of journals from approximately seventy international labor unions. Ibid., pp. 190–193.

29. There is a substantial body of literature consistently showing positive correlation between class and political participation. For example, Robert Agger et al., *The Rulers and the Ruled: Political Power and Impotence in American Com-*

munities (New York: Wiley, 1964); Campbell et al., *American Voter*; Robert Dahl, *Who Governs? Democracy and Power in an American City* (New Haven, Conn.: Yale University Press, 1961); and Heinz Eulau, *Class and Party in the Eisenhower Years* (New York: The Free Press, 1962).

30. For a definition of socioeconomic class and its role in social behavior in general and political participation in particular, see note 29 and Lester Milbrath, *Political Participation: How and Why Do People Get Involved in Politics?* (Chicago: Rand McNally, 1965), pp. 118–120.

31. The positive relationship between income and political participation is a well-established fact. See Ibid., pp. 120–122.

32. Ibid., pp. 124–128.

33. Unfortunately for our purpose, the variables representing group forces do not appear in all four sets of election data. In addition, the years in which one variable appears is not coincidental with the year in which another is included so that we are here forced to use only the 1956 data in which all the variables appear.

34. Philip E. Converse, "Political Standards in Secondary Groups," in Herbert H. Hyman and Eleanor Singer, eds., *Readings in Reference Group Theory and Research* (New York: The Free Press, 1968), pp. 473–489.

35. For a good description of canonical correlation and its principles, see John P. Van de Geer, *Introduction to Multivariate Analysis for the Social Sciences* (San Francisco: W. H. Freeman, 1971), ch. 14, pp. 156–170, and Norman Nie and C. Hadlai Hull, *Statistical Package for the Social Sciences: Update Manual* (Chicago: National Opinion Research Center, University of Chicago, 1971).

36. This is, in statistical terms, equivalent to error variance.

Chapter 5

1. Angus Campbell and Homer C. Cooper, *Group Differences in Attitudes and Votes* (Ann Arbor, Mich.: Survey Research Center, University of Michigan, 1956), p. 35.

2. Max Beloff, *The American Federal Government* (New York: Oxford University Press, 1959), pp. 157–158.

3. Angus Campbell et al., *The American Voter* (New York: Wiley, 1966), p. 357. Another scholar shares this view of class voting as a waning phenomenon, noting the extent to which the Republican candidate captured the support of the lower-income groups in 1952 and 1956. V. O. Key, *Politics, Parties and Pressure Groups*, 5th ed. (New York: Crowell, 1964), pp. 249–250.

4. Alford's data are derived from a variety of sources—the CPS data for 1948 and 1952, the Gallup and Roper survey data for other years, and others. See his "The Role of Social Class in Voting Behavior," *Western Political Quarterly* 26 (1963), pp. 180–194.

5. Ibid., p. 194.

6. Samuel Lubell, *The Future of American Politics* (New York: Doubleday Anchor Books, 1965), pp. 69–70.

7. Arthur Kornhauser et al., *When Labor Votes* (New York: University Books, 1956), p. 281.

8. See Chapter 4.

9. William H. Whyte, *The Organization Man* (New York: Doubleday Anchor Books, 1957), pp. 331–332. For an excellent source of reviews of journalists' predictions in this direction, see Bennett M. Berger, *Working Class Suburb: A Study of Auto Workers in Suburbia* (Berkeley, California: University of California Press, 1969), pp. 28–33.

10. *American Political Science Review* 59 (1965), pp. 874–895.

11. For comments on these measures and the concept of affluence used by Lane, see below.

12. Lane, "The Politics," p. 879.

13. The so-called age of affluence to which Lane refers covers the period from 1946 to 1965.

14. Most notably, a group of European studies fall in this category. See, for example, John H. Goldthorpe et al., *The Affluent Worker: Political Attitudes and Behavior* (London: Cambridge University Press, 1968), ch. 3, pp. 33–48.

15. Kornhauser et al., *When Labor Votes,* p. 47.

16. For example, Joseph Lopreato, "Upward Social Mobility and Political Orientation," *American Sociological Review* 32 (1967), pp. 586–592.

17. Goldthorpe et al., *Affluent Worker,* p. 48.

18. For example, the idea of "movement" has often been incorporated into the measurement process in social psychology. For a good example of this, see R. S. Crutchfield, "Conformity and Creative Thinking," in H. E. Gruber, G. Terrell, and M. Werthermer, eds., *Contemporary Approaches to Creative Thinking* (New York: Atherton, 1962), pp. 120–140.

19. Kenneth H. Thompson, "Upward Social Mobility and Political Orientation: A Reevaluation of the Evidence," *American Sociological Review* 36 (1971), pp. 223–235.

20. Unfortunately we cannot test this because of absence of a variable that would enable us to answer this question of exactly when the social mobility occurred. For methodological problems pertaining to this kind of measurement of the degree of social mobility, see Leo A. Goodman, "On the Measurement of Social Mobility: An Index of Status Persistence," *American Sociological Review* 34 (1969), pp. 831–850.

21. Also, these figures are much smaller than the corresponding percentage figures for the case of straight classes, for example, 17.7 percent and 22.0 percent for white-collar union and nonunion members, respectively.

22. The question used here as the dependent variable is, "Was there ever a time when you thought of yourself as a member of the other party?" This asks about the party identification and not party vote. An answer of "Yes, Republican," was interpreted to mean a switch of identification to the Democratic party. We are aware that the respondent might have changed to a third party, but we take into consideration the marginal probability of this event.

23. All we are suggesting is that affluence as a feeling, though not measurable in a strict behavioral sense, has been *assumed* to accompany occupational ascendancy.

24. Lane, "The Politics," pp. 874–875. Methodologically speaking, Lane is exempt from criticism since he defines affluence as the gross increase measured in five ways.

25. What impoverished villagers in India undergo for their survival is largely out-

side the consideration of those who set out to evaluate their status relative to "the next-door neighbor."

26. See, for example, Herman Miller, *Income Distribution in the United States* (Washington, D.C.: Bureau of the Census, U.S. Department of Commerce, 1976).

27. However, the impact of the federal income tax is considerably more moderate than formerly presumed. See Richard C. Edwards et al., *The Capitalist System* (Englewood Cliffs, New Jersey: Prentice-Hall, 1972), pp. 235–238.

28. Ibid., pp. 236–237.

29. "Consumer and Wholesale Indexes, Annual Averages and Changes, 1949 to Date," in *Monthly Labor Review* 93 (1970), pp. 112–119.

30. Another way of incorporating cost of living is to measure income and re-calculate it by adjusting it for three levels of living: high class, comfortable, and barely surviving. See, for example, "Spring 1969 Cost Estimates for Urban Family Budgets," *Monthly Labor Review* 93 (1970), pp. 62–64. Again, the entries represent the 1960s compared with the 1950s for the theoretical reason in our study.

31. Frank Ackerman et al., "The Extent of Income Inequality in the United States," in Edwards et al., *Capitalist System*, p. 208.

32. For two views on the question, see Irving B. Kravis, "Relative Income Shares in Fact and Theory," *American Economic Reveiw* 49 (1959), pp. 917–949; and Robert M. Solow, "A Skeptical Note on the Constancy of Relative Shares," *American Economic Review* 48 (1958), pp. 618–631.

33. C. E. Ferguson and John R. Moroney, "The Sources of Change in Labor's Relative Share: A Neoclassical Analysis," *Southern Economic Journal* 35 (1969), p. 308.

34. Ibid., p. 320.

35. For an elaborate discussion of the topic in regard to class, occupation, and tax, see Ackerman et al., "Income Inequality," pp. 212–218.

36. Ibid., p. 213.

37. See, for example, (1) John Gurley, "Federal Tax Policy," *National Tax Journal,* September 1967; (2) W. Lee Hansen and Burton A. Weisbrod, *Benefits, Costs, and Finance of Public Higher Education* (Chicago: Markham, 1969); (3) Gabriel Kolko, *Wealth and Power in America* (New York: Praeger, 1962); (4) James Meade, *Efficiency, Equity, and the Ownership of Property* (Cambridge, Mass.: Harvard University Press, 1965); (5) Stephan Michelson, "The Economics of Real Income Distribution," *Review of Radical Political Economics,* II, No. 1 (Spring 1970); (6) Herman P. Miller, *Rich Man, Poor Man* (New York: New American Library, 1964); (7) Patricia C. Sexton, *Education and Income* (New York: Viking, 1961); (8) William Spady, "Educational Mobility and Access: Growth and Paradoxes," *American Journal of Sociology,* November 1967; (9) Maurice Zeitlin, *American Society, Inc.* (Chicago: Markham, 1970).

38. Ackerman et al., "Income Inequality," p. 211; and Richard C. Edwards, "Who Fares Well in the Welfare State?" in Edwards et al., *Capitalist System,* pp. 244–251.

Chapter 6

1. The CPS used the following item for the purpose of measuring class consciousness: "There is a bit of talk these days about different social classes. Most people say they belong either to the middle class or to the working class. Do you ever think of yourself as being in one of these classes?"
2. See Chapter 3.
3. For the continuum of satisfaction–dissatisfaction, the SRC includes an item: "We are ... interested in how people are getting along financially these days. So far as you and your family are concerned, would you say that you are pretty well satisfied with your present financial situation, more-or-less satisfied, or not satisfied at all?"
4. The kind of variables necessary for measuring relative deprivation would include not only the state of deprivation but the comparative group that serves as the evaluative standard, e.g., membership as opposed to nonmembership group. In addition, there would have to be a variable measuring the primary dimension of the respondent's comparison. See G. W. Runciman, "Problems of Research on Relative Deprivation," in Herbert H. Hyman and Eleanor Singer, eds., *Readings in Reference Group Theory and Research* (New York: The Free Press, 1968), pp. 69–76.
5. See Chapter 3.
6. Note that different classes of mobility do not necessarily coincide with the dichotomous scale we established: low-class and high-class mobility. However, there is a statistical probability of lower-class mobility among those who move up one occupational level and, given the three-point item in our case, the mobility-by-two class has to be the high-class mobility.
7. Angus Campbell et al., *The American Voter* (New York: Wiley, 1960), especially ch. 9.
8. V. O. Key, *The Responsible Electorate* (New York: Vintage Books, 1968), especially chs. 1 and 2.
9. David E. RePass, "Issue Salience and Party Choice," *American Political Science Review* 65 (1971), p. 400.
10. Ibid., p. 400.
11. Gerald Pomper, "Toward a More Responsible Two-Party System? What, Again?" *Journal of Politics* 33 (1961), p. 929.
12. Ibid., pp. 934–936.
13. The maximum possible combination is: $n!/2(n-2)!$
14. Wright's rule can be summarized as follows: (1) Compound path is equal to a product of simple paths within it, e.g., $P_{21} \cdot P_{42} = P_{41}$. (2) Correlation of any two variables is equal to the sum of the simple and compound path that connects them, e.g.: $r_{14} = P_{31} \cdot P_{43} + P_{21} \cdot P_{42}$. Sewall Wright, "The Treatment of Reciprocal Interaction with or without Lag in Path Analysis," *Biometrics* 16 (1960), pp. 213–219.

Chapter 7

1. Bernard Berelson et al., *Voting* (Chicago: University of Chicago Press, 1954), pp. 46–47.

2. V. O. Key, Jr., *Public Opinion and American Democracy* (New York: Knopf, 1961), p. 523.

3. Angus Campbell et al., *The American Voter* (New York: Wiley, 1966), p. 304.

4. Harry M. Scoble, "Organized Labor in Electoral Politics: Some Questions for the Discipline," *Western Political Quarterly* 16 (1963), p. 674.

5. Note that all the nonunion figures here cited both by Scoble and Schattschneider refer to nonunion voters in general and not un-unionized workers. Again, for the purpose of consistency, the data used for this analysis come from the presidential elections of 1952 to 1964.

6. One exception is in 1960 for the Strong Democrats. The inflated figure of Democratic votes among nonunion Strong Democratic Identifiers may be due to the religious character of the election.

7. Arthur Kornhauser et al., *When Labor Votes: A Study of Auto Workers* (New York: University Books, 1956), p. 261.

8. New York: Norton, 1970.

9. Walter Dean Burnham, "The End of American Party Politics," *Transaction* 7 (1969), p. 17. For a fuller technical discussion, see Walter Dean Burnham, "The Changing Shape of the American Political Universe," *American Political Science Review* 59 (1965), pp. 7–28. Much of this article was later incorporated in his work cited in note 8. See also Jerrold G. Rusk, "The Effect of the Australian Ballot Reform on Split Ticket Voting: 1876–1908," *American Political Science Review* 64 (1970), pp. 1220–1238; a letter by Walter Dean Burnham, *American Political Science Review* 65 (1971), pp. 1149–1152; and a reply by Jerrold G. Rusk, pp. 1152–1157.

10. Burnham, "End of American Party Politics," p. 20.

11. Ibid.

12. See Chapters 5 and 6.

13. David Apter, "Ideology and Discontent," in David Apter, ed., *Ideology and Discontent* (Glencoe, Ill.: The Free Press, 1964), pp. 15–43, as cited in Burnham, *Critical Elections,* p. 138.

Chapter 8

1. Norman H. Nie et al., *The Changing American Voter* (Cambridge, Mass.: Harvard University Press, 1976), p. 94.

2. See Chapter 8, note 9.

3. "Election Study Notes New Trend in Voter Behavior, Attributes Close Race to Well-Run Campaign," Institute for Social Research, University of Michigan, *ISR Newsletter* (Winter 1977), p. 4.

4. U.S. Bureau of Census, *Statistical Abstract of the United States: 1960* (Washington, D.C., 1969), p. 370; Robert Lane, *Political Life* (New York: Free Press of Glencoe, 1959), p. 20.

5. The other year is 1924 when only 43.9 percent of the eligible voters actually voted. U.S. Bureau of Census, *Statistical Abstract of the United States: 1971,* p. 364.

6. U.S. Bureau of Census, *Statistical Abstract of the United States: 1975,* p. 450. We have reason to believe that this figure may be slightly exaggerated since it is based on the sample data collected by the U.S. Bureau of Census and there

may be differences in percentage between the same and the current population statistics collected by the Bureau "due to overreporting of voting by persons in the
sample." See the note to Table 728, Ibid., p. 450. To approximate "generously"
another figure assuming an overreporting, we can subtract the reported 48.3
percent (a very generous proportion) of the first-time voters (5.3 million)
from the census total (not based on the sample), and divide by the total
eligible voters minus the total first-time voters (11 million). The resulting rate
is 56.1 percent, a figure still higher than any one year during the 1932–1952
period. As of this writing, a similar information is not available on the 1976
turnout rate, but since we are dealing with the observations on the trend
during the period 1968–1972, the most recent figure is not necessary.

7. V. O. Key, *Politics, Parties and Pressure Groups,* 5th ed. (New York: Thomas
Y. Crowell, 1964), p. 164. Key attributes the term *party-in-the-electorate* to
Ralph M. Goldman. See Goldman's "Party Chairman and Party Factions, 1789–
1900" (unpublished Ph.D. dissertation, University of Chicago, 1951), ch. 17.

8. Gerald M. Pomper, *Voter's Choice: Varieties of American Electoral Behavior*
(New York: Harper & Row, 1975), pp. 20–22.

9. *Transformations of the American Party System: Political Coalitions from the
New Deal to the 1970s* (New York: Norton, 1975), pp. 291–292.

10. Three percent according to the Gallup poll and 6 percent according to the
CPS data. See *The Gallup Opinion Index,* Report No. 137 (December 1976),
p. 50; *ISR Newsletter,* p. 4. If one takes the plurality figure (percent Democrat
identifiers — percent Republican identifiers) as an indication, then the plurality
figure for 1976 is, according to the CPS data, 28 (51 − 23) which is even
higher than that of 1964.

11. *The Gallup Opinion Index,* Report No. 137 (December 1970), p. 50.

12. Nie et al., *American Voter,* p. 94.

13. Angus Campbell et al., *The American Voter* (New York: Wiley, 1966), p. 143.

14. Pomper, *Voter's Choice,* p. 32; see also note 26, p. 230; Nie et al., *American
Voter,* ch. 26; Walter Dean Burnham, *Critical Elections and the Mainsprings
of American Politics* (New York: Norton, 1970), pp. 130ff; William H. Flanigan, *Political Behavior of the American Electorate,* 2d ed. (Boston: Allyn and
Bacon, 1973), pp. 45–48.

15. Ladd and Hadley, *Transformations,* pp. 15–16.

16. The breakdown by Strong Democrat, Weak (or Not So Strong) Democrat,
Independent Leaning to the Democratic Party, Independent, Independent Leaning to the Republican Party, Weak (or Not So Strong) Republican, Strong Republican, is not available as yet.

17. Nie et al., *American Voter,* p. 95.

18. For the data on the increase of split-ticket voting, see Walter DeVries and
V. Lance Tarrance, *The Ticket Splitter: A New Force in American Politics*
(Grand Rapids, Mich.: William B. Eerdmans, 1972); for Congressional elections, see Burnham, *Critical Elections,* p. 109; for a general discussion of this
topic, see also Ladd and Hadley, *Transformations,* pp. 293–299.

19. Richard W. Boyd, "Popular Control of Public Policy: A Normal Vote Analysis
of the 1968 Election," *American Political Science Review* 66 (June 1972), pp.
429–4491.

20. Gerald M. Pomper, "From Confusion to Clarity: Issue and American Voters,
1956–1968," *American Political Science Review* 66 (June 1972), pp. 415–428;

for the election of 1968, see Philip Converse et al., "Continuity and Change in American Politics: Parties and Issues in the 1968 Election," *American Political Science Review* 63 (December 1969), pp. 1083–1105; for the election of 1972, see Arthur H. Miller et al., "A Majority Party in Disarray: Policy Polarization in the 1972 Election," *American Political Science Review* 70 (September 1976), pp. 753–778; for a good overview of the recent treatment, see Nie et al., *American Voter*, chs. 8, 9, and 10; for an excellent bibliography of both published and unpublished sources on this topic, see John H. Kessel, "Comment: The Issue in Issue Voting," *American Political Science Review* 66 (June 1972), p. 459; for additional comments, see Boyd, "Popular Control," and comments and reviews by Richard A. Brody, Benjamin I. Page, pp. 450–458. In addition, for a recent rebuttal of the theme of issue awareness, see Michael Margolis, "From Confusion to Confusion: Issues and the American Voter (1956–1972)," *American Political Science Review* 71 (March 1977), pp. 31–43.

21. Ladd and Hadley, *Transformations*, p. 195. Emphasis is mine.

22. V. O. Key, "Theory of Critical Elections," *Journal of Politics* 17 (February 1955), p. 4.

23. V. O. Key, "Secular Realignment and the Party System," *Journal of Politics* 21 (May 1959), p. 207. This modification is obviously what Ladd and Hadley consider "major." See Ladd and Hadley, *Transformations*, p. 24.

24. V. O. Key, "Secular Realignment," p. 199.

25. For an excellent critique of these two methods, see Gerald M. Pomper, "Classification of Presidential Elections," *Journal of Politics* 29 (August 1967), pp. 535–566. For Key's comprehensive scheme, see *Politics*, pp. 522–536. We believe that one of the chief weaknesses of Key's definition is its vulnerability to an ex post facto generalization. By defining a realignment with the use of the aggregate vote statistics, Key severely limits the use of his definition to a retrospective description of a period that must span at least fifty years.

26. Nie et al. note: "There seems to be considerable casualness in the exact definition of realignment. Key is quite consistent in using this notion of the party bias change as the characteristic of realignment.... James Sundquist is a bit less careful about keeping to his explicit definition...." *American Voter*, p. 213, note 4.

27. For an attempt at a systematic treatment, see Ladd and Hadley, *Transformations*, "Introduction," pp. 1–27.

28. Arthur H. Miller et al., "A Majority Party in Disarray: Policy Polarization" (unpublished paper, Institute for Social Research, University of Michigan, 1974), p. 82. Emphasis is mine.

29. Nie et al., *American Voter*, p. 352.

30. Ibid., pp. 353ff.

31. Walter Dean Burnham, "The Changing Shape of American Political Universe," *American Political Science Review* 64 (1970), pp. 1220–1238; Burnham, *Critical Elections*; Burnham, "The End of Party Politics," *Transaction* (1969), p. 17; Burnham, "Beyond American Party in the 1970's" (Beverly Hills: Sage Publications, 1975), especially pp. 238–237.

32. Ladd and Hadley, *Transformations*, p. 344.

33. Ibid.; see especially chs. 4 and 5.

34. Kevin Phillips, *The Emerging Republican Majority* (New York: Doubleday, 1970).

35. Arthur Schlesinger, Jr., "How McGovern Will Win," *New York Times Magazine* (July 30, 1972), pp. 10–11, 28–34, as quoted in Ladd and Hadley, *Transformations,* p. 8.

36. Richard M. Scammon and Ben J. Wattenberg, *The Real Majority: An Extraordinary Examination of the American Electorate* (New York: Coward, McCann & Geoghegan, 1971), p. 280.

37. Paul Abramson, "Generational Change in American Electoral Behavior," *American Political Science Review* 68 (March 1974), pp. 93–105.

38. Ladd and Hadley, *Transformations,* p. 19.

39. James Sundquist, *Dynamics of the Party System: Alignment and Realignment of Political Parties in the United States* (Washington, D.C.: The Brookings Institution, 1973). See especially various scenarios of realignment in ch. 2 and his projections in ch. 17.

40. Jae-On Kim, "Changing Bases of Party Identification in the United States, 1952–1972," *Sociology Work Paper Series* 74-3 (Iowa City, Iowa, University of Iowa, 1975), p. 26.

41. John Stewart, *One Last Chance: The Democratic Party, 1974–1976* (New York: Praeger, 1974), p. 96.

42. As in the case of Lubell, Burnham, Phillips, Schlesinger, and Stewart on the one hand, and Kim, Miller et al., Boy, and Abramson on the other.

43. See Ladd and Hadley, *Transformations,* for example.

44. For example, the "classical sense of massive defection" in Miller et al., "Majority Party" (unpublished paper).

45. However, the mean proportion of the labor union members and their families identified as Democrats for the period 1968–1976 does not show a deviation from the previous period. For example, the mean for the period 1968–1972 is 53.9 percent while the corresponding figure for 1952–1964 is 56.9 percent which generates a difference of 3.5 percent. (We do not have the figure for 1930–1952). This deviation is not, however, a deviation from the general pattern of the party identification distribution. The difference between the period 1952–1964 and the period 1968–1972 for the entire electorate is 3.5 percent also (i.e., 47.5 percent for 1952–1964 minus 44 percent for 1936–1952). We can expect, therefore, that if the data for the period 1930–1952 were available, the mean for 1968–1976 would reflect no deviation from the previous New Deal era.

46. Needless to mention, we are often forced to limit our analysis in this chapter to "consequent phenomena" or hypothesis implications of a hypothesis implication of the original hypothesis, mainly due to a low N's from the separate election-to-election analyses such as this and even when two years are merged.

47. All the data used in this section are the CPS election data of 1968 and 1972 unless otherwise noted.

48. The union votes for George Wallace were as follows: 13 percent from $5000–7999, 11.9 percent from $8000–9999, 10.1 percent from over $10,000.

49. See Chapter 5, especially Table 23.

50. Nie et al., *American Voter,* p. 232, note 20. What is claimed in note 19, p. 231, is not, however, entirely consistent with our analysis.

51. Miller et al., "Majority Party," *American Poltical Science Review* 70 (September 1976), pp. 753–779. For the election of 1976, see Gerald M. Pomper et al.,

The Election of 1976: Reports and Interpretations (New York: McKay, 1977), especially chs. 2 and 3.

52. Stewart, *Last Chance,* p. 100.
53. Miller et al., "Majority Party" (unpublished paper), p. 30; see also Henry A. Plotkin, "Issues in the 1976 Presidential Campaign," in Pomper, *Election of 1976,* pp. 35–53.
54. Stewart, *Last Chance.* See also a similar differentiation made in a study for Potomac Associates in which the respondents were asked their opinion in nine areas of social spending. They were asked, for example, if the present amount should be reduced, increased, or retained; in only one instance (welfare program for welfare families) was the response for reduction or termination of a specific program more than 20 percent. William Watts and Lloyd A. Free, eds., *State of the Nation* (New York: Universe Books, 1973), pp. 294–297.
55. As reported in the *Wall Street Journal,* August 6, 1976, p. 1.
56. The literature on income distribution is, as usual, mountainous. However, "data on distribution of personal income of adult males in the United States indicate that relative inequality declined between 1939 and the early postwar years but has subsequently remained almost unchanged." B. R. Chiswick and J. Mincer, "Time Series Changes in Personal Income Inequality in the United States from 1939 with Projections to 1985," *Journal of Political Economy* 80 (May/June 1972), pp. S34–S73; see also the chapter on income distribution in President's Council of Economic Advisers. *President Nixon's Annual Report to Congress* as reported in the *New York Times,* February 2, 1974, p. 10 in which the Council reports no change in income distribution during the previous twenty-five years. For labor's share, see P. C. Nystrom and C. C. Johnson, "Labor's Share: New Evidence on Old Controversy," *Quarterly Review of Economics and Business* 16 (Spring 1976), pp. 23–32. The literature on the income trend in terms of the net spendable take-home pay is also voluminous. See, for example, the U.S. Bureau of Census Report as summarized in the *New York Times,* February 2, 1974, p. 13.
57. For a similar but broad treatment of this theme, see Fred Hirsch, *Social Limits to Growth* (Cambridge, Mass.: Harvard University Press, 1976).
58. Ladd and Hadley, *Transformations,* pp. 277ff.
59. This essentially is the assessment of the 1976 election by Norman Nie which contrasts sharply with that of Warren Miller who saw in it a return of the party vote. A roundtable discussion, "Perspectives on the 1976 Presidential Election," at the 35th Annual Meeting of Midwest Political Science Association, April 21–23, Chicago, Illinois. The third discussant was Walter Dean Burnham.
60. For an outstanding analysis of why the elections of 1952 and 1956 could not be construed as the clues that portended the coming of a "new realignment of the 1960's," see Campbell et al., *American Voter,* p. 537.
61. Institute for Social Research, University of Michigan. *Newsletter,* Winter 1977, p. 4.

Bibliography

Books

Agger, Robert. *The Rulers and the Ruled: Political Power and Impotence in American Communities.* New York: John Wiley, 1964.

Barbash, Jack. *Labor's Grass Roots.* New York: Harper and Brothers, 1961.

———. *The Practice of Unionism.* New York: Harper and Brothers, 1956.

———, ed. *Unions and Union Leadership.* New York: Harper and Brothers, 1959.

Bean, Louis. *Ballot Behavior.* Washington, D.C.: American Council on Public Affairs, 1946.

———. *How to Predict Elections.* New York: Alfred A. Knopf, 1948.

Bell, Daniel, ed. *The New American Right.* New York: Criterion Books, 1955.

Beloff, Max. *The American Federal Government.* New York: Oxford University Press, 1959.

Berelson, Bernard, et al. *Voting.* Chicago: University of Chicago Press, 1954.

Berger, Bennett M. *Working Class Suburb: A Study of Auto Workers in Suburbia.* Berkeley: University of California Press, 1969.

Blaisdell, Donald C. *American Democracy Under Pressure.* New York: Ronald Press, 1957.

Blalock, Hubert M. *Causal Inferences in Nonexperimental Research.* Chapel Hill: University of North Carolina Press, 1964.

———. *Social Statistics.* New York: McGraw-Hill Book Co., 1960.

———, and Blalock, Ann B. *Methodology in Social Research.* New York: McGraw-Hill, 1968.

Blau, Peter. *Exchange and Power in Social Life.* New York: John Wiley, 1964.

Bone, Hugh A. *American Politics and the Party System.* New York: McGraw-Hill, 1955.

Bornet, Vaughan D. *Labor Politics in the Democratic Republic.* Washington, D.C.: Spartan Books, 1964.

Burnham, Walter Dean. *Beyond American Party in the 1970s.* Beverly Hills: Sage Publications, 1975.

———. *Critical Elections and the Mainspring of American Politics.* New York: W. W. Norton, 1970.

Butler, D. E. *The Study of Political Behavior.* New York: Humanities Press, 1959.

Calkins, Fay. *The CIO and the Democratic Party.* Chicago: The University of Chicago Press, 1952.

Campbell, Angus, et al. *The American Voter.* New York: John Wiley, 1966.

———. *Elections and the Political Order.* New York: John Wiley, 1966.

———. *The Voter Decides.* Evanston, Illinois: Row, Peterson and Co., 1954.

———, and Cooper, Homer C. *Group Differences in Attitudes and Votes.* Ann Arbor: Institute for Social Research, University of Michigan, 1956.

———, and Kahn, Robert. *The People Elect a President.* Ann Arbor: Survey Research Center, University of Michigan, 1952.

Cartwright, Dorwin, and Zander, Alvin, eds. *Group Dynamics: Research and Theory.* Evanston, Illinois: Row, Peterson and Co., 1953.

Centers, Richard. *Psychology of Social Classes.* Princeton: Princeton University Press, 1949.

Coleman, James. *Community Conflict.* Glencoe, Illinois: The Free Press, 1957.

Commons, John R., et al. *History of Labor in the United States.* New York: Macmillan, 1936.

Crick, Bernard. *The American Science of Politics: Its Origins and Conditions.* Berkeley: University of California Press, 1959.

Dahl, Robert. *Who Governs? Democracy and Power in an American City.* New Haven, Connecticut: Yale University Press, 1961.

Dahrendorf, Ralf. *Class, and Class Conflict in Industrial Society.* Stanford, California: Stanford University Press, 1959.

Deutsch, Morton, and Kraus, Robert M. *Theories in Social Psychology.* New York: Basic Books, 1965.

DeVries, Walter, and Lance, Tarrance, V. *The Ticket Splitter: A New Force in American Politics.* Grand Rapids, Mich.: William B. Eerdmans, 1972.

Down, Anthony. *An Economic Theory of Democracy.* New York: Harper and Row, 1957.

Duncan, Dudley, et al. *Statistical Geography.* Glencoe, Illinois: The Free Press, 1961.

Durkheim, Emile. *The Division of Labor in Society.* New York: The Free Press, 1960.

Edelman, Murray. *The Symbolic Uses of Politics.* Urbana: University of Illinois Press, 1967.

Edwards, Richard C., et al. *The Capitalist System.* Englewood-Cliffs, New Jersey: Prentice-Hall, 1972.

Eulau, Heinz. *Class and Party in the Eisenhower Years.* New York: The Free Press, 1962.

Flanigan, William H. *Political Behavior of the American Electorate.* 2d ed., Boston: Allyn and Bacon, 1973.

Geiger, Theodore. *Sozaile Umschichtungen in einter dänischen Mittelstadt.* Aahrus Universitet, 1951.

Gibbs, Jack P., and Martin, T. *Status Integration and Suicide.* Eugene: University of Oregon Press, 1964.

Glass, David, ed. *Social Mobility in Britain.* London: Rutledge and Kegan Paul, 1954.

Goldthorpe, John H., et al., *The Affluent Worker: Political Attitudes and Behavior.* London: Cambridge University Press, 1968.

Gosnell, H. F. *Getting Out the Vote.* Chicago: University of Chicago Press, 1927.
———. *Machine Politics: Chicago Style.* Chicago: University of Chicago Press, 1937.
———. *Non-Voting.* Chicago: University of Chicago Press, 1924.

Greenstone, J. David. *Labor in American Politics.* New York: Alfred A. Knopf, 1969.

Grob, Gerald N. *Workers and Utopia.* Evanston: Northwestern University Press. 1961.

Gross, Llewellyn, ed. *Symposium on Sociological Theory.* New York: Harper and Row, 1959.

Hansen, W. Lee, and Weisbrod, Burton A. *Benefits, Costs, and Finance of Public Higher Education.* Chicago: Markham, 1969.

Hartz, Louis. *The Liberal Tradition in America.* New York: Harcourt, Brace and World, 1955.

Heard, Alexander. *The Costs of Democracy.* Chapel Hill, North Carolina: University of North Carolina Press, 1960.

Hempel, Carl J. *The Philosophy of Natural Science.* Englewood Cliffs, New Jersey: Prentice-Hall, 1966.

Hirsch, Fred. *Social Limits to Growth*. Cambridge, Mass.: Harvard University Press, 1976.

Hofstadter, Richard. *The Age of Reform*. New York: Alfred A. Knopf, 1955.

Homans, George C. *The Human Group*. New York: Harcourt-Brace, 1950.

Hoover, Herbert. *Memories of Herbert Hoover, 1920–1933*. New York: Macmillan, 1952.

Hyman, Herbert H., and Singer, Eleanor, eds. *Readings in Reference Group Theory and Research*. New York: The Free Press, 1968.

Karson, Marc. *American Labor Unions and Politics*. Carbondale: Southern Illinois University Press, 1958.

Key, V. O. *Politics, Parties and Pressure Groups*. 5th ed. New York: Thomas Y. Crowell, 1964.

———. *Public Opinion and American Democracy*. New York: Alfred A. Knopf, 1949.

———. *The Responsible Electorate: Rationality in Presidential Voting, 1936–1960*. New York: Vintage Books, 1968.

———. *Southern Politics*. New York: Alfred A. Knopf, 1949.

Kish, Leslie. *Survey Sampling*. New York: John Wiley, 1967.

Kolko, Gabriel. *Wealth and Power in America*. New York: Praeger, 1962.

Kornhauser, Arthur, et al. *When Labor Votes: A Study of Auto Workers*. New York: University Books, 1956.

Kim, Jae-On, "Changing Bases of Party Identification in the United States, 1952–1972," *Sociology Work Paper Series*, 74-3. Iowa City, Iowa: University of Iowa, 1975.

Ladd, Everett Carl, Jr., with Hadley, Charles D. *Transformations of the American Party System: Political Coalitions from the New Deal to the 1970s*. New York: W. W. Norton & Co., 1975.

Lazarsfeld, Paul, et al. *The People's Choice*. 2d ed. New York: Columbia University Press, 1948.

Lorwin, Lewis L. *The American Federation of Labor*. Washington, D.C.: The Brookings Institution, 1933.

Lubell, Samuel. *The Future of American Politics*. New York: Doubleday Anchor Books, 1965.

McConnell, Grant. *Private Powers and American Democracy*. New York: Alfred A. Knopf, 1966.

McPhee, William N. *Formal Theories of Mass Behavior*. New York: The Free Press, 1963.

Matthews, Donald R., and Prothro, James. *Negroes and the New Southern Politics*. New York: Harcourt, Brace, and World, 1966.

Meade, James. *Efficiency, Equity, and the Ownership of Property*. Cambridge, Mass.: Harvard University Press, 1965.

Michels, Robert. *Political Parties*. Glencoe, Illinois: The Free Press, 1949.

Milbrath, Lester. *Political Participation: How and Why Do People Get Involved in Politics?* Chicago: Rand McNally and Company, 1965.

Miller, Herman P. *Rich Man, Poor Man*. New York: New American Library, 1964.

Nagel, Ernest. *Structure of Science*. New York: Harcourt, Brace, and World, 1961.

New Jersey State CIO Council. *The Effectiveness of CIO-PAC in New Jersey in 1950*. Newark, 1951.

Nie, Norman H., et al. *The Changing American Voter*. Cambridge, Mass.: Harvard University Press, 1976.

――――, and Hull, C. Hadlai. *Statistical Package for the Social Sciences: Update Manual*. Chicago: National Opinion Research Center, University of Chicago, 1971.

Parsons, Talcott. *Essays in Sociological Theory*. Glencoe, Illinois: The Free Press, 1954.

Patchen, Martin. *The Choice of Wage Comparisons*. Englewood Cliffs, New Jersey: Prentice-Hall, 1961.

Perlman, Selig. *A Theory of the Labor Movement*. New York: Macmillan, 1928.

Phillips, Kevin. *The Emerging Republican Majority*. New York: Doubleday, 1970.

Polsby, Nelson W., et al., eds. *Politics and Social Life*. Boston: Houghton Mifflin, 1963.

Pomper, Gerald M. *Elections in America: Control and Influence in Democratic Politics*. New York: Dodd, Mead and Co., 1968.

――――, et al. *The Election of 1976: Reports and Interpretations*. New York: David McKay Co., 1977.

――――. *Voter's Choice: Varieties of American Electoral Behavior*. New York: Harper & Row, 1975.

Ranney, Austen, ed. *Essays on the Behavioral Study of Politics*. Urbana: University of Illinois Press, 1962.

Raybeck, Joseph G. *A History of American Labor*. New York: Macmillan, 1961.

Redford, Emmette S., et al. *Politics and Government in the United States*, 2d ed. New York: Harcourt, Brace and World, 1968.

Rice, Stuart. *Farmers and Workers in American Politics*. New York: Columbia University Press, 1924.

――――. *Quantitative Methods in Politics*. New York: Alfred A. Knopf, 1928.

Rogers, Lindsay. *The Pollsters: Public Opinion, Politics, and Democratic Leadership*. New York: Alfred A. Knopf, 1949.

Rose, Arnold M. *Union Solidarity*. Minneapolis: University of Minnesota Press, 1952.

Rudner, Richard S. *Philosophy of Social Science*. Englewood Cliffs, New Jersey: Prentice-Hall, 1966.

Runciman, W. G. *Relative Deprivation and Social Justice*. Berkeley: University of California Press, 1966.

Schlesinger, Arthur, Jr. *The Crisis of the Old Order*. Boston: Houghton Mifflin, 1957.

――――. *The Politics of Upheaval*. Boston: Houghton Mifflin, 1967.

Scammon, Richard M., and Wattenberg, Ben J. *The Real Majority: An Extraordinary Examination of the American Electorate*. New York: Coward, McCann & Geoghegan, 1971.

Seidman, Joel. *The Needle Trades*. New York: Farrar and Rinehart, 1943.

Sexton, Patricia C. *Education and Income*. New York: Viking, 1961.

Simon, Herbert, *Models of Man*. New York: John Wiley, 1957.

Stewart, John. *One Last Chance: The Democratic Party, 1974–1976*. New York: Praeger, 1974.

Storing, Herbert J., et al., eds. *Essays on the Scientific Study of Politics*. New York: Holt, Rinehart and Winston, 1962.

Stouffer, Samuel A., et al. *The American Soldier*. Princeton, New Jersey: Princeton University Press, 1949.

Sundquist, James. *Dynamics of the Party System: Alignment and Realignment of Political Parties in the United States*. Washington, D.C.: The Brookings Institution, 1973.

Taft, Philip. *The A. F. of L. in the Time of Gompers*. New York: Harper Brothers, 1957.

Van de Geer, John P. *Introduction to Multivariate Analysis for the Social Sciences*. San Francisco: W. H. Freeman and Co., 1971.

Veblen, Thorstein. *The Theory of the Leisure Class*. New York: Modern Library, 1934.

Vorse, Mary H. *Labor's New Millions*. New York: Modern Age Books, 1938.

Walsh, Raymond. *CIO: Industrial Unionism in Action*. New York: Norton, 1937.

Warner, W. Lloyd, and Low, J. O. *The Social System of the Modern Factory*. New Haven, Conn.: Yale University Press, 1947.

Watts, William, and Free, Lloyd A., eds. *State of the Nation*. New York: Universe Books, 1973.

Weber, Max. *The Theory of Social and Economic Organization*. New York: Oxford University Press, 1947.

White, L. D., ed. *The State of the Social Science*. Chicago: University of Chicago Press, 1956.

Whyte, William H. *The Organization Man*. New York: Doubleday Anchor Books, 1957.

Wolfe, Leon. *Lookout*. New York: Harper and Row, 1965.

Zeitlin, Maurice. *American Society, Inc*. Chicago: Markham, 1970.

Component Part of a Collection

Ackerman, Frank, et al. "The Extent of Income Inequality in the United States." *The Capitalist System*. Edited by Richard C. Edwards et al. Englewood Cliffs, New Jersey: Prentice-Hall, 1972.

Apter, David. "Ideology and Discontent." *Ideology and Discontent*. Edited by David Apter. Glencoe, Illinois: The Free Press, 1964.

Bernstein, Irving. "The Politics of the West Coast Teamsters and Truckers." *Unions and Union Leadership*. Edited by Jack Barbash. New York: Harper and Brothers, 1959.

Brodbeck, May. "Models, Meanings, and Theories." *Symposium on Sociological Theory*. Edited by Llewellyn Gross. New York: Harper and Row, 1959.

Campbell, Angus. "Recent Development in Survey Studies of Political Behavior." *Essays on the Behavioral Study of Politics*. Edited by Austin Ranney. Urbana: University of Illinois Press, 1962.

Converse, Philip E., et al. "Stability and Change in 1960: A Reinstating Election." *Elections and the Political Order*. Edited by Angus Campbell et al. New York: John Wiley, 1966.

———, and Campbell, Angus. "Political Standards in Secondary Groups." *Readings in Reference Group Theory and Research*. Edited by Herbert H. Hyman and Eleanor Singer. New York: The Free Press, 1968.

Crutchfield, R. S. "Conformity and Creative Thinking." *Contemporary Approaches to Creative Thinking*. Edited by H. E. Gruber, G. Terrell, and M. Werthermer. New York: Atherton, 1962.

Derber, Milton. "Growth and Expansion." *Labor and the New Deal*. Edited by Milton Derber and Erwin Young. Madison: The University of Wisconsin Press, 1957.

Duncan, O. D. "Methodological Issues in the Analysis of Social Mobility." *Social Structure and Mobility in Economic Development*. Edited by Neil J. Smelser and Seymour Martin Lipset. Chicago: Aldine Publishing Co., 1966.

Edelman, Murray. "New Deal Sensitivity to Labor Interests." *Labor and the New Deal*. Edited by Milton Derber and Erwin Young. Madison: University of Wisconsin Press, 1957.

Eulau, Heinz. "Identification with Class and Political Role Behavior." *Readings in Reference Group Theory and Research*. Edited by Herbert H. Hyman and Eleanor Singer. New York: The Free Press, 1968.

Festinger, Leon. "A Theory of Social Comparison Process." *Readings in Reference Group Theory and Research*. Edited by Herbert H. Hyman and Eleanor Singer. New York: The Free Press, 1968.

French, John R. P., and Raven, Bertram. "The Bases of Social Power." *Studies in Social Power*. Edited by Dorwin Cartright. Ann Arbor: University of Michigan Press, 1959.

Hempel, Carl G. "Explanatory Incompleteness." *Readings in the Philosophy of Social Science*. Edited by May Brodbeck. New York: Macmillan, 1968.

Jackson, Elton F., and Curtin, Richard F. "Conceptualization and Measurement in the Study of Social Stratification." *Methodology in Social Research*. Edited by Herbert M. Blalock and Ann B. Blalock. New York: McGraw-Hill, 1968.

Kaplan, Norman. "Reference Groups and Interest Group Theories of Voting." *Readings in Reference Group Theory and Research*. Edited by Herbert H. Hyman and Eleanor Singer. New York: The Free Press, 1968.

Karsh, Bernard, and Garman, Philip L. "The Impact of the Political Left." *Labor and the New Deal*. Edited by Milton Derber and Erwin Young. Madison: University of Wisconsin Press, 1957.

Key, V. O. "A Theory of Critical Elections." *American Party Politics: Essays and Readings*. Edited by Donald G. Herzberg and Gerald M. Pomper. New York: Holt, Rinehart and Winston, 1966.

————, and Munger, Frank. "Social Determinism and Electoral Decision: The Case of Indiana." *American Voting Behavior*. Edited by Eugene Burdick and Arthur Brodbeck. Glencoe, Ill.: The Free Press, 1959.

Kirkpatrick, E. M. "The Impact of the Behavioral Approach on Traditional Political Science." *Essays on the Behavioral Study of Politics*. Edited by Austin Ranney. Urbana: University of Illinois Press, 1962.

Lazarsfeld, P. F., and Barton, A. H. "Quantitative Measurement in the Social Sciences." *The Policy Sciences*. Edited by D. Lerner and H. D. Lasswell. Stanford: Stanford University Press, 1951.

Lipset, Seymour M., et al., "The Psychology of Voting: An Analysis of Political Behavior." *Handbook of Social Psychology*, 2. Edited by Gardner Lindsey. Cambridge, Mass.: Addison-Wesley, 1954.

————, and Zetterberg, Hans L. "A Theory of Social Mobility." *Class, Status, and Power: Social Stratification in Comparative Perspective*. 2nd ed. Edited by Seymour Martin Lipset and Reinhard Bendix. New York: The Free Press, 1966.

Littell, Robert. "Undercover Man." *Public Opinion and Steel Strike*. Edited by Heber Blankenhorn. New York: Harcourt, Brace and World, 1921.

Marx, Karl, and Engels, Friedrich. "Manifesto of the Communist Party." *Basic Writings on Politics and Philosophy*. Edited by Lewis S. Feuer. Garden City, New York: Doubleday, 1959.

Merton, Robert K. "Continuities in the Theory of Reference Groups and Social Structure." *Social Theory and Social Structure*. Edited by Robert K. Merton. New York: The Free Press, 1957.

————, and Rossi, Alice Kitt. "Contributions to the Theory of Reference Group Behavior." *Readings in Reference Group Theory and Research*. Edited by Herbert H. Hyman and Eleanor Singer. New York: The Free Press, 1968.

Patchen, Martin. "A Conceptual Framework and Some Empirical Data Regarding Comparisons of Social Rewards." *Readings in Reference Group Theory and Research*. Edited by Herbert H. Hyman and Eleanor Singer. New York: The Free Press, 1968.

Perlman, Selig. "Labor and the New Deal in Historical Perspective." *Labor and the New Deal*. Edited by Milton Derber and Erwin Young. Madison: The University of Wisconsin Press, 1957.

Ranney, Austin. "The Utility and Limitations of Aggregate Data in the Study of Electoral Behavior." *Essays on The Behavioral Study of Politics*. Edited by Austin Ranney. Urbana, Ill.: University of Illinois Press, 1962.

Riesman, David, and Glazer, Nathan. "The Intellectuals and the Discontented Class." *The New American Right*. Edited by Daniel Bell. New York: Criterion Books, 1955.

Rossi, Peter H. "Four Landmarks in Voting Research." *American Voting Behavior*. Edited by Eugene Burdick and Arthur Brodbeck. Glencoe, Illinois: The Free Press, 1959.

————. "Trends in Voting Behavior Research: 1933–1963." *Political Opinion and Electoral Behavior: Essays and Studies*. Edited by Edward Dreyer and Walter Rosenbaum. Belmont, California: Wadsworth, 1966.

Runciman, G. W. "Problems of Research on Relative Deprivation." *Readings in Reference Group Theory and Research*. Edited by Herbert H. Hyman and Eleanor Singer. New York: The Free Press, 1968.

Stokes, Donald E., and Iversen, Gudmund R. "On the Existence of Forces Restoring Party Competition." *Elections and the Political Order*. Edited by Angus Campbell et al. New York: John Wiley, 1966.

Weber, Max. "Politics as a Vacation," and "Class, Status, Party." *From Max Weber*. Edited by H. H. Gerth and C. Wright Mills. New York: Oxford University Press, 1959.

Articles in Periodicals

Abramson, Paul. "Generational Change in American Electoral Behavior," *American Political Science Review* 68 (March 1974), 93–105.

Albig, William. "Two Decades of Opinion Study: 1936–1956." *Public Opinion Quarterly* 21 (1957), 14–22.

Alford, Robert R. "The Role of Social Class in Voting Behavior." *Western Political Quarterly* 26 (1963), 180–194.

Anderson, Bo. "Some Problems of Change in the Swedish Electorate." *Acta Sociologica* 6 (1963), 241–255.

Back, Kurt. "Influence through Social Communication." *Journal of Abnormal and Social Psychology* 46 (1951), 9–23.

Barkin, Solomon, and Blum, Albert A. "Is There a Crisis in the American Trade-Union Movement? The Trade Unionists' Views." *Annals of the American Academy of Political and Social Science* 350 (1963), 16–24.

Bay, Christian. "Politics and Pseudo-politics: A Critical Evaluation of Some Behavioral Literature." *American Political Science Review* 59 (1965), 39–51.

Bennett, Stephen E., and Klecka, William R. "Social Status and Political Participation: A Multivariate Analysis of Predictive Power." *Midwest Journal of Political Science* 14 (1970), 355–382.

Bernstein, Irving. "The Growth of American Unions." *American Economic Review* 44 (1954), 301–318.

Blalock, Hubert M. "Status Inconsistency and Interaction: Some Alternative Models." *American Journal of Sociology* 73 (1967), 305–315.

———. "Status Inconsistency, Social Mobility, Status Integration and Structural Effects." *American Sociological Review* 32 (1967), 790–801.

Blau, P. M. "Structural Effects." *American Sociological Review* 25 (1960), 178–193.

Blume, Norman. "The Impact of a Local Union on Its Membership in a Local Election." *Western Political Quarterly* 23 (1970), 138–150.

Bott, Elizabeth. "The Concept of Class as a Reference Group." *Human Relations* 7 (1954), 259–285.

Boyd, Richard. "Popular Control of Public Policy: A Normal Vote Analysis of the 1968 Election." *American Political Science Review* 66 (June 1972), 429–449.

Burnham, Walter Dean. (A letter) *American Political Science Review* 64 (1970), 1220–1238.

———. "The Changing Shape of the American Political Universe." *American Political Science Review* 65 (1965), 7.

———. "The End of American Party Politics." *Transaction* (1969), 17.

Cable, J. A. "Labor's Political Duty." *American Federationist* 15 (1908), 839.

Charities and the Commons 21 (1908), 149–150.

Chiswick, B. R., and Mincer, J., "Time Series Changes in Personal Income Inequality in the United States from 1939 with Projections to 1985." *Journal of Political Economy* 80 (May/June 1972), S34–S73.

"Consumer and Wholesale Indexes." *Monthly Labor Review* 93 (1970), 112–119.

Converse, Philip E., et al., "Continuity and Change in American Politics: Parties and Issues in the 1968 Election." *American Political Science Review* 63 (1969), 1083–1105.

Dahrendorf, Ralf. "Symposia on Political Behavior." *American Sociological Review* 29 (1964), 734–736.

Davis, James A. "A Formal Interpretation of the Theory of Relative Deprivation." *Sociometry* 22 (1959), 287–288.

Duncan, O. Dudley, and Davis, Beverly. "An Alternative to Ecological Correlations." *American Sociological Review* 18 (1953), 665–666.

Eldersveld, Samuel J. "Theory and Method in Voting Behavior Research." *Journal of Politics* 18 (1951), 70–87.

"Election Study Notes New Trend in Voter Behavior, Attributes Close Race to Well-

Run Campaign," Institute for Social Research, University of Michigan. *ISR Newsletter* (Winter 1977), 4.

Fenton, John H. "The Right-to-Work Vote in Ohio." *Midwest Journal of Political Science* 3 (1959), 241–253.

Festinger, Leon. "The Role of Group Belongingness in the Voting Situation." *Human Relations* 1 (1947), 154–180.

Fuchs, Lawrence A. "American Jews and the Presidential Vote." *American Political Science Review* 49 (1955), 385–401.

Gallup, George. "How Labor Votes." *Annals of the American Academy of Political and Social Science* 274 (1951).

The Gallup Opinion Index, Report No. 137 (December 1976).

Gerard, Harold B. "The Anchorage of Opinions in Face-to-Face Groups." *Human Relations* 7 (1954), 314ff.

Glazer, Nathan. " 'The American Soldiers' as Science." *Commentary* 8 (1949), 493.

Goldberg, Arthur S. "Discerning a Causal Pattern Among Data on Voting Behavior." *American Political Science Review* 60 (1966), 916.

Gompers, Samuel. "The Campaign and Labor's Future." *American Federationist* (Dec. 1908), 1065.

Goodman, Leo A. "Ecological Regressions and the Behavior of Individuals." *American Sociological Review* 18 (1953), 663–664.

———. "On the Measurement of Social Mobility: An Index of Status Persistence." *American Sociological Review* 34 (1969), 831–850.

———. "Some Alternatives to Ecological Correlations." *American Journal of Sociology* 44 (1959), 610–625.

Greenstein, Fred, and Wolfinger, Raymond. "The Suburbs and Shifting Party Loyalties." *Public Opinion Quarterly* 22 (1958), 473–483.

"The Growth of American Unions, 1945–1960." *Labor History* 2 (1961), 131–157.

Gurley, John. "Federal Tax Policy." *National Tax Journal,* September 1967.

Hoxie, Robert F. "President Gompers and the Labor Vote," *Journal of Political Economy* 16 (1908), 700.

Hyman, Herbert H. "The Psychology of Status." *Archives of Psychology* 269 (1942), 147–165.

Jackson, Elton F. "Status Consistency and Symptoms of Stress." *American Sociological Review* 27 (1962), 469–480.

Jaffe, A. J., and Adams, Walter. "College Education for U.S. Youth: The Attitudes of Parents and Children." *American Journal of Economics and Sociology* 23 (1964), 269–283.

Kessel, John H. "Comment: The Issue in Issue Voting," *American Political Science Review* 66 (June 1972), 459–465.

Key, V. O. "The Politically Relevant in Surveys," *Public Opinion Quarterly* 24 (1960), 54–61.

———. "Secular Realignment and the Party System," *Journal of Politics* 21 (May 1959), 198–210.

———. "A Theory of Critical Elections." *Journal of Politics* 17 (1955), 3–18.

Kravis, Irving B. "Relative Income Shares in Fact and Theory." *American Economic Review* 49 (1959), 917–949.

Kroll, Jack. "Labor's Political Role." *Annals of the American Academy of Political and Social Science* 274 (1951), 118–122.

Leiserson, Avery. "Organized Labor as a Pressure Group." *Annals of the American Academy of Political and Social Science* 274 (1951), 108–117.

Lens, Sidney. "Labor and the Election." *Yale Review* (Summer 1952), 577.

Lopreato, Joseph. "Upward Social Mobility and Political Orientation." *American Sociological Review* 32 (1967), 586–592.

Maccoby, Eleanor E., et al. "Youth and Political Choice." *Public Opinion Quarterly* 18 (1954), 35.

MacRae, Duncan, and Meldrum, James A. "Critical Elections in Illinois." *American Political Science Review* 54 (1960), 669–683.

Margolis, Michael. "From Confusion to Confusion: Issues and the American Voter (1956–1972)," *American Political Science Review* 71 (March 1977), 31–43.

Martin, Walter T. "Socially Induced Stress: Some Converging Theories." *Pacific Sociological Review* 8 (1965), 63–69.

Michelson, Stephan. "The Economics of Real Income Distribution." *Review of Radical Political Economics.* Vol. II, No. 1, Spring 1970.

Miller, Arthur H., et al., "A Majority Party in Disarray: Policy Polarization in the 1972 Election," *American Political Science Review* 70 (September 1976), 753–778.

Nystrom, P. C., and Johnson, C. C., "Labor's Share: New Evidence on Old Controversy," *Quarterly Review of Economics and Business* 16 (Spring 1976), 23–32.

Overacker, Louise. "Labor's Political Contributions." *Political Science Quarterly* 14 (1939), 58.

Pomper, Gerald M. "Classification of Presidential Elections," *Journal of Politics* 29 (August 1967), 535–566.

——. "From Confusion to Clarity: Issue and American Voters, 1956–1968," *American Political Science Review* 66 (June 1972), 415–428.

——. "Toward a More Responsible Two-Party System? What, Again?" *Journal of Politics* 33 (1961), 929.

RePass, David E. "Issue Salience and Party Choice." *American Political Science Review* 65 (1971), 400.

Robinson, W. S. "Ecological Correlations and the Behavior of Individuals." *American Sociological Review* 15 (1950), 351–357.

Rosenfarb, Joseph. "Labor's Role in the Election." *Public Opinion Quarterly* 8 (1944), 384.

Runciman, W. G. "Embourgeoisement, Self-Rated Class and Party Preference." *Sociological Review* 7 (1964), 137–153.

Rusk, Jerrold G. "The Effect of the Australian Ballot Reform on Split Ticket Voting: 1876–1908." *American Political Science Review* 64 (1970), 1220–1238.

——. (A letter) *American Political Science Review* 65 (1971), 1152–1157.

Schlesinger, Arthur, Jr., "How McGovern Will Win," *New York Times Magazine* (July 30, 1972), 10–11, 28–34.

Scoble, Harry M. "Organized Labor in the Electoral Process: Some Questions for the Discipline." *Western Political Quarterly* 16 (1963), 675.

Seidman, Joel, et al. "Political Consciousness in a Local Union." *The Public Opinion Quarterly* 15 (1951), 692–702.

Sheppard, Harold L., and Masters, Nicholas A. "Political Attitudes of Union Members: The Case of the Detroit Auto Workers." *American Political Science Review* 53 (1959), 447.

Shively, W. Phillips. " 'Ecological' Inference: The Use of Aggregate Data to Study Individuals." *American Political Science Review* 63 (1969), 1183–1196.

Solow, Robert M. "A Skeptical Note on the Constancy of Relative Shares." *American Economic Review* 48 (1958), 618–631.

Spady, William. "Educational Mobility and Access: Growth and Paradoxes." *American Journal of Sociology* (November 1967).

"Spring 1969 Cost Estimates for Urban Family Budgets." *Monthly Labor Review* 93 (1970), 62–64.

Stokes, Donald, et al. "Components of Electoral Decision." *American Political Science Review* 52 (1958), 367–387.

Taft, Philip. "Is There a Crisis in the Labor Movement? No." *Annals of the American Academy of Political and Social Science* 350 (1963), 15.

————. "Labor's Changing Political Life." *Journal of Political Economy* 45 (1937), 637–638.

Thompson, Kenneth, H. "Upward Social Mobility and Political Orientation: A Reevaluation of the Evidence." *American Sociological Review* 36 (1971), 223–235.

Thompson, Dorothy A., and Arrowood, A. John. "Self-Evaluation, Self-Enhancement, and the Laws of Social Comparison." *Journal of Experimental Psychology,* Supplement 1 (1966), 46.

Townsend, Edward T. "Is There a Crisis in the American Trade-Union Movement? Yes." *Annals of the American Academy of Political and Social Science* 350 (1963), 3.

Turner, Ralph H. "Reference Groups of Future-Oriented Men." *Social Forces* 36 (1955), 130–136.

Wheeler, Ladd. "Motivation as a Determinant of Upward Comparison." *Journal of Experimental Social Psychology,* Supplement 1 (1966), 27–31.

Wilensky, Harold L. "The Labor Vote: A Local Union's Impact on the Political Conduct of Its Members." *Social Forces* 35 (1956–57), 113.

Wright, Sewall. "The Treatment of Reciprocal Interaction with or without Lab in Path Analysis." *Biometrics* 16 (1960), 213–219.

Public Documents

U. S. Bureau of Census. *Statistical Abstract of the United States: 1960.* Washington, D.C.: 1969.

————. *Statistical Abstract of the United States: 1971.* Washington, D.C.

————. *Statistical Abstract of the United States: 1975.* Washington, D.C.

U. S. Department of Commerce, Bureau of the Census. *Income Distribution in the United States,* by Herman P. Miller. Washington, D.C.: Government Printing Office, 1966.

U. S. Department of Labor, Bureau of Labor Statistics. *Directory of National and International Labor Unions in the United States.*

Illinois. *Blue Book of the State of Illinois.* Springfield, biennial.

Reports and Proceedings

Lipset, S. M., and Bendix, Reinhard. "Ideological Equalitarianism and Social Mobility in the United States." *Transactions of the Second Congress of Sociology,* II. London: International Sociological Association, 1954, 33–54.

The Report of the First, Second, Third, and Ninth Annual Convention of the American Federation of Labor.

Report of the Proceedings of the Twelfth Annual Convention of the American Federation of Labor.

Report of the Forty-Fourth Annual Convention of the American Federation of Labor.

Report of the Forty-Sixth Annual Convention of the American Federation of Labor.

Unpublished Materials

Anson, Charles P. "A History of Labor Movement in West Virginia" (unpublished Ph.D. dissertation, University of North Carolina, 1940).

Converse, Philip E. "Group Influence in Voting Behavior." (unpublished Ph.D. dissertation, University of Michigan, 1958), 173–180.

Dodge, R. W. "Some Aspects of the Political Behavior of Labor Union Members in the Detroit Metropolitan Area." (unpublished Ph.D. dissertation, University of Michigan, 1958), 18ff.

Fishbein, Martin, and Coombs, Fred S. "Modern Attitude Theory and the Explanation of Voting Choice." (unpublished paper delivered at the annual meeting of the American Political Science Association, Chicago, 1971).

Goldman, Ralph. "Party Chairman and Party Factions, 1789–1900" (unpublished Ph.D. dissertation, University of Chicago, 1951).

Goodman, T. Wilbain. "The Presidential Campaign of 1920" (unpublished Ph.D. dissertation, Ohio University, 1951), 295, 396.

Harris, Avril E. "Organized Labor in Party Politics: 1906–1932." (unpublished Ph.D. dissertation, University of Iowa, 1937).

Iversen, Gudmund R. "Estimation of Cell Entries in Continuity Tables When Only Margins Are Observed" (unpublished Ph.D. dissertation, Harvard University, 1969).

Kreps, Juanita M. "Developments in the Political and Legislative Policies of Organized Labor: 1920–1947" (unpublished Ph.D. dissertation, Duke University, 1947).

Rogin, Michael. "Voluntarism as an Organizational Ideology in the American Federation of Labor: 1886–1932" (unpublished M.A. thesis, University of Chicago, 1959).

Stokes, Donald E. "Ecological Regression as a Game with Nature" (unpublished manuscript).

Index

Abramson, Paul, 125

AFL: "Bill of Grievances," 16; building trade in, 16; and Communists, 19; compared with CIO, 67–68; Convention of 1881, 16; Convention of 1923, 19; Convention of 1924, 19; and election of 1936, 24; and homogeneity of membership, 19; before 1906, 15; in 1906–1922, 16–19; in 1922–1928, 19–21; in 1928–1955, 21–25; in 1955–1964, 25–27; and Railroad Brotherhood, 16, 19; and traditional economic issues, 23. *See also* Labor unions

AFL-CIO: and Adlai Stevenson, 25; merging of, 24

Alford, Robert R., 78

American Institute of Public Opinion (AIPO). *See* Gallup poll

Apter, David, 115

Berelson, Bernard, 28–29

Berger, Bennett M., 80

Bernstein, Irving, 28

Bryan, William Jennings, 17

Burnham, Walter Dean, 113–114, 118, 124

Calkins, Fay, 28

Campbell, Angus, 4, 57, 59

Carter, Jimmy, 134

Catholics: clergy's role in laissez-faire doctrine, 16; and election of 1928, 20

Center for Political Studies (CPS): election data from, 8, 10–12; interpretation by, of recent elections, 123–124, 134, 136

Child labor law, 17. *See also* Economic issues

CIO: compared with AFL, 67–68; and election of 1936, 24; members' perception of politics, 27; militancy of, 24, 25; in Ohio, 28

Civil rights, 35, 125, 135. *See also* Social issues

Class and politics, 45, 69, 78, 79–81

Class consciousness: decline of, in 1940s, 25; and early labor movement, 14; of labor union members, 97, 133; and

New Deal era, 23; and occupational mobility, 96; and satisfaction, 98–99, 133

Collective bargaining, 15

Communication industries, nationalization of, 17. *See also* Social issues

Comparative reference group: and in-group comparison, 47; and out-group comparison, 47; theory of, 34, 45–51. *See also* Reference group, theory of; Relative deprivation, theory of

Consumerism, 52, 125, 135

Converse, Phillip, 37, 71

Crime, 135. *See also* Social issues

Critical elections, 20–21, 123. *See also* Election of 1928

Davis, James A., 47

Democratic Party: and distribution of wealth, 78; and labor, 17, 20, 24, 25, 27, 35, 61, 80, 111; platform of 1924, 20

Derber, Milton, 21

Dewey, Thomas E., 80

Economic issues, 27, 99, 134, 136. *See also entries under individual economic issues*

Educational aid, 35. *See also* Social issues

Eisenhower, Dwight D., 59

Election of 1906, 17

Election of 1924, 20

Election of 1928, 20. *See also* Critical elections

Election of 1936, 24

Election of 1944, 24

Election of 1948, 24, 28

Election of 1952, 7, 8, 9, 25, 116

Election of 1956, 7, 8, 9, 27, 59, 116

Election of 1960, 7, 8, 9, 118

Election of 1964, 7, 8, 9, 116

Election of 1968, 7, 12, 115, 116, 133

Election of 1972, 7, 12, 115, 116, 123, 124, 131, 133

Election of 1976, 7, 12, 115, 116, 118, 134

Embourgeoisement, thesis of, 82–85

Voluntarism, 14, 16, 19. *See also* Labor
  unions, and laissez-faire doctrine
Voting behavior: aggregate studies of, 1,
  5; analytic, systemic studies of, 4, 5;
  profiles of, 3, 118–122; social psychological surveys of, 2–4; and turnout
  rate, 118–119; of union members, studies on, 26–29; of women, 119; of
  youths, 119

Watergate issue, 124. *See also* Social issues
Weber, Max, 39

Whyte, William H., 81
Wilke, Wendell, 28
Women voters, 119
Women's suffrage, 17. *See also* Social is-
  sues
Women's work hours, 17. *See also* Social
  issues
Work relief program, 24. *See also* Eco-
  nomic issues
Workers, income level of, 91–96, 135.
  See also Labor union members
World War I, 16, 17, 19

Library of Congress Cataloging in Publication Data
Ra, Jong Oh.
Labor at the polls.
Bibliography: p.
Includes index.
    1. Trade-unions—United States—Political activity—
History. 2. Presidents—United States—Election—
History. 3. Voting—United States—History. I. Title.
HD8076.R3   324   77–90729
ISBN 0–87023–026–3